D1596412

Land Tenure among the Amhara of Ethiopia

Land Tenure among the Amhara of Ethiopia

The Dynamics of Cognatic Descent

Allan Hoben

The University of Chicago Press
Chicago and London

This volume is presented also as volume 4 in the series MONOGRAPHS IN ETHIOPIAN LAND TENURE, sponsored by the Institute of Ethiopian Studies and the Faculty of Law of Haile Selassie I University, Addis Ababa. All other volumes in the series are published by the sponsoring institutions.

The University of Chicago Press, Chicago 60637
The University of Chicago Press, Ltd., London
 Published 1973
Printed in the United States of America
International Standard Book Number: 0–226–34548–3
Library of Congress Catalog Card Number: 72–97666

This book is dedicated to the many good people of Dega Damot who gave me hospitality and helped me with this study, in the hope that this presentation of the knowledge with which they entrusted me will contribute to the wise and just administration of their beloved land, and to my teacher and friend Lloyd Fallers.

contents

tables and illustrations

Tables

Maps

Figures

note on amharic transcription

The transliteration of Amharic terms and names in this book utilizes an orthography intended to be readable for non-specialists. Amharic is written in a syllabary alphabet primarily consisting of thirty-three basic characters representing consonants, each having seven variant forms, referred to as "orders," to express the seven vowel phonemes of Amharic. These vowels have been rendered in the following manner:

Order in Ethiopic script	*Transcription*	*Pronunciation*
First order	e	as in *e*ver
Second order	u	as in r*u*de
Third order	ī	as in el*i*te
Fourth order	a	as in f*a*ther
Fifth order	é	as in touch*é*
Sixth order	i	as in f*i*t
Seventh order	o	as in h*o*pe

In the transcription of consonants, a dot under *ṭ*, *ṣ*, or *c̣h* indicates that the stop or affricate is a glottalized explosive; in accordance with many Semiticists' usage, *q* has been used to represent glottalized *k*. The letter *j* is pronounced as in the word "judge," and *ž* is pronounced like the *z* of "azure." Palatalized *n* is written *ñ*, as in Spanish "cañon." The rest of the consonants have approximately their English values. Double consonants indicate gemination. For a rigorous phonemic description of Amharic, see, for example, Bender (1968).

The plural of most Amharic nouns is formed by adding the suffix *-och* (*-yoch* or *-woch* after vowels) to the singular stem. However, with Amharic words used as technical terms in the text, such as *fej*, plurals have been formed in the English, rather than the Amharic, manner; for example, *fejs* instead of *fejoch*.

preface

The material in this book is based on twenty months of fieldwork conducted in 1961 and 1962 with the generous financial support of the Ford Foundation Foreign Area Training Fellowship Program and three months of additional research in 1966 supported by the Wenner-Gren Foundation and the University of Rochester. A limited amount of comparative data was also gathered between 1968 and 1970, when I was conducting fieldwork in a different area on another topic. For its support in this last field trip I am grateful to the National Science Foundation.

I would like to take this opportunity to thank the Imperial Ethiopian Government for facilitating and encouraging my research. I would also like to express my deep gratitude to the Haile Selassie I University and the Institute of Ethiopian Studies for the great assistance they have given me.

It is not possible to mention all those to whom I am indebted. I am particularly grateful, however, to Dejazmatch Tsehay Inqo Selassie, Ato Million Neqniq, His Excellency Bellete Gebre-Tsadik, Ato Gebre Hiwot Welde Hawariat, Ato Alemu Ambe, Ato Tafesse Bekkele, Dejazmatch Desta Biru, Ato Taye Retta, Fitawrari Ayalew Bezabih, and the many other officials of the Imperial Ethiopian Government who enabled me to live and work in Gojjam Province. I am also indebted to Stanislaw Chojnacki, Abraham Demoz, Asmarom Legesse, Donald Levine, Richard Pankhurst, James Paul, Georges Savard, Arnold Green, Dan Bauer, Harrison Dunning, Bill Ewing, Robert Merrill, and Paul Baxter for their suggestions concerning research and analysis;

to Andrea Williams and Susan Hoben for editorial suggestions; and to Nicky Harmon, Sandy Shufler, David Mallach, and Patty Pessar for their help in the preparation of the manuscript for this book. Finally, I would like to thank my assistant, Tilahun Ingida, for his patient help with research, his constant companionship, and his suggestions for revisions in the completed manuscript.

The names of living persons who appear in this book have been altered. The names of key ancestors and of descent corporations have also been changed. It is impossible, however, to disguise entirely the identity of these ancestors and the lands which bear their names, for many of them are well known in Dega Damot. For this reason, I wish to state emphatically that the genealogical information in this book is subject to error and should not, under any circumstances whatsoever, be introduced as evidence in legal disputes concerning land.

1. Introduction

The subject of this book is land tenure in a remote peasant community on the highlands of the Ethiopian plateau. To all but the died-in-the-wool Ethiopianist the topic may well sound esoteric. For this reason I will begin by trying to answer the question that should be asked of any anthropological monograph: what of general and comparative interest can be learned from this finely focused case study? The answer to the question, and hence my object in writing this book, is fourfold.

First, I believe the book represents a substantial ethnographic contribution to our understanding of land tenure, one of the central institutions of Amhara civilization past and present. In this respect it will be of interest both to historians interested in the comparative study of feudal[1]

1. The term "feudal" has been used rather loosely with respect to sub-Saharan African kingdoms. The Ruanda (Maquet 1961, 1970), the Ashanti (Rattray 1929), and the Nupe (Nadel 1942), for example, have all been called feudal. Recently Goody (1963) and Beattie (1964) have argued that such uncritical usage obscures important institutional differences between African and medieval European kingdoms. Following Marc Bloch in his discussion of feudalism as a type of society (Bloch 1961: 441–47), these writers hold that to be called feudal a society should be characterized by: a subject peasantry; widespread use of the fief instead of salary; the supremacy of a class of specialized warriors; ties of obedience and protection which bind man to man within the warrior class, that is, personal bonds of political dependence; the fragmentation of authority; and reference to the survival in some form of the idea of a former state. Goody and Beattie find that some but not all of these characteristics are found in the African kingdoms with which they are concerned. In the Amhara case, by contrast, it seems to me (see also Gamst 1970) that all of them fit rather well. Amhara cultivators, unlike most sub-Saharan African cultivators (Fallers 1961), are peasants. The ideal image to

peasant societies and to anyone interested in understanding contemporary rural Amhara society.

Second, the book is concerned with the relationship between social status, land tenure, and peasant attitudes towards land reform. In this respect I believe that the study confronts some widely accepted generalizations about peasant society, land tenure, and modernization. In particular it confronts the assumption of some social scientists and politicians that peasant populations in third-world countries inevitably live in a depressed condition with respect to land rights; and that significant economic development and social reform only await a drastic overhauling of the extant rules of land tenure.

Third, the book is directed towards anthropologists interested in cognatic descent, for it is through a rather complex system of cognatic descent groups and their political manipulation that land is acquired, lost, and held. The central puzzle in understanding cognatic descent systems like that of the Amhara concerns the restriction of overlapping claims to scarce resources. I believe the most important contribution of this book to the comparative anthropological study of cognatic descent is that it presents the first well-documented description and analysis of this process of restriction in a social system that has not been greatly altered by the administrative impositions of a colonial regime.

Fourth, though my aim is not theoretical, I think the book demonstrates the usefulness of a particular kind of anthropological perspective. The key point of this perspective is that the observed pattern of behavior—in this case, of landholding—cannot be understood as the product of customary rules alone. It must instead be seen as the cumulative product of a great many individual decisions. The anthropologist's task is to understand the contexts in which, and the processes through which, these decisions are reached. In this chapter I will discuss further each of these objectives.

---

which Amhara lords aspired was that of the man who was at once a fiefholder, a warrior, a vassal, and a governor. (This point is discussed in Levine 1965:155–67.) Finally, the high culture of Amhara civilization is oriented to the former glory of the Axumite empire.

The Amhara

The Amhara are an ethnic group with approximately five million members. Today they occupy a central position on the highlands of the Ethiopian massif. Most rural Amhara presently live between 7,000 and 12,000 feet above sea level in adjacent parts of four Ethiopian provinces: Begemdir, Gojjam, Shoa, and Wello (map 1). Culturally and politically, however, the Amhara are the dominant group in Ethiopia as a whole.

Since their emergence as a self-conscious ethnic and linguistic group in the beginning of the second millennium A.D., the Amhara have been the main political heirs of Axum, the ancient Semitic kingdom that flourished on the northern reaches of the Ethiopian plateau from several centuries before Christ until well after the rise of Islam. Of paramount importance in the heritage of Axum were a plow-based, mixed-farming agricultural pattern, the Ethiopic Christian church, and the venerated tradition of the Imperial throne, standing above and symbolically uniting the great regional rulers and their lower vassals. The land-based feudal pattern of social and political organization with which this book is concerned, however, developed, or at least took its present form, during the centuries of comparative isolation since the decline of Axum and the emergence of Amhara civilization.

Traditionally Amhara society,[2] like other peasant societies, was composed of a number of distinct segments differentiated from one another by occupation, power, and honor. The great majority of Amhara were (and still are) peasants living in scattered hamlets in the mountain fastness of the

2. The changes that mark the end of what may be called the traditional period in Ethiopian history began, in most respects, in the last part of the nineteenth century during the reign of Emperor Menilek (1889–1913) and have accelerated rapidly since the Second World War. In a sense the very idea of a traditional period is misleading in the Ethiopian context, for, at least in its popular sense, the term suggests an essentially static era, which Ethiopian history prior to the late nineteenth century was certainly not. The major divisions of Amhara society with which I am concerned here, however, endured throughout the period of Amhara ascendancy.

Ethiopian plateau and tilling the soil with iron-tipped ox-drawn plows. This farming population supported or, in the Amhara idiom, "carried on their backs" a much smaller ruling elite. The division of Amhara society into tax-paying peasants (*gebar*, sing.) and a nonfarming elite (*mekwanint*) was crosscut by a distinction between laymen and churchmen. The elite was thus divided into men who held secular, essentially military, titles on the one hand, and high ecclesiastic officials on the other.[3] Correspondingly, the farming population was (and is) divided into lay peasants (usually called *c̣hewa* in the region I studied) and clergy (*kahinat*) who also engage in agriculture. Above both the secular and ecclesiastic branches of the elite, at the apex of the stratification system, was the Emperor, the Conquering Lion of the Tribe of Judah, the King of Kings of Ethiopia.[4] Finally, at the other end of the social spectrum were endogamous groups of artisans, slaves, and non-Amhara peoples under Amhara domination.

Though there were great differences in power, honor, and wealth between the peasantry and the elite, the cultural distance between them was not so great as in most other agrarian civilizations.[5] Most important, in this regard, was the fact that the elite was not an urban elite; for there were in Ethiopia prior to the present century virtually no cities, with their attendant occupational specialization, their doubting intellectuals, their scholastic skeptics, and their independent commercial classes.[6]

3. This book is concerned with the elites only insofar as they are a part of the institutional environment of the peasant community. An excellent characterization of the elites, past and present, is to be found in Levine (1965:chap. 5). Other relevant discussions are to be found in Perham (1948), Clapham (1969), and Hoben (1970a). Titles and their significance are discussed in the Appendix.

4. For an excellent discussion of the position of the throne and its sources of legitimacy, see Levine (1964). See also Caquot (1957).

5. This point is elaborated in Hoben (1970a).

6. The only exception to this generalization was the city of Gondar to the north of Lake Ṭana where the court of the Emperors flourished briefly in the seventeenth and eighteenth centuries while their dominions were eroded by subinfeudation, internecine strife, and the inroads of Galla tribesmen from the south. The absence of urban centers since the Axumite period is discussed by Pankhurst (1961:chap. 6).

Nor was the geographical distance between the peasants and their elites great. The sprawling military camps of the secular elite, with their active courtly life, their displays of martial pomp, and their extravagant feasting, circulated periodically throughout the realm; while in old Amhara areas it is seldom more than a day's walk to the nearest great monastery, a cynosure of the more quiescent and contemplative life and a center of religious learning.

Land rights and Amhara society: gwilt and rist

Land tenure is of fundamental importance to any agrarian civilization. It is of particular importance for an understanding of Amhara civilization, for in traditional Amhara society most kinds of political and social, as well as material, relations were expressed through and reflected in the distribution of rights over land.

Traditionally, there were two basic principles of land tenure: *gwilt* and *rist*. For the present, gwilt rights may be thought of as fief-holding rights, and rist rights may be thought of as land-use rights. Gwilt (fief) rights provided economic and political support for the elite and in their territorial aspect constituted the framework for the administration of the peasantry. Rist (land-use) rights, on the other hand, played an important role in the social and economic organization of the local community.

Gwilt rights over land were given to members of the ruling elite as a reward for loyal service to their lord, and to religious institutions as endowments. The individual or institution that held land as gwilt had the right to collect taxes from those who farmed it, and also had judicial and administrative authority over those who lived on it. Gwilt rights were thus far more than just a type of land tenure. They were an integral part of the Amhara feudal polity; they represented the granting away by a regional ruler of an important part of his taxing, judicial, and administrative authority.

Virtually all arable and inhabited land was held by someone or some institution as gwilt. There was "no land without a master." The individual units of land held as estates of gwilt were from one to three or four square miles in area. A particular great lord or monastery might hold many estates of gwilt, and some of these might be contiguous. However, from an administrative standpoint, and in the eyes of the peasants, each estate of gwilt was a distinct unit with its own internal organization. Indeed these estates were the minimal and most enduring units of secular administrative organization in traditional Amhara society.

Rist rights, in contrast to gwilt rights, were (and are) land-use rights. In principle they were hereditary and could be held by lord and peasant alike. It is of fundamental importance to remember that rist and gwilt are not different types of land but distinct and complementary types of land rights. Normally, they extended over the same land. A single estate of gwilt land, comprising a few square miles, included within its boundaries strip fields held as rist by scores or even hundreds of farmers. The gwilt-holder might also hold some fields as rist within his estate of gwilt land.

A person who held a field as rist could cultivate it as he wished, subject only to the limitations imposed by the fallowing pattern of his neighbors. He was not a tenant. Nevertheless, his hereditary rist right to use the field was conditional on his meeting tax and service obligations associated with it. The most important of these were to the holder of gwilt rights over the estate in which the field was located. Other obligations might be to help maintain the local church or some part of its service.

There were privileges as well as obligations associated with having rist land within a particular estate. Paramount among these were the right to hold minor offices of secular and ecclesiastical administration and the right to be counted among the elders when matters of public concern were discussed.

The full significance of rist rights for the Amhara will become clear in the following chapters. It will be seen that even today these rights are of far more than economic value. A man uses them to select his house site, to validate his claim to office, to expand his control over land and people, to further his cause in court whatever the specific issue at hand,

and to judge the fitness and desirability of his son's or daughter's marriage partner. Land rights provide some of the most basic categories by which Amhara peasants have conceptualized, and to a large extent still do, their political, economic, and social relationships with one another.

Since the Second World War the feudal Amhara polity has been largely replaced by a bureaucratic form of government (see below, chapter 10). Inevitably the role of gwilt rights and of the gwilt-holder has been greatly diminished by these changes. This book, however, is not primarily concerned with regional government and politics, past or present. Its main focus is not on the activities of the gwilt-holding elite of yesterday or the world of the provincial functionary today. The members of both these groups enter my story only insofar as they affect the local community of intensive study.

Rist rights, and more generally the complex of ideas and activities which I will refer to as the rist system, appear to have changed relatively little since the war; nevertheless, even the small changes which have occurred will be examined. The rist system is of central importance to the social organization of the community I studied, and is the subject of this book.

Land tenure and social status in Amhara society

The close association of political authority, social status, and the hereditary control of land has fostered a static image of Amhara class structure which my research does not support. Despite the peasants' insistence that all land-use rights, or rist rights, are hereditary, it was found that the amount of land held by individual household heads, and the social status of these heads, may change markedly over the course of their lifetime. This fact has important implications for peasant attitudes towards land reform and, at the same time, raises some apparent paradoxes concerning the "hereditary" nature of rist.

Social status, as well as political authority, has always been closely related to land tenure in Amhara society (Hoben 1970a). Differences between major classes have corresponded to differences in the type of land rights potentially available to their members. Thus, at least in Amhara theory, low caste artisans or *ṭayb* (including smiths, weavers, and tanners) have had access to land only through tenancy. They have not held rist or gwilt. Ordinary peasant farmers, lay and clergy alike, have held land as rist but not as gwilt. Members of the elite, or *mekwanint*, have controlled land both as rist and gwilt. Moreover, a person's standing within his respective class also has corresponded quite closely to the extent of his control over land, a change in his social status usually being accompanied by a change in his control over land. Finally, and of great importance to this book, his attitude towards changes in the land-tenure system has been based, for the most part, on his assessment of how they will affect his status and his chances of improving it.

In light of this association between authority, status, and land tenure in Amhara society it is not surprising that many foreign observers and an increasing number of educated, urban Ethiopians have come to call the land-tenure system feudal, and have cast it somewhat uncritically in an image thought appropriate to other feudal, agrarian societies. This image generally rests on four assumptions. First, it is assumed that power and social status are based on the hereditary control of land. Second, Amhara society is thought to consist of numerous land-poor or even landless peasant families dominated by a small, land-holding gentry by means of tenancy. Third, it is assumed that there is little social mobility; status is thought to derive from land, and land is thought to be hereditary. A man's social standing is thus presumably more or less determined by chance of birth. The peasant farmer is seen as toiling year after year on the lands held by his father before him with little incentive to improve his techniques and little hope of improving his social standing. Disputes over land rights, which are indeed frequent, are held to be senseless and wasteful squabbles resulting from insecurity of title and the absence of a cadastral survey. Fourth, it is thought to follow from these assumptions that most peasants will welcome a program of land reform once its objectives are properly understood.

My fieldwork does not bear out these assumptions. While power and status are certainly related to control over land, it is inaccurate to say they are based on it. It would be at least as true to say that control over land is based on power, for, as will be seen, individuals who increase their political power are able to increase their holding of "hereditary" land.

Nor does my research support the assumption that the Amhara peasantry is land-poor and that the domination of the elite rests in large part on its control of land-use rights. With the exception of artisans, former slaves, and strangers, all of whom together generally constitute well under 10 percent of the population, most farmers are able to obtain substantial amounts of their land rent-free. Very few are altogether landless. Tenancy arrangements are of great importance to some individuals, but tenants do not constitute a distinct class. Many tenants are young men who will eventually obtain additional fields in their own right. Others are comparatively wealthy men who, having sufficient oxen and labor, rent additional land from their less fortunate neighbors and kinsmen. "Landlords," on the other hand, include the poor, the sick, and the aged, as well as the great.

The assumption that there is little social mobility, that a man can do little to improve his social status because it is largely determined by the amount of land he inherits, is also unwarranted. On the contrary, there are marked differences in status not only between fathers and their only sons, but also between full brothers who initially inherited equal shares of land. Most men are able gradually to increase the size of their landholding as their household grows and matures. Men who gain political prominence acquire additional land more rapidly. These spectacular gains are almost inevitably secured by means of litigation. From the upwardly mobile man's point of view at least, court disputes over land are not a waste of time.

Contrary to the fourth assumption, the Amhara farmer does not want to see his rights in land modernized. In fact, the vigor with which the Amhara peasants of Gojjam, the province in which I carried out my research, oppose land reform has been demonstrated by armed rebellion three times since the Second World War. The most recent of these violent protests, which reportedly took the lives of several hundred persons in 1967–68, was in response to tax reforms representing only a feeble first step towards land reform (see below, chapter 10). It has been argued by some, most notably by officials of the Ethiopian government, that this uprising, like those before it, resulted from misunderstanding. The peasants, it is argued, did not understand the true objectives of government policy or the benefits they would ultimately derive from a cadastral survey, individual registration of titles, and individual taxation. It is undoubtedly true that the recent revolt reflects, in part, a lack of confidence in the government. Nevertheless, as I believe will become clear in the following chapters, many peasants, particularly those who are most ambitious and who are leaders in their local communities, do oppose precisely the reform measures the government actually hopes to implement. Paradoxically their opposition is based on their fear that the measures will bring about the very state of affairs they are intended to correct. In particular it is feared that the introduction of freehold tenure and land sale will increase the economic dominance of powerful men and cut off avenues of upward social mobility now available to every young man.

When I began my research it was only gradually and after several months of fieldwork that I became aware that there was something puzzling about the sense in which rist rights in land are hereditary. Finding the solution to the puzzle took much longer and led me in directions I had not anticipated.

During the first part of my research, I found little to contradict the "static" view of Amhara society which, at that time, I accepted as more or less accurate. Men spoke frequently and with fervor of their ancestral rist, the land of their forefathers. Their sentiments about land were also evident as a recurrent theme in song and verse. Above all, the strength of their attachment to land was brought home to me by their willingness to fight about it and, if need be, to die for it.

People also insisted that all rist is hereditary; that it cannot be bought or sold. My questions about inheritance were met with the apparently simple statement that when a person dies his (or her) land is divided equally among all his children regardless of sex or birth order. When I asked about a specific field I was invariably told by the owner that it was his father's rist, his mother's rist, or his wife's rist.

As the months passed, however, I found myself confronted with an increasing amount of anomalous data. Despite their strong attachment to ancestral land, most peasants did not seem to know just where their ancestors, including great-grandparents and often even grandparents, had lived. They were even less certain as to the exact location of their ancestors' fields. It also became apparent that a number of the largest landholders in the area, including gwilt-holding members of the elite, were born of humble parents. Yet they claimed, and others agreed, that all of their land, even land acquired through litigation, was their ancestral rist. Even more anomalous was the fact that almost half of all the fields in the community I lived in had been acquired by their present owners from men or women who were not their parents or persons whom they considered to be significant kinsmen!

It thus became evident that land might legitimately be considered hereditary rist whether or not it was inherited. More generally, I found that the status and legitimacy of a person's right to a field are not determined by the way in which he acquires it or from whom he acquires it. Paradoxically, a man might inherit a field from his father only to later have it taken from him on the grounds that it was not his hereditary rist; conversely, he might obtain it through litigation or clearing forest land only to later defend it against the claims of others by arguing that it was his ancestor's rist!

The more I came to appreciate the central importance of rist in the lives of the people I was studying, the more I began to understand that the basic ideas, rights, interests, and processes associated with rist differ fundamentally from those associated with freehold tenure in the modern West. At the same time I found that the rist system, as I came to understand it, did not appear to resemble systems of kin-group or village ownership common in other parts of Africa. What, then, are the major characteristics of rist rights in contrast with freehold?

Most of the distinctive characteristics of rist are related to the fact that a field held by rist right is not thought of as an enduring unit with fixed boundaries and a permanent location. It is not an object, like a cow or a gun, which a person can dispose of as he pleases. Instead, it represents a share of a much larger tract of land held corporately by the descendents, *through any combination of male and female ancestors,* of a legendary figure who is believed to have first held the tract of land as his rist. The individual's rights in a particular field are always limited by the rights of other descendents of the first holder, and his ability to obtain or maintain possession of the field is subject to the control of a corporation composed of all those recognized descendents who hold land in the tract. The rules which are supposed to determine a descendent's share of the ancestral tract, and the organization and regulatory functions of the landholding corporation will be described in considerable detail in the following chapters. For the moment, however, let me anticipate by suggesting, in broad outline, how the corporate characteristics of the rist system resolve the apparent paradoxes and anomalies in the data I have discussed in this section.

The peculiar sense in which rist is hereditary can now be understood. All land held as rist is held by hereditary right since the holder is ipso facto a descendent of the ancestral first holder. It does not matter how the individual actually obtained possession of the field—through inheritance, litigation, clearing, or even tenancy, so long as his pedigree of descent from the first holder is accepted by the corporation leaders.

The flexible relationship between rist land and social status, the high level of conflict over land, and the peasants' deep commitment to the rist system are all related to a fundamental ambiguity in the concept of rist which is reflected in the semantics of the term itself. In its most general sense, rist refers to the right a person has to a share of the land first held by any of his or her ancestors in any line of descent. In its most restricted sense, by contrast, it refers to a specific field held by virtue of such a recognized right. In this book, for clarity, I shall refer to rist in the first sense as rist right and in the second sense as rist land. In Amharic, however, no lexemic distinction is made between rist rights a person believes he has in an ancestral tract of land, and a field he actually possesses. The context in which the term is used may, of course, restrict its meaning, but it is striking that it is often impossible to tell whether a person is speaking of land he possesses or of rights which he feels may some day enable him or his children to obtain land.

The ambiguity of the term "rist" is not a mere ethnographic oddity or a sign of conceptual confusion. It is an accurate reflection of a fluid land-tenure system in which it is a person's hereditary rights, not his fields, which are his most enduring possession, his real birthright.

The dual reference of rist also points to a basic condition of the rist system that simultaneously creates conflict within it and commitment to it. This is that *a person's rist rights always far exceed his rist land.* In other words he is always able to trace pedigrees to some ancestral first holders in whose land tracts he does not yet have any fields. This is assured by the fact that pedigrees are traced bilaterally, that is, through both male and female ancestors, and are from eight to twelve generations deep. To put it another way, there are always more legitimate descendents of an ancestral first holder than there are men who hold fields in his land tract. Whenever a right holder who has not previously held rist land tries to obtain land, he comes into conflict with the men already using the land. Yet it is precisely by entering into conflicts of this type successfully that a man can increase his holding of "hereditary" land and improve his social status. Thus by assigning to each individual a large array of bilaterally traced pedigrees through which he may be able to claim land at the expense of other men, the rist system fosters a pattern of endemic suspicion and conflict which tends to mask the underlying commitment of the peasantry to preserving their land-tenure system in its present form.

Cognatic descent groups and the rist system

The men and women who share an ancestral land tract because they believe they are descendents of its first holder constitute what is known to anthropologists as a cognatic or ambilineal descent group. Groups of this type, which are fairly common in the Pacific and quite unusual in Africa, present, in principle, some distinctive organizational problems. There are a number of ways in which these problems are solved. The Amhara solution, which is somewhat different from others that have been described, serves the function of allocating land to people more or less in accordance with their achieved social and political prominence, while at the same time it is compatible with the stabilizng doctrine that one's basic rights are hereditary and inalienable.

The Amhara cognatic descent group

The nature of the Amhara cognatic descent group must be understood in relation to the land tract over which it exercises corporate control; it is only with respect to their shared interest in this land that the individual landholders constitute a group. A descent group's land tract is usually from one-half to one and one-half square miles in area. It bears the name of its legendary first holder, a titled noble, a famed warrior, or a priest, who is thought to have received it from his superior when the Amhara first settled in the region. The land tract is divided into sections which are said to represent the shares of the first holder's sons and daughters. Each section is named after one of these children. The process of subdivision may be repeated at the generational level of the first holder's grandchildren and subsequent descending generations. Regardless of the number of generations to which subdivision has been carried, the smallest units of land division are plots and strips from one to ten acres (three acres is the average and the most common size). Altogether, there are several hundred of these plots and strips in a single first holder's land tract. These are the fields that are individually held as rist, and their holders are the members of the cognatic descent group.

The size, segmentation, and organization of the descent group corresponds quite closely to the division of its land tract. Typically, the number of members in an Amhara descent group, that is, of people who hold fields in its land tract as rist, varies from 50 to more than 150. All of these people consider themselves to be descendents of the ancestral first holder. They refer to him (or her) as the first father or ancestor (*wanna abbat*) of the land. One of the members is selected to act as representative (*fej*) of the group as a whole, or literally of the first father, in situations that involve the land tract in its entirety.

A descent group is internally divided into segments, one for each of the land sections divided in the name of the first holder's children. Members of a segment refer to the child who first held their land section as its divisional father (*minzir abbat*). The segments of the descent group, in turn, may each be divided into subsegments in the name of their respective first holders' children. The degree to which the descent group is segmented corresponds to the extent to which the land tract is subdivided. Like the descent group as a whole, each segment has a representative who acts for it when its section of land is involved.

There is an element of situational relativity in the way names are applied to sections of the land tract and segments of the descent group. A field may be referred to as land of the first holder of the entire tract, or of any of his descendents within whose section or subsection it happens to lie. It may also be referred to as the field of the living holder. Similarly, a member of the descent group may refer to himself as a descendent of the first holder or of any of the first holder's descendents who founded segments of which he counts himself a member.

The Amhara descent group differs from most descent groups or lineages found in African societies in five important respects. First, the Amhara descent group is not a solidary or cohesive group. Its members have no esprit de corps, no emblems, totems, or honorific names to symbolize their unity. Nor are their relations with one another, even ideally, characterized by affect, cooperation, or good will. If, upon occasion, they act with unity of purpose, it is because they individually think it is in their best interest to do so, not because of loyalty to the idea or ideals of the group.

Second, the Amhara descent group is not, except in a nominal sense, a kinship group. To be sure, the members of the group are consanguineal kinsmen by Amhara definition since they are codescendents (*dirrib*) of the same ancestor; but they are not expected to behave towards one another as kinsmen (*zemed*). Some members of the descent group may happen to be close kin and will treat each other accordingly. Most, however, cannot trace the kind of close kinship ties with one another which are of significance in Amhara social life. Similarly, the descent group is not in any way responsible for its members' marriages, nor is it, as such, an exogamous group.

Third, the Amhara descent group is not a ritual group. The members do not constitute a congregation. They do not perform any religious ceremonies together. There is no ancestor cult and no ancestral shrine. Furthermore, there is no belief that the welfare of the members is affected by their ancestors, and no belief that the actions of the living are judged by the dead.

Fourth, the Amhara descent group is not a multipurpose group. It controls land and the rotation of certain minor administrative offices among its members; it has no other functions. It is not used as a framework for the organization of intermittent or unusual cooperative tasks in the community.

Fifth, membership in Amhara descent groups is not mutually exclusive, but overlapping. Most men are members of several descent groups. This pattern of overlapping membership is closely related to the weak sentiments of attachment people feel towards the descent group and towards their fellow members, for people who are united by their interest in one descent group's land may be divided from one another by their interests in other descent groups. Overlapping membership is a characteristic of cognatic descent groups in general, and is the source of the distinctive organizational problems of systems based on cognatic descent.

The organizational problems of cognatic descent systems

Descent is a way of recruiting people to socially significant groups, groups that serve to order people's relationships to one another and to property. Cognatic descent, unlike unilineal descent, recruits an individual to more than one group and thus may introduce an element of disorder, ambiguity, or conflict into social organization. For this reason, systems of cognatic descent always restrict membership in descent groups by some other means in addition to rules of descent. A description of a system of cognatic descent groups and analysis of their function is not complete unless it includes a description of these additional ways in which membership is restricted.[7]

The rules that anthropologists refer to as rules of descent are rules that place children in social groups in accordance with the membership of their parents. The groups of living people formed and maintained in this way are called descent groups because they are composed, or are thought to be composed, of the lineal descendents of a particular ancestor. The significance of descent groups to the members of a society depends on the extent to which a person's status as a descent group member gives him access to scarce resources, such as land, and important rights and duties towards other members of his own group and members of other groups.

It would be more accurate to say that descent rules place

7. My object in this section is to place the Amhara descent-group system in a broader comparative perspective and not to engage in a critical or exhaustive discussion of cognatic descent. Important works that have influenced my remarks include: Coult (1964); Davenport (1959); Firth (1963); Freeman (1961); Goodenough (1955, 1961); Keesing (1968, 1970); Murdock (1960b); Peranio (1961); Scheffler (1965). The contribution of the Amhara case to the literature on cognatic descent and the analytical usefulness of the concept of cognatic descent will be discussed at greater length in the conclusion.

children in social *categories* or *groups* in accordance with the categorization or membership of their parents. This distinction between descent category and descent group is required by the fact that, though being "born into" the right category may be a necessary condition for active participation in a particular descent group,[8] it may not, as in the Amhara case, be a sufficient condition. It is one thing to have the qualifications for membership in the group and it is another to have the rights, responsibilities, and interests associated with the status of group member. This is precisely the difference, in the Amhara case, between having rist rights and having rist land.

Anthropologists have distinguished several classes of descent rules, each with certain broad structural implications for social organization. For the purposes of this discussion it is useful to compare and contrast two of these classes of descent rules: unilineal and cognatic. Unilineal descent rules are those which place children (regardless of their sex) in the descent category of parents of one sex only. There are thus two types of unilineal descent: patrilineal, in which children are placed in the descent category of their father only; and matrilineal, in which children are placed in the descent category of their mother only. Cognatic descent rules, which are also sometimes termed ambilineal or nonunilineal, place children (regardless of their sex) in the descent categories of both their mother and father.

The structural significance of the distinction between unilineal and cognatic descent is that unilineal descent is compatible with the partitioning of a society's members into mutually exclusive groups, while a rule of cognatic descent, in itself, is not. In a society with patrilineal descent groups, for example, a man's son is placed in the same descent category as the man himself. The son is not placed in the descent category of his mother, for membership cannot be passed through a female. A man's daughter also is placed in the same category as himself. She cannot, however, pass on this

8. The phrase "born into" must be taken in a metaphorical sense; many descent systems permit adoption into the descent group.

membership to her children who will, instead, be placed exclusively in the category of her husband. Unilineal descent thus makes it possible for each individual to be placed in only one descent category and group. Cognatic descent places children in the descent categories of both parents and thus, in principle, with exogamy, could double the number of descent categories to which people belong in each generation.

The organizational significance of the distinction between unilineal and cognatic descent is related to the way in which the two kinds of descent structure people's rights in relation to property and to one another. By placing people in only one descent group, unilineal descent gives them clear-cut rights in the property of their descent group and unambiguous relationships to one another either as members of the same group or of different groups. With cognatic descent the situation is different. Unless there is some other way in which membership in descent groups is limited, property rights associated with each group become so widely diffused as to be meaningless. At the same time social relationships in respect to descent group membership become ambiguous, since individuals may be related to one another in several different ways at once.[9]

Because of these inherent organizational difficulties, cognatic descent systems alway restrict membership in descent groups by some additional means. There is considerable variation in the ways that restriction is achieved and in the extent to which it reduces or eliminates overlapping membership. Both of these variables are related to the function of

9. These statements are ideal-typical. They are about the logical properties of descent rules as recruitment principles and not about ethnographic reality. Men living outside the territory politically associated with their natal patrilineage, for example, may be in a highly ambiguous position in relation to their neighbors and their agnates, as is the case among the Konds of highland Orissa (Bailey 1960). On the other hand, a cognatic descent system may structure people's social relationships without ambiguity if, as among the Iban of Borneo (Freeman 1960), there is an additional rule of restriction based on the choice of residence made by people at marriage. My statements are about the way descent rules are capable of ordering relationships, "other things being equal." Other things are seldom equal, of course, because the affairs governed by descent are usually too important to be left to the chance of birth alone.

cognatic descent, to its organizational role in a particular society.

The restriction of membership in cognatic descent groups is often related to the territorial localization of each group's economic resources, the most common resource being, as in the Amhara case, land. The descent group's land is concentrated in one locality. Members of the descent category associated with the land are widely dispersed over a much larger area. The probability of their participating in the affairs of the descent group and holding a share of its land decreases with the distance of their residence from the group's land.

Membership in the group and participation in its affairs need not be an all-or-nothing proposition. There may be degrees of participation in the group's political, economic, social, and ritual affairs corresponding, more or less, to degrees of residential distance from the group's land. People who live near the land, for example, may still use some of it. People who live at a greater distance may attend weddings, funerals, and other social events; while people who live still farther away may maintain only a ritual connection with the group's more active members. Geographically and socially, then, the cognatic descent group is frequently composed of a series of concentric rings centered on the group's estate.

The restriction of descent group membership by geographical proximity, that is, distance from the descent group's resources, may result from purely pragmatic considerations. In the absence of modern transportation and economic and legal conditions that make it profitable to rent or share-crop land, it may be impractical for people to maintain active membership in descent groups whose estates are very far from their homes.

There may also be formalized rules restricting membership in relation to geographical proximity. Residence on the descent group's land as well as descent from its founder may, for example, be a prerequisite to holding land, as is the case in parts of Eritrea in northern Ethiopia (S.F. Nadel 1946).

There may be restrictive rules pertaining to genealogical proximity as well as geographical proximity. For example, there may be a statute of limitations on claims to land; a rule that limits people's claims to land to descent groups where their parents and grandparents lived, held land, or perhaps participated in group rituals. Marriage rules favoring or prescribing descent-group endogamy also serve to limit or eliminate overlapping membership in some cognatic descent systems.

Whether the result of pragmatic considerations or formal rules, restriction of active membership in the cognatic group leads to restriction of the descent category of which the active membership is a subset; for descent lines which can no longer be used, have been long dormant, or only validate claims to distant resources tend to be forgotten in favor of lines of more immediate relevance. Through this continuing process of progressive genealogical amnesia, inactive collateral lines are lost to memory and the number of remembered descendents in a descent category, instead of doubling in each generation, remains essentially stable.

There is much variation in the extent to which overlapping membership in descent groups is restricted and in the ways this restriction is accomplished. Even in cognatic descent systems with no overlapping of active membership, however, individuals have some choice of affiliation.[10] The cumulative effect of this choice is to introduce a characteristic element of flexibility into the functioning of institutions organized by cognatic descent.

Even cognatic descent systems that restrict an individual to active membership in only one group give him some choice as to which group that will be. Less narrowly restricted systems give him a wider range of choice and perhaps the opportunity to be active in more than one descent group as well, for the obverse of multiple membership in groups is multiple affiliation of the individual.

10. This does not mean that the individual himself is always in a position to choose his affiliation. He may be a minor bound by his parents' decision. A woman may be bound by her husband's decision. Furthermore, in a particular case all but one choice of affiliation may happen to be quite impractical. The point is that, from a structural point of view, alternatives of affiliation are available.

Cognatic descent is often described as a more flexible form of social organization than unilineal descent. In one sense this is misleading. Enduring unilineal descent systems are also flexible in response to ecological, demographic, or political imbalance, no matter how rigid their formal rules of recruitment. In another sense, however, cognatic descent systems do exhibit a characteristic type of flexibility or fluidity. It is a flexibility related to the ability of the individual to alter or increase his affiliations, rather than to group action or the use of genealogical fictions. If a man's descent group does not have enough land, for example, he may have the option of reaffiliating himself with a descent group with land to spare. If he does not like his neighbors he may be able to change his residence. An able and ambitious person may be able to profit by obtaining access to economic or political resources in several descent groups at once.

The cumulative effect of many people making choices like these gives cognatic descent systems their characteristic flexibility of function. In an egalitarian society cognatic descent may serve to allocate people more or less evenly to available land. In a society marked by political inequalities it may concentrate available resources in the hands of a powerful minority. It may function to keep the size of descent groups more or less constant relative to one another or to facilitate the rapid expansion of descent groups led by unusually gifted and powerful men.

The function of a cognatic descent system, its organizational role in a particular society, must be understood through the kinds of options its mode of restriction makes available to individuals, the kinds of interests these individuals are pursuing through descent-group affiliation, and the wider institutional context in which decisions affecting membership in descent groups are made.

Restriction, option, and function in Amhara descent

Membership in Amhara cognatic descent groups is comparatively unrestricted. There are no formal cultural rules to prevent any descendent of the founding ancestor from claiming active membership in the descent group and a share of its rist land. He is not required to live on the land or to farm it himself. Nor is there any statute of limitations on the validity of an unused pedigree. A person may claim membership in a group even though none of the ancestors in the pedigree, except the founder himself, have done so. Rist rights do not die.

There is a considerable degree of overlapping membership in descent groups and descent categories. An ordinary farmer is a rist landholding member of two or three descent groups. An influential elder may be active in five or ten groups, while a leading political figure in the district may be active in twenty or thirty groups. The number of descent groups in which a man thinks he has potential rights, that is, rist rights as opposed to rist land, always far exceeds the number of groups in which he is active. In fact there is virtually no limit to the number of descent groups to which a man can trace pedigrees with the help of relatives and genealogical experts, should he think it in his interest to do so.

Though an Amhara's rist rights are almost boundless, his chances of holding rist land in a particular descent group or of obtaining it from the members of the landholding group are, in practice, restricted in several ways. Most important among these are his genealogical proximity to a previous landholder, his geographical proximity to the descent group's land, and the extent of his political influence.

Restriction by genealogical proximity refers to the fact that, though a pedigree does not legally become less valid through disuse, it becomes less effective. A person can almost always obtain rist land in a descent group in which either of his parents held land. Usually he does this through simple inheritance, a process which need not affect the land rights of other members of the descent group. A person also can usually obtain rist land in a descent group in which any of his grandparents were active members. He may not choose to do so, however, if pressing his claim brings him into conflict with collateral relatives with whom he or his parents have reached an informal agreement about land division. Beyond the grandparental level, other things being equal, it becomes increasingly difficult for a man to activate rist rights that have been unused in the intermediate generations. His formal right to rist land, however, is never thought to be extinguished, and this is of real significance, for other things are not always equal.

Restriction by geographical proximity refers, in part, to the fact that, other things being equal, a man can obtain and retain rist land more easily if he resides in the parish in which the land is located. This is not because of a formal rule, but because locally resident descent-group members favor the claims of men who are their friends and neighbors and who share with them the collective obligations of church support and statute labor that rest on the residents of a parish. In part, too, the restriction of geographical proximity is simply a function of distance, of the time and effort a man must expend to cultivate distant fields and of the difficulty he will have collecting and transporting his share of the crop, should he give the land to a tenant.

Political influence, usually derived directly or indirectly from political office, makes it easier for a man to obtain rist land through pedigrees that have been unused for many generations or that is distant from his homestead. To put it another way, political influence enables him to extend the genealogical and geographical range of his ability to obtain rist land through his rist rights. There are several reasons for this. A powerful person can litigate more successfully than an ordinary farmer because of his ability to mobilize favorable witnesses, influence the judge, and sustain the cost, in time and money, of a protracted court case. In some instances landholding members of a descent group are willing or even eager to recognize an influential man's claim because they think he will prove to be a powerful ally in their struggle against a rapacious local leader or a rival segment of the group. Finally, an influential man can find tenants to sharecrop his distant fields—tenants who are also, in a sense, clients and who regard him as a patron as well as a landlord.

To summarize, the Amhara cognatic descent system provides each individual with a comparatively wide range of optional affiliations in the form of rist rights. These affiliations almost always enable a man to obtain rist land in his residential parish. They usually enable him to obtain land in some nearby parishes where his parents or grandparents held rist land. They also enable him to take up residence in another parish with the expectation that, as a resident, he will be able to expand his holding of rist land in local descent-groups' land sections. Finally, they enable him to substantially increase his holding of rist land both within his residential parish and in other parishes as he improves his political standing.

The picture of the rist system I have presented in this section is, of necessity, incomplete and oversimplified. It will be filled in with more detail in the remaining chapters. In the final section of this chapter I would like to comment briefly on the point of view I have adopted in this book.

Perspective, methods, and data

The pattern of landholding in the area I studied cannot be understood as the result of customary rules of land tenure alone. Instead, it must be seen as the cumulative product of a great many individual decisions concerning land. My task is to describe the situations in which these decisions are made and the factors that affect the way they are made. This perspective, which is particularly useful for understanding changes in the landholding pattern, has influenced the methods I used in my research, the kinds of data I gathered, and the way I have organized this book.

Customary rules of land tenure, however important, are only one of several considerations that influence the way people make decisions about land. In response to questions, to be sure, Amhara elders usually formulate the principles of their land-tenure system as immutable and unambiguous rules for action rather than as a series of contingent possibilities. It is universally held, for example, that a man's children inherit his land equally, that a man can claim his rist land even if neither he, his father, nor his grandparents have held it, and that a son should build his homestead next to his father's. It is evident from even a cursory inspection of case material that when, to what extent, and in what way these general rules are implemented depends on a number of additional considerations. An older son who becomes an influential and respected elder may, in fact, hold more of his father's fields than his younger, wastrel brother. Whether a man's claims to land once held by his great-grandfather or a more remote ancestor will be recognized depends on his residence and his influence in regional politics. Whether a son actually builds his homestead near his father's depends on the extent of the father's lands, the number of his sons, and the availability of uncleared or unused land in the community. Rules about land are important because they help define a man's possibilities and influence his choice of strategies in pursuing these possibilities; but, in themselves, they do not determine the outcome of decisions about land.

In order to understand how decisions about land are made and the factors that affect them, it is also necessary to understand the situations or institutional contexts in which they are made. For example, the decisions that result in what I have termed restriction by genealogical proximity are decisions about the inheritance and division of parental lands. They are made in the context of household and kinship relations, and they may be influenced by norms, interests, and sentiments associated with these institutions. The decisions that result in what I have called restriction by geographical proximity are made in the context of hamlet and parish relations. These decisions are influenced by people's ideas about the amity of neighbors, the equity of allowing nonresidents to hold land without sharing the burdens of statute labor, and the expedience of attracting clergymen who are needed to offer mass in the parish church. The decisions that enable a powerful man to extend the genealogical and geographical range of his claims to rist land are made in the context of regional political relations. When contested in government court, the decisions are argued in the formal, narrowly legalistic idiom of descent-group rules. The outcome of these contests, however, depends on the litigants' ability to mobilize their supporters and influence the court. It is the realities of power politics in the regional arena and not norms or sentiments about family or community that are of paramount importance here.

The decision-making perspective I have adopted has implications for the analysis of stability and change. It cannot be assumed that the landholding pattern I observed in the 1960s is one that has persisted unchanged from the remote past. It is not a pattern that endures through the sheer weight of tradition, but rather is constantly coming into being. It is generated by a multitude of decisions about land. To the extent that the holding pattern has remained unchanged, it is because the same factors are determining the way these decisions about land are being made. In fact, some of these factors appear to have changed in the present century. Further and accelerating changes seem inevitable in the future.

The factors that affect decisions about land can be viewed as the parameters of the land-holding pattern. Some of them, such as normative and pragmatic rules about land, are a part of the cultural tradition of the local Amhara community.[11] Others, such as the system of land taxation, the operation of government courts, and the penetration of national markets for agricultural produce, are exogenous to the local social system; the conditions which affect these factors are national conditions, and the decisions which control them are made in Addis Ababa by the national government. Finally, there are natural parameters, such as the density of population and the fertility of the soil, which also affect the way people make decisions concerning land.

Changes in any of these parameters can bring about changes in the pattern of landholding. They can, for example, alter the size or fragmentation of the typical household estate. They can affect the relative frequency of land acquisition through inheritance and litigation. They can increase the importance of tenancy or lead to a greater concentration of land in the hands of the powerful.

When I undertook to write this book, one of my objectives was to explore these relationships of change in greater detail. I was particularly interested in the effects that changes

11. The distinction I have in mind here is between rules which are considered morally or legally sanctioned on the one hand, and those which are purely pragmatic guides about the selection of effective strategies on the other. The distinction is based on Bailey (1970: 4–6).

in land law, land taxation, market conditions, and population density have had or will have on the landholding pattern in the area I studied and hence on the lives of its people. The results of my inquiry, which are presented in chapter 10, are tentative and suggestive rather than conclusive, as they must be in the absence of far more quantitative data than is currently available. Nevertheless, I believe they will be of both practical and analytical interest.

Much of the material in this book is based on the intensive study of a few communities rather than on an extensive survey. This method of research, which is consistent with my analytical perspective, was dictated by the absence of government records about land and the difficulty of gathering accurate data from peasants through interviews or questionnaires.

The communities I studied most intensively are a cluster of parishes located 150 air miles to the northwest of Addis Ababa in Dega Damot district of Gojjam province. My first period of fieldwork lasted eighteen months, beginning in the fall of 1960. I was able to return to the area in April of 1966 for three months of additional research. Finally, between November 1968 and January 1970, I was able to gather additional data used in this book, although I devoted most of my time to fieldwork in another Amhara region.

At the beginning of my first field trip I had only a rather unfocused interest in Amhara peasant social organization and its relationship to church and state elites. I was not specifically interested in land tenure and was not even aware of the cognatic descent groups, which had not previously been described in the literature on the Amhara. Nevertheless, I spent more and more of my time investigating the descent system as I came to understand its central role in Amhara social and political organization.

During the first period of field research I relied heavily on the participant-observer techniques ordinarily used by anthropologists in intensive microstudies. I spent most of my time in the same communities among the same people and tried to establish personal ties with as many of them as was practical. I talked with farmers and priests, with low-caste artisans and titled gwilt-holders, with government officials and learned monks, with women and children. I asked them about themselves and about each other, about what they did and thought and felt and hoped and feared.

Most important, perhaps, I tried to relate what people told me about themselves with what they did. Sometimes I could do this by participating in their activities, as when I attended a wedding, a land dispute, or church festival. Sometimes the best I could do was to record case histories of events from what various people told me. In this way, I was able to gather a large fund of information about the lives and actions of a limited number of people. As I did so, I began to see how people were constrained by customary rules and how they were able to manipulate them. I was able to see how the total complex of rights and duties, of interests and sentiments a person had in virtue of all his many roles could affect his decisions in specific situations, including situations involving land. Indeed one of the major goals of the participant-observer technique and the microstudy method is to enable the analyst to understand the point of view of the individual actors in the society he is studying—to understand the way they classify their experience, evaluate it, and make decisions concerning what to do about it.

When I returned to Dega Damot in 1966 my specific goal was to gather more data for this book. My main objective was to obtain more quantitative data concerning the cumulative effects of the kinds of decisions people make with regard to land under various social, demographic, and economic circumstances, effects on both individual holdings and on the general distribution of land among people through time.

It was very difficult to get accurate information about landholding in Dega Damot, as in all traditional Amhara areas with the rist system. There has been no cadastral survey. There are no land maps and there is no individual registration of title. Government tax records in Dega Damot do not list individuals or their holdings, but instead contain only the names of the founding ancestors of descent groups or their children. Similarly, court records do not indicate the size or exact location of disputed land but only its "genealogical position" within the descent group and the locality in which it is situated.

People were very suspicious of inquiries about their land. Attempts to count or measure fields are seen, at best, as the prelude to higher taxes and, at worst, as the harbingers of dreaded land reform. It was necessary to gain each farmer's confidence before questioning him in any systematic fashion about his fields, a circumstance that severely limited the number of interviews conducted.

Insofar as I could, I tried to cross-check the information about land gathered in interviews against maps constructed from aerial photographs and against unofficial tax lists kept by descent-group representatives. These attempts were only partially successful, particularly with respect to fields held in distant parishes which I was unable to study or map. There are undoubtedly many errors in the quantitative data I have been able to gather. These will be corrected, I hope, by further research in the future. For the present, however, I believe that the quantitative information I have used in this book is considerably more complete and accurate than that which has been previously available for Amhara rist-holding areas.

The organization of the following chapters is intended to reflect the goals, interests, and analytical perspective I have outlined in this introductory discussion. Chapters 2 through 5 provide an introduction to the geographical and institutional setting of the book. Chapter 6 is about the descent group and its estate. Chapter 7 is concerned with the way the individual landholder conceptualizes and classifies his rist rights in many estates and the secondary rights through which the use of rist land can be temporarily transferred. Chapter 8 is about the diverse processes and strategies through which a man can acquire rist land and build up his personal household holding. Chapter 9 examines the dynamics of social stratification, land, and power. Chapter 10 is concerned with problems of change and land reform, and chapter 11 returns to some of the comparative issues raised in this introductory discussion and attempts to assess the general significance of the detailed case study presented in this book.

2. The Setting

Eastern Gojjam province, in which Dega Damot is located, is bounded on three sides by the mile-deep canyon of the Blue Nile (map 1). The Blue Nile leaves Lake Ṭana near Bahir Dar and flows to the southeast for ninety miles. It then turns to the south for sixty miles and finally swings around to the west where it leaves the Ethiopian highlands and enters the Sudan. The region thus enfolded in the great bend of the Blue Nile is bisected by a mountainous plateau running from a peak to the south of Lake Ṭana to another peak seventy miles to the southeast. At its highest point in the southeast the massif rises to over 13,000 feet above sea level, and its slender central plateau is almost everywhere over 10,000 feet. Long ridges drop away on both sides of this central plateau spine, extending as much as thirty miles into the plains thousands of feet below.

The high plateau, the ridge tops, the valley floors, and the plains beyond are a patchwork of field, fallow, and pasture. The steep mountain slopes between highland and lowland are blanketed with scrub thorn, and the rushing rivers in the narrow valley headlands flow through a dense growth of moss-coated rain forest.

The color of the landscape varies with the season. During the rains, from May through October, the land is a lush green. During the dry season, from November until April, it gradually changes from green to gold to brown with the harvest of the grains and then the gradual drying of the soil. Temperature varies with both season and altitude. In the lowlands, just before the rains begin, daytime temperatures are often

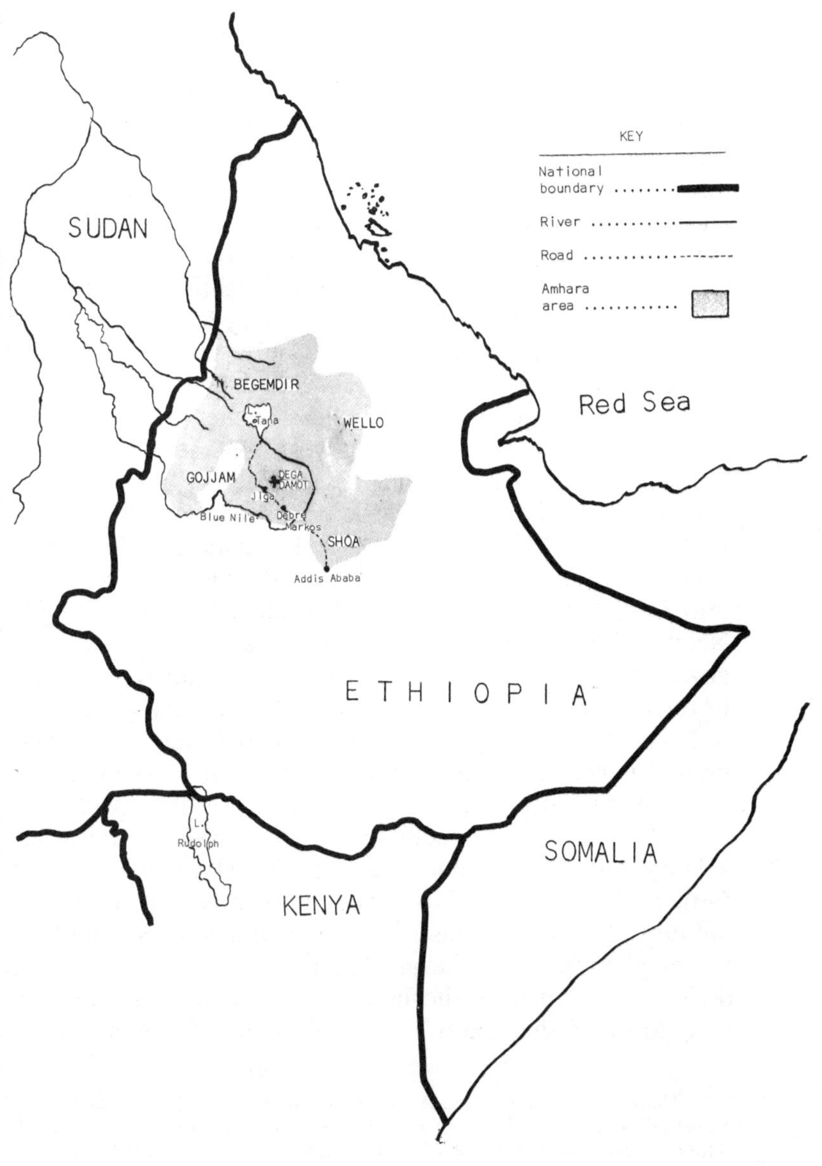

Map 1. Ethiopia

over 90° F. On the high plateau there is frost on cold December nights, and even at noonday the wind carries a chill.

Dega Damot district straddles this central mountain plateau and extends into the plains on both sides. Its altitude ranges from under 6,000 to over 12,000 feet above sea level. Its area is approximately 700 square miles and it has an estimated population of between 50,000 and 60,000. The overall population density is thus around 80 people per square mile, but there is considerable local variation; in some densely settled and intensely farmed localities it was found to be over 130 per square mile.[1] With very few exceptions all the inhabitants of the district speak only Amharic, are strict adherents of the Ethiopic Christian church and consider themselves to be members of the Amhara ethnic group.

At the present time (1970) Dega Damot is one of six administrative districts that make up Qolla-Dega Damot subprovince of Gojjam province. It is divided into four subdistricts: Feres Bét, Berqeñ, Arefa, and Inamora. Each of these subdistricts, in turn, is divided for administrative purposes into from twenty to forty "neighborhoods" (*aṭībya*, sing.). Neighborhoods are currently the minimal territorial units of governmental administration. They are ordinarily from two to three square miles in area, and usually have a population of from 150 to 250 people. Neighborhoods were given their present names and administrative statuses in 1947 by a central government proclamation establishing a nationwide system of neighborhood courts.[2] In Dega Damot, however, neighborhoods correspond exactly to the estates of gwilt land formerly held as fiefs or benefices by members of the ruling military elite and monasteries. Approximately one-third of the neighborhoods of Dega Damot are coextensive with a parish, the minimal territorial unit of ecclesiastic administration. Most of the others consist of some part of a parish,

1. There has been no census in Dega Damot, nor has its land been measured. The figures I have used here are based on projections of data I gathered, made with the aid of aerial photographs. The figures are thus only crude approximations useful in that they indicate an order of magnitude.

2. Proclamation 90 of 1947.

while in a few exceptional cases a single neighborhood encompasses more than one parish.

The present-day district of Dega Damot represents the last remnant of a larger, rather little known, kingdom called Damot. The first reliable mention of the kingdom of Damot, made by the Portuguese monk Francisco Alvares who visited Ethiopia in the first quarter of the sixteenth century, places it to the west of the kingdom of Shoa, south of the Blue Nile (Alvares 1961: 455). As the result of Galla invasions, Damot as a political entity retreated to the north of the Blue Nile to its present mountain-backed position.

James Bruce, who visited Ethiopia in the last quarter of the eighteenth century, a century and a half after Alvares, reached the springs of Gīsh Abbay in Agau country only thirty miles northwest of the present administrative center of Damot.[3] Bruce places Damot in its present location and estimates it to be forty miles by twenty miles in size (Bruce 1790: 3:257). According to him, Damot was in his time tributary to the imperial throne at Gondar across Lake Ṭana to the north. Nevertheless, because of its location on the southern marches of Amhara domination and because the monarchy was nearing the nadir of its influence, Damot seems to have enjoyed some degree of autonomy in Bruce's day. The fertile region of Agau Midir to the southwest of Lake Ṭana, for example, paid tribute to the governor of Damot as well as directly to the emperor.

During much of the troubled nineteenth century, most of Gojjam, including Damot, was virtually independent of political control from the centers of Amhara power beyond the Blue Nile. More than once during this period Damot served as a retreat for the great independent lords of Gojjam and their armies when invaders from the north of the Blue Nile

3. Bruce's avowed purpose in visiting Ethiopia was to discover the source of the Nile. His visit to the Gīsh Abbay springs, the source of a tributary of Lake Ṭana known as the "little Blue Nile" to the people of Gojjam, was thus the high point of his entire six-year journey. In reality the Gīsh Abbay had been "discovered" a century earlier by the Portuguese. This fact, which Bruce never accepted, fortunately did not deter him from recording his impressions of Ethiopia, or as it was then known, Abyssinia, in four fascinating volumes.

occupied the plains below;[4] its rugged cloud-enshrouded terrain offered protection and military advantage to those who knew it well.

Today Dega Damot has lost most of its former political autonomy. It has not, however, been very effectively integrated into the political and economic institutions of modern Ethiopia. Modern forms of communication and transportation do not presently penetrate the district, and there is no road or track connecting any part of the district with the newly rebuilt all-weather road that skirts the massif to the south on its way from the provincial capital at Debre Markos to Bahir Dar on Lake Ṭana.[5] No form of telecommunication or postal service links Feres Bét wth the rest of the country. The district governor, the judge, the police chief, and the tax collector who represent the central administration in Feres Bét are hampered in their work by their dependence on hand-carried messages for routine communication with their superiors at the subprovincial capital of Finote Selam on the road beyond Jiga.

For the outsider who wishes to travel to Feres Bét, the trip begins in Debre Markos. The first part of the trip, and the easiest, is made by car or bus to the roadside marketing and administrative center of Jiga. For the most part the road runs straight through open, flat, or gently inclined plains. At several points it snakes upwards to cross the outermost extensions of the ridges reaching down from the distant mountain massif that dominates the skyline to the north.

At Jiga the traveler must procure a saddle horse or mule, and, if he has any baggage, he must assemble pack animals and men to drive them. Unless arrangements have been made

4. Gojjam here refers to the modern province. Formerly it was restricted to the region to the north of Damot.

5. The present isolation of Dega Damot represents, in some respects, a regression from earlier days. During the brief Italian occupation, a cantonment in the Dega Damot district center of Feres Bét was supplied by trucks brought over a rough track from Debre Markos. Yet earlier, in the 1920s, when Gojjam was under the rule of its last independent governor, Ras Hailu Tekle Haymanot, Feres Bét was connected to Debre Markos by telephone. The telephone operator's emoluments characteristically included a land grant.

in advance, organizing the pack train usually takes a day or two of negotiation and hard bargaining. On the morning of the journey to Feres Bét everyone must be up early, preferably before sunrise. There is much to be done and there are many opinions about how best to do it. The loads must be apportioned among the pack animals by rival owners, each vying for the lightest loads. This accomplished, the foreigners' oddly-shaped packages and boxes must be slung and strapped in equal loads on both sides of the traditional packsaddle. The delays and the confusion seem endless, but at last, by eight or nine in the morning, all is in readiness. The last of many kind offers of coffee and breakfast has been declined and the procession files out along Jiga's main trail. Soon the rows of square, tin-roofed wattle-and-daub houses have been left behind. The trail rises gently through the less densely populated groves of eucalyptus trees that surround most modern Ethiopian towns, providing a ready supply of firewood and building timber. Leaving the trees, the broad earthen trail comes out on the open farmlands.

The air is clear and cool. Spirits are high. The trek across the low plains to the foothills will be over before midday, when the heat of the sun becomes intense and the ever-present flies most bothersome. If all goes well, the party will reach Feres Bét before dark; and an uncomfortable night in the open or on the floor of the hut of some half-unwilling peasant will be avoided. This thought cheers the merchants who have joined the party to enjoy the safety of numbers, for in Dega Damot banditry is not yet a thing of the past.[6] The pace is brisk. A driver to the rear sings out at a laggard pack horse trying to supplement his breakfast from a farmer's unfenced barley field.

6. The leading bandits in the Dega Damot region at the time of fieldwork were outlaws (*shifta*, sing.); usually men who had fallen afoul of the law while defending their property or their honor. Not all outlaws, to be sure, engaged in banditry, some being content to stay home and tend their farms, secure in the knowledge that they could slip off into the forested ravines in the unlikely event that the undermanned police force should actually venture out of Feres Bét in search of them. During the entire period of my fieldwork a pack train carrying my goods was robbed only once. According to custom, I was fully recompensed by the members of the community where the robbery occurred.

A mile or so out of Jiga the procession passes a recently built church surrounded by a grove of young eucalyptus trees. The church is round, as are all the churches of Gojjam, but its tin roof testifies to its recent origin. It was built by a man of Jiga who attained great success as a merchant. Formerly most churches were built by successful military lords.

The procession travels on across the rolling plain. The sun is well above the ridge that rises across the Silver (*Birr*) River to the east. The mountains ahead do not seem to get much closer. Here and there amidst the farmlands and pastures are scattered hamlets, the houses set apart from one another by from fifty to a few hundred yards. Most of the houses are round now, with thatched roofs, but a few glinting tin roofs are still to be seen. Fewer than the hamlets are the plumes of sacred trees, often cedar, that mark the presence of a parish church. The trail does not often approach a settlement, for Gojjam farmers do not like to build near a major thoroughfare unless they are forced by nature to do so.

Sometime before noon the travelers ford the Silver River near the site where British and Italian forces skirmished during the liberation of Ethiopia in 1940. The "time of the enemy," as it is known, is past but not forgotten. In 1966 five people were killed by a bomb that had lain in the soft ground near the Silver River for a quarter-century before the farmer who discovered it tried to open it with his ploughshare. The war was a period of critical importance in Gojjam, for its end marked the end of traditional rule and the beginning of modern administration in the province. It was also a politically formative period, for many of the men who have held political power in the postwar period as district governors, subdistrict governors, and neighborhood judges are men who carried on guerrilla warfare against the Italians and who were rewarded with rank and office by Emperor Haile Selassie upon his return from exile in England.

After crossing the Silver River, the trail rises gently into a deep valley lying between the steep slopes of two mountain ridges. The valley floor narrows and the trail passes close to a number of homesteads. A trail branches to the left, to Mahidera Maryam, one of Dega Damot's numerous small monasteries, perched on a ledge halfway up the ridge. The main trail slopes up more steeply, passes the last settlements, and enters a forested ravine that rises abruptly from the end of the valley floor where the two ridges meet.

In the forest it is always dark and cool. Shaggy gray moss hangs from the limbs of the giant trees, and ferns abound on the ground. The bird calls are different here from those of the open countryside. The colobus monkey may be seen, and the leopard though not seen is present. The Amhara, however, are more apprehensive of the invisible beings they believe inhabit the forest than of its animals. These include the invisible spirit-people (*zar*, sing.) who occasionally leap on humans in wild places like forests, and possess them; and anchoritic monks who have become so holy that they can turn themselves into animals.[7] In the presence of the forest, men are less given to shouting and singing out the songs of the trail. They are also short of breath; the trail is too steep and slippery for a mounted horse or mule, and everyone must proceed on foot.

After an hour or so of steady climbing, the trail emerges from the valley onto the slopes of the central plateau, and the heavy forest ends. There follows what seems like an endless succession of farmed terraces and steeper slopes of scrub thorn. On the terraces are isolated homesteads, each well guarded by a dog or two which raise the hue and cry with their barking at the approach of the travelers. Each steep incline seems the last, but proves not to be once the terrace edge is reached.

At last, as the afternoon wears on, the trail comes out on the high plateau, 9,000 feet above sea level and 4,000 feet above Jiga. For the first time on the trip there is a sense of

7. There are countless tales of hunters whose rifles refused to fire upon an unusually colored animal, often a white bushbuck or a colobus monkey, therefore presumed to be in reality a transformed monk. Considering the state of some vintage rifles in the area, the frequency of these tales should perhaps not be surprising.

complete openness; there is no longer any higher ground ahead. The wind is chilling and carries with it none of the rich odors of the lowlands or the forest. To the south, the view is magnificent. The sprawling hamlets, the patchwork fields, the long ridges all spread out below. In the distance the tin roofs of Jiga glint in the late afternoon sun, while etched against the southern horizon are the Galla-inhabited mountains of Wellega province.

The settlement pattern on the high plateau is the same as that on the plains below; again, most homesteads are away from the trail. The pattern of fields is also similar in appearance but there is lush pasturage along the numerous rivulets and streams that drain off the plateau into the wooded ravines.

The trail turns to the east and continues over rolling countryside cut through at several points by the watercourses of larger streams. Finally, in the late afternoon, or, if the trip has been a slow one, after sunset in the gathering dusk, Feres Bét comes into view.

When I first saw it in 1960, Feres Bét with its 101 thatched mud huts huddled together on a knoll astride the plateau watershed was hardly an impressive sight. Yet it was and still is the only nucleated settlement in Dega Damot. The town was "founded" in the early part of this century as a storage center for grains raised on state fields (*hudad*, sing.) in the region. During the Italian occupation, Feres Bét was a walled cantonment from which Italian soldiers sallied forth to skirmish inconclusively with the patriots. It was only after the war that the town became an effective administrative center.

By 1961 Feres Bét, with a total population of just over three hundred people, was beginning to outgrow its low stone walls. Only its five government buildings had tin roofs. About one-third of the town's households were those of administrative officials, policemen, or schoolteachers. Another third of the households belonged to tailors and market traders, while the remaining households were those of single women catering to the needs of men who came to town on administrative matters. There were no stores or shops in the town, and the weekly market, held every Saturday, met, as it still does, on a rocky hillside half a mile outside town.

When I returned to Feres Bét in 1966, the town had expanded well beyond its walls; there were a dozen or so square, tin-roofed new buildings along its main trail, and several self-styled shopkeepers who sold goods in their homes. Most striking of all was a thick growth of twenty-foot-high eucalyptus trees, formerly absent, which gave the town a modern cast. For the most part, however, this book is not concerned with the people of Feres Bét but with the farmers who live in the countryside beyond its walls.

An elder of Dega Damot making the journey from Jiga to Feres Bét can see in the natural and man-made features of the local landscape many tangible manifestations of the institutions through which he and his neighbors are united with and divided from one another, as well as manifestations of the legendary events which they believe account for the origins and interrelations of these institutions.

To him each homestead is a household, the most important unit of social and economic organization in the day-to-day life of the peasant. Each group of scattered homesteads is a hamlet (*mender*), a clustering of neighbors bound to one another by many interwoven ties of voluntary cooperation, friendship, and god-parenthood. Each church represents to him the abode of a holy ark symbolizing one of the religious figures of the Ethiopic church and influencing by its peculiar character the tempo and quality of life in the parish it defines. In a barren rock-strewn hillside he sees an important marketplace where once a week great throngs from the mountains and the plains gather to exchange their produce, their greetings, and their news. In the networks of broad and narrow paths that interlace homestead, hamlet, church, and market he sees the repetitive movement of people as they ebb and flow across the countryside in accordance with the daily, weekly, monthly, and yearly cycles of their lives. Finally, if he knows the locality well, an elder can see in the paths, streams, and other features of the landscape the historically chartered boundaries of parishes, neighborhoods (corresponding to estates of gwilt), and the complex, nesting land divisions of the rist system.

Not all of these institutions through which Damotians are tied to one another are equally relevant to a discussion of the rist system, though few are untouched by it. In the following two chapters, however, I am particularly concerned with an elder's position in the household and in the institutions that define his relationship with the local community, parish, and neighborhood. My primary object throughout the discussion is to show how his position in each of these fields of social relations generates and shapes his interest in acquiring rist land and sets bounds on his ability to do so.

3. The Household

The household is the social group that most affects the personal welfare, the day-to-day activities, and the community standing of the people of Dega Damot. It is of particular importance to this book because it is the organizational unit by which land is managed and exploited. In Amhara land-theory, of course, rist rights are ultimately vested in the descent group and are held by its individual living members. In practice, however, it is normally only those members who are household heads who actually control the use of rist land.

The Amharic word *béteseb*, which I am translating as household or domestic group, literally means "house of people." In Dega Damot it refers to any group of people who live together in a single homestead and who depend on a common source for food. Households, in this most general sense, vary considerably in size, composition, and source of income. It might be possible to construct an "average" or "typical" household on the basis of this observable variation, but to do so would be to misrepresent the Amhara view and, I believe, social reality as well. In an important sense, the only type of household considered complete is the farming household with its own homestead, oxen, equipment, lands, and labor force. Households which lack one or more of these elements because of poverty or position in the domestic cycle may still be households in the minimal sense of the word, but they are incomplete.

A single house is sufficient to constitute a homestead, though two or three are preferred. A yoke of oxen can plough the ordinary holding, but unless the household has other cattle, including calves and perhaps a third ox as well, its agricultural situation is precarious. The most expensive and important agricultural implement is the iron-tipped scratch-plow, though the homestead must be fitted out with the numerous mortars, mills, baskets, mats, jars, pots, and other utensils necessary in food preparation. It is more difficult to specify minimal land requirements, but I would estimate that the produce of between two and a half and three acres of land is required to support an adult for a year in a household.[1]

The minimal labor force required by a complete farming household must include a man who is responsible for ploughing and most other agricultural tasks, and a woman who is responsible for the management of food preparation and most other routine activities at the homestead as well as for the provision of firewood and water. If the household is to thrive and its head is to take his place in the community as an elder, it is only slightly less essential that the household have three other positions in its labor force. It should have a boy between the age of seven and twelve (a girl, though not favored, can be substituted) to herd the household's livestock; a girl over seven or a young divorcée to help the mistress of the house with her work; and a young man between twelve and about twenty to assist the man of the house with the arduous year-round task of ploughing.

Ideally, the household is also the type of kinship unit anthropologists call a nuclear family. First marriage, the only marriage which is marked with a large celebration, is expected to result in the creation of a new household through the pooling of the new couple's labor, the cattle given to them in equal value by their respective parental households, and eventually by the pooling of their rist rights as well. The master and mistress of the household are thus expected to be husband and wife. The herdboy and the plowboy are ideally

1. This estimate is based on observations of household size and land utilization in households that appeared to be near the lower limit of viability. It was not based on the estimated consumption of food since this method would result in an unrealistically low figure which does not reflect the many other expenses involved in support.

sons, and the girl who helps the mistress of the house is her daughter. Other children may, of course, be born to the couple, but the family remains nuclear in structure, for marriage is monogamous; married children, with a few exceptions discussed below, do not remain in the household of their parents.[2]

Despite the fact that the core members of a household are ideally, and often in reality, the members of a nuclear family, there are several reasons why it would be misleading to merge the concepts and refer to the Damotian household as a family.[3] One reason is that, as will become clear, the Amharic term *béteseb* has no direct reference to kinship ties or to a unit with transgenerational continuity. Another reason is that familial kinship roles must be analytically distinguished from household roles even though the former frequently serve as recruitment roles for the latter. A boy brought into a household to fill the vacant role of herdboy may hope to be generously rewarded for his service when he marries, but he does not, by entering the household, become the son of the household's head.

A final, closely related reason for not identifying the household as a family, and one that is particularly germane to this book, is that the composition of a household, the strength of its labor force, and its community standing in relation to other households are not determined or limited by familial or kinship considerations. The composition, the standing, and, to some degree, the size of the household are dependent on the managerial talents of its head, on his ability to maintain orderly relations among its members, to organize its agricultural activities, and to gain and retain control over rist land.

2. The neolocal residence pattern of Gojjam contrasts with that of some other Amhara regions such as the Menz distinct of Shoa province, where patri-virilocal extended families predominate.

3. The confusion of household and family in the anthropological literature is widespread. It is well exemplified in G. P. Murdock's influential discussion of the nuclear family (1949: 1–12). At the same time the importance of maintaining the distinction between family and household has been noted by a number of writers including Fortes (1966) and Bender (1967, 1971).

No matter how talented its head may be, a farming household does not become very large. In a group of 282 households representing entire hamlets from four parishes it was found that only six, or slightly over 2 percent, had more than seven members; none had more than twelve.[4] The fact that married children do not remain in parental households contributes to the limitation of household size, but it does not account for it, since household heads with sufficient resources can bring additional members into their households if they wish. Nevertheless, even household heads with from two to three times the mean or modal holding of rist land and two or more good teams of plow oxen seldom have households exceeding seven members.

Most men, including lay farmers, clerics, and even neighborhood judges, hope to head the type of complete farming household I have described; indeed many men realize this aspiration during at least a part of their elderhood. Nevertheless, there is another type of household that is far more admirable and prestigious in the eyes of Damotians than the farming household. This is the household of the officeholding lord. Traditionally these vastly expanded households, modeled ultimately on the courtly household of the emperor, had a central place in Amhara political organization. They varied from scores to hundreds of members, according to the authority and hence the greatness of the household's master, and their internal organization was intimately bound up with the way he administered the land and people under his control.

Today these vast domestic establishments, like the tribute system that supported them and the political system of which they were an integral part, are but a fading memory. At the time of my fieldwork the only household in Dega Damot that took the great man's household as its model was that of the district governor, and it, with its two dozen or so members

4. In a survey of 282 households, it was found that 12 had 1 member, 58 had 2 members, 60 had 3 members, 63 had 4 members, 49 had 5 members, 17 had 6 members, 12 had 7 members, 3 had 8 members, 1 had 9 members, none had 10 or 11 members, and 2 had 12 or more members.

and its sporadic feasts, was often the object of invidious comparisons with the households of prewar governors. It is thus the less glorious farming household that is of primary interest in this book. The remainder of this section presents a more concrete ethnographic picture of the farming household; of its homestead, of its lands, of its farming, of the routine activities of its members, and of its cyclical development through time.

Though geographically some homesteads stand in isolation, most are loosely grouped or strung out along some minor pathway. In any case homesteads are set apart from one another beyond the range of normal conversation. Usually, too, they are so situated that their dooryard areas are hidden from one another by a grove of trees, a rocky outcropping, or the orientation of their buildings.

The homestead of a successful elder ideally includes three buildings: a cattle house (*yekebt bét*), a reception house (*ilfiñ*), and a living house (*menorīa bét*). Usually, however, the functions of all three buildings are combined in the living house. This circular, wattle and daub, all-purpose structure has two concentric walls dividing it into an inner room and an outer doughnut-shaped area between the walls. The inner room serves both as a general living quarter and as a reception room. The outer area is divided into sections used for sheltering livestock, storage, cooking, and sleeping.

An adult must stoop to enter the doorway in the outer wall of the house, for the eaves of the thatched roof are brought low against the driving dampness of the rainy-season winds. Inside the outer doorway to the right is the entrance to the *gwada,* the section of the outer area where calves, lambs, and other young livestock are housed. To the left is the entrance of the *gaṭ*, the section where the larger animals are kept at night. Ahead is the windowless, dimly lit central room where the members of the household spend most of their indoor hours. A hearth sunken in the earthen floor marks the center of the room. Beyond it, recessed in the wall opposite the doorway, is the bed where the household head and his wife sleep. A low mud bench runs along the wall, from the right of the doorway to the bed halfway around the room.

It is on this bench that visitors are carefully seated in accordance with their secular authority, their church office, and their age, the highest-ranking guests nearest the bed and the lowest near the door. When honored guests are present, members of the household other than adult men leave the area between the bench and the central hearth. Young men may move across to the less prestigious "lower" bench that runs a quarter of the way around the room to the left of the door. Women, children, and young boys retreat into the kitchen area of the room, the quadrant running from the bed to the end of the lower-ranking bench. In part this symbolizes the lower status of women and children in formal situations, and in part it is required by the fact that, when guests visit, a meal must be prepared for them.

In the kitchen area of the house and in the section of the outer room adjacent to it, foodstuffs and the many utensils employed in their preparation are kept. Here, too, are the water jars that must be filled daily at the nearest spring and, in festive season, a great jar of barley beer or of hydromel. A few hundred pounds of grain are also kept in the kitchen area ready to be ground into flour and baked into the thin, flat, pancake-like bread that, along with many varieties of stew, constitutes the major part of the household's diet. Most of the household's grain supply, however, is stored outside the house in small thatched granaries and subterranean storage pits.

The land cultivated by a household consists of a number of dispersed strip-fields scattered over the countryside within two or three miles of the homestead. Most farming households cultivate at least four fields that average about three acres each.[5] One household in four cultivates more than eighteen acres, and one out of seven cultivates more than thirty acres, while probably not more than one out of fifty households cultivates more than forty-five acres.

The significance of a field to the household depends on whether the field is held in tenancy and on the quality of its

5. By farming household I mean a household with at least an adult man and woman, a pair of oxen and a plough, and one which derives the major part of its subsistence from farming.

soil, as well as on its size. For most farming households tenancy is not of great importance; in a given year only one household in four cultivates any fields in tenancy.[6] Thus for most farming households land cultivated and land held do not differ greatly. For some household heads, however, tenancy arrangements assume greater importance. Young men who have not gained control over much land, and energetic men with healthy oxen and perhaps a plowboy to help them, may cultivate several fields in tenancy, while households without oxen or a ploughman are forced to give their fields to tenants. Men with large holdings characteristically give much of their land to tenants. The main disadvantage of cultivating land in tenancy is, of course, the lower rate of return. In the commonest arrangement, the tenant, who must supply half the seed, both oxen, and all the labor, receives from one-half to three-quarters of the harvest depending on the type of grain being raised.

The farmers of Dega Damot, like farmers everywhere, carefully distinguish differences in the fertility, quality, drainage, and exposure of their fields. Here, however, I am concerned with only those Damotian categorizations of land which have major ecological significance and which are explicitly recognized in customary land law. The most important distinction in these respects is between fertilized (*kels*) land which has been enriched with manure, ashes, and other house refuse, and unfertilized or unimproved land (*bodda*). Fertilized fields are usually located in the vicinity of homesteads in long-settled hamlets, while unfertilized land is usually farther away from homesteads, often in former pastureland that has more recently been brought into cultivation. In the highland area I surveyed, 30 percent of all fields were fertilized and 60 percent were unfertilized.

About half of the other fields are newly cleared land on which trees have beeen felled and burned to produce a soil that is very productive for a few seasons. Such land constitutes a distinct category, termed *jibasid* after the grain which

6. Young married sons often cultivate fields of their father in return for a share of the crop. Following Amhara usage, I am not considering this arrangement tenancy.

is normally grown on it. *Jibasid* is of ecological importance only in those few parishes which are still partly forested, and today is usually found only on slopes too steep to cultivate except with the hoe. Most of the remaining fields (only about 3 percent of all highland fields) are kitchen gardens adjacent to homesteads and small, spring-irrigated onion patches.

The ecological importance of fertilized land to the household rests on the land's higher annual yield and the fact that it can be cultivated continuously, without fallowing. Farmers estimated that the type of barley they usually sow on their fertilized fields in the highlands yields from five to seven times the seed sown in a year, while the only kind of barley that will grow on unfertilized fields yields three to five times the seed sown. Fertilized land thus produces on the average about one and one-half times more barley, the staple crop used for both bread and beer in the highlands, than unfertilized land.

The most important advantage of fertilized land is that it can produce a crop every year while unfertilized land must be fallowed every other year or, if the land is very poor, two years out of three. Fertilized land thus contributes more to most households' grain supply over the years than unfertilized land. There is variation in this respect, however, from household to household, and there is also variation in some households from year to year as they alternately have the larger portion of their unfertilized land in cultivation or in fallow. This is due to the fact that a farmer cannot choose when to fallow a field but must submit to the regime of fallowing established for the larger tract in which his field is located. A final advantage of fertilized land is that in recognition of the value added by the holder it is not as likely as is unfertilized land to be reassigned to someone else by descent corporation leaders.

The crops a Damotian household grows on its land vary with soil type, drainage, exposure, and, above all, altitude, but the basic pattern of agriculture is the same throughout the district. Staple cereals are cultivated everywhere on land that has been plowed three or four times to ensure depth of cultivation and sufficient granulation of the earth. In the lowlands the successive plowings must follow upon one another within a few weeks or the ground will become caked and hard again. In the highlands, where I carried out most of my intensive research, the preparation of a field may be spread over as long as ten months in unfertilized fields. Weeding most crops once or twice during their growth is held to be desirable, but many households do not weed their fields at all in a normal year. After they mature, the cereals are reaped by groups of men and women using hand sickles, threshed under the feet of oxen or horses, winnowed, and stored.

In Dega Damot, as everywhere in Amhara country, three altitude zones are recognized: lowlands (*qolla*), midlands (*weyna dega*), and highlands (*dega*).[7] In the lowland zone the staple crops are maize (*zea mays*), pearl millet (*pennisetum typhoideum*), and sorghum (*sorghum vulgare*). In the midlands these crops give way to wheat (*triticum* sp.); numerous varieties of barley (*hordeum* sp.); and *ṭéff* (*eragrostis teff*), a type of domesticated grass seed universally favored by upper-class Amhara for bread flour. In the highlands several species of barley and the Irish potato reign supreme. In addition to the cereals and the potato, a number of pulses, oil seeds, vegetables, and spices are grown in Dega Damot, the highland zone once again having the least variety.

Higher-status household heads try to obtain fields in more than one altitude zone in order to diversify their crops and add variety to their meals. Less fortunate household heads obtain some produce from other zones at the weekly markets and through private exchange agreements with trade partners.

Though a household head's status is closely related to his control over land, and his diet to the types of crops he raises, he is accounted wealthy (*habtam*) or poor (*deha*) primarily by his livestock. In part this is because livestock are a more visible and tangible manifestation of material success than widely scattered plots of land. In part it is due to the fact that livestock, unlike land, can be readily converted to cash

7. All the land of Dega Damot district falls into these three zones. In addition to them, however, two other zones are recognized: *choqé*, the frequently frost-covered high mountains to the east; and *berha*, which in Damot refers to the sweltering climatic zone found at the floor of the Blue Nile gorge.

through sale. Wealth, or perhaps more accurately riches, is desired, but is considered in a sense to be illicit or illegitimate unless it is accompanied by high status based on the possession of authority and, usually, of land.

The most important type of livestock, as has been noted, are cattle, without which a household cannot plow its lands. They are kept at all three altitude zones of Dega Damot. The herds of farming households are small; a man who has two pairs of oxen and three or four cows is accounted wealthy in cattle. It is not cattle, however, but sheep and goats that are most commonly sold for cash. Both kinds of animals are kept in all parts of the district, but sheep predominate on the grassy highlands while goats thrive on the browse of the middle and lower zones. Household flocks of these animals commonly vary from five to twenty head. Donkeys, which are used as pack animals, and horses, used for pack and saddle, are kept by some households, while mules are regularly kept only by men of substance. Chickens, cats, dogs, and bees are also kept by most households though they are of minor importance.

Many household heads keep a small stretch of land near their homesteads in pasture for the supplemental grazing of their cattle, particularly of their plow oxen during periods of hard work. Most pastures, however, are used in common by all the households of a hamlet. These larger pastures always belong to the estate of a descent group but they are usually land which has not been divided in the name of the first ancestral holder's children. Such undivided descent-group lands are referred to as *shī belo* or "[that which is] eaten by one thousand."

Finally, in addition to arable land for cultivation and pasturage for its livestock, a household must have access to wood for cooking and construction. Wood from the thorn forest of the mountainside may be cut by anyone resident in the parish in which the forest is located. Trees and bamboo planted on the cleared land, often near homesteads, are held by individual households. Most firewood is gathered in the forest, and most of the larger trees used in house construction have been planted.

As an economic unit the household is dependent on other households for the exchange of labor and on the market for the exchange of goods. At the time of my fieldwork, the household had not yet been caught up to any great extent in the cash nexus of the modern Ethiopian economy. Most of the staple crops raised by a household are consumed by its members and their guests. The sale of crops has not been regarded as an important source of cash in most of the district because of the high cost of transportation by pack train. One of the most successful elders in the Feres Bét area, who cultivates over seventy acres, reported that he had sold Eth. $80 ($32 U.S.) worth of barley in 1961 but added ruefully that he did not expect to sell much in 1962 "because it is a good year and everyone will have enough."[8]

The most important sources of cash in Dega Damot are honey, hides, skins, a little *nug* seed (an indigenous oil seed), and, at the approach of major holidays, sheep and goats. These forms of produce are bought by local part-time traders and sold either in the towns along the road or, in the case of honey, directly to traders in Addis Ababa.

The cash expenditures of most households are rather low even by African standards. One of the few fixed expenses for most households is the land tax, of which more will be said in chapter 10. The principal manufactured items bought by the ordinary household are soap, a few utensils, and, for men and boys, pants and jackets. Most households have one or two glasses, a few spoons, a demitasse or two for coffee, and an iron dish for cooking stew. In 1960 only government officials, teachers, and a few noblemen had diesel fuel burning lamps, fashioned of tin cans, and only the district governor had a radio, which did not work. In 1966 there was a marked increase in the number of oil lamps and there were perhaps a dozen transistor radios, most of them owned by government workers in the town of Feres Bét.

Small amounts of cash are also required for certain other items, the most important of which are bars of rock salt and coffee beans. Cash is also used to buy baskets, pottery, condi-

8. One Ethopian dollar was worth $.40 U.S.

ments, cotton (from the lowlands), and other regional products. The cotton is carded, combed, and spun by the women of most households in their spare time. The thread thus produced is then taken to members of the low-status weaver community where, in return for a payment, it is woven into the white cloth invariably used for women's clothing and men's capes. The household head must arrange in similar fashion to have his leather work done by a tanner and his iron work done by the local smith.

The daily activities of the household head and his dependents are shaped by the demands of agriculture and by the holiday calendar of the parish church. On an ordinary weekday a man rises between six and seven in the morning. If he attended church school as a boy and is therefore quasi-literate, he may begin his day by reading a psalm. After this he sends his livestock to pasture with his herdboy or, if he has none, drives them to join the larger hamlet herd he tends by turn with his neighbors. Upon returning to his homestead, he takes his breakfast, unless it is a Wednesday, a Friday, or one of the many other fast days prescribed by the church.[9] By eight or nine o'clock he is ready to prepare for the main work of the day. If he goes to the fields to plow or reap, or to the forest to cut wood, he is likely to remain away from the homestead until three or four in the afternoon. He may have his midday meal brought to him in the fields or he may eat upon his return, but in either case he is likely to rest for a while after returning to his house. In the late afternoon or early evening he must see to the return of the livestock. He takes his evening meal after dark and usually retires for the night by nine or nine-thirty.

There are many days on which plowing, reaping, cutting wood, and digging in the ground are forbidden by religious

9. The Wednesday and Friday fasts as well as the Lenten fast are kept by everyone above the age of about twelve except new mothers and the sick. There are a number of other major fasts that are kept only by clerics and older people. Those who adhere strictly to all the fasts of the Ethiopic church must fast over two hundred days a year! On a fast day no meat or other animal product, including milk, butter, and eggs, may be taken at any time, and no food at all may be eaten before about one in the afternoon.

rules. These include every Saturday and Sunday, the nine major saints' days a month, the saint's day of the local parish even if it is not one of these nine, and the major annual holydays. Heavy work is also forbidden within a parish from the time any parishioner dies until he is buried, which should be on the day of death if possible. On these days a man may occupy himself in many ways. He may attend church or go to market. He may enjoy himself as a spectator or advisor at some local neighborhood judge's court. He may attend one of the frequent large mourning ceremonies held on holidays to commemorate recent deaths in an area of five or ten parishes. He may also go to discuss matters of business with one of his artisans, visit with his friends, or simply do light work around the homestead.

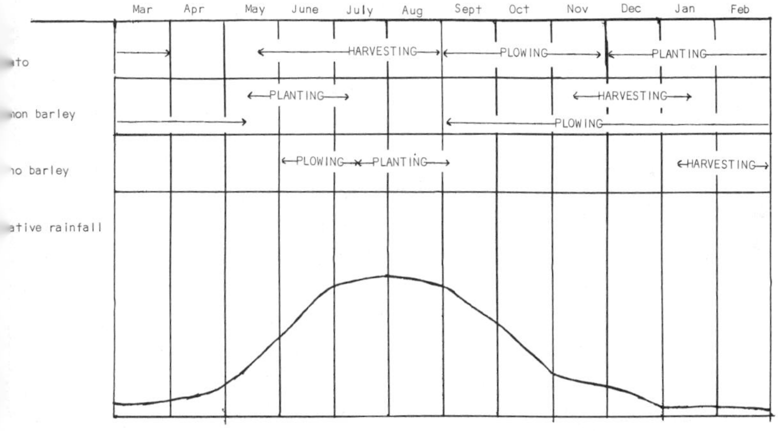

Fig. 1. Major seasonal agricultural activities on the high plateau

The rhythm of social life, like agricultural activity, changes with the seasons and is punctuated by the annual cycle of religious fasts, feasts, and holidays. The major seasonal division of the year is into a dry season (*bega*) and a rainy season (*kremt*) (see fig. 1). In the *dega*, or highlands, showers may occur in any month, but rainfall is insignificant for agricultural purposes until sometime in late April. By the latter part of June the heavy rains have commenced and will continue until mid-September. Rainy season downpours are not usually violent in the highlands, but the rain falls for weeks on end with little respite. Warmer, moisture-laden winds from the lowlands sweep up the valleys and condense into a thick mist, precipitating a steady, bone-chilling drizzle, even on days when the sun is shining below. In the lowlands there is seldom rainfall before April. From mid-June on, it may rain continuously for several days at a time, but normally mornings are sunny, with heavy downpours in the afternoons and evenings.

The onset of the rains marks the end of the post-Easter period of feasts and weddings. The first part of the rainy season, from mid-May till early June, brings with it a time of hard work. The fields which are to receive common barley have already been plowed three or four times in the dry season months (see fig. 1). Now they must be plowed again in preparation for sowing. When the soil it ready, a strip of land ten feet wide and as long as the field is marked out with the plow. Members of the household move down the strip, breaking large clumps of soil and spreading the barley broadcast. After two or three traces have been sown, they are plowed again to cover the seed. Even before all his common barley is in the ground, a farmer must begin plowing other fields in preparation for planting his other important staple crop, *mesno* barley.

At the height of the rains, during July and August, work is lighter. The only important agricultural activity is plowing land for *mesno* barley. Flatlands turn to mud, marshlands are flooded, each ravine becomes a brook, and each brook a raging torrent to be forded only in the right places and with care. Travel is difficult and unpleasant, though never impossible. There is much less visiting than during the dry season. Long hours are spent in the smoky hut enjoying the comparative warmth of the small fire in the middle of the dirt floor. The only major religious holiday that marks this period is the Assumption of the Virgin Mary, preceded by sixteen days of fasting and worship.

In poorer households the latter part of the rainy season is a hungry time of year; there may be only one meal a day. Potatoes, not a highly favored food, constitute an important part of the humble household's diet.

In September the rains begin to abate. Heavy showers continue sporadically until November, or even December in the highlands, but their frequency and duration decrease. Food is still not abundant. The joy expressed on the two great holidays that fall at this time of the year, New Year's, or St. John's, day and Mesqel, the celebration of the finding of the true cross by St. Helena, is associated more with a sense of relief and of renewal "with the flowers," than with the feasting that normally accompanies all major holidays. In the midlands and lowlands the harvest has already begun.

From mid-November until February is the coldest time of the year. At 11,000 feet in Feres Bét, ice is occasionally found on pools of water on crisp December mornings. With the end of the rains the crops mature, and by mid-November the first fields of common barley are ready for reaping. From then until mid-February, when the last of the *mesno* barley has been harvested and the potatoes planted, is the second period of hard work in the year.

The early part of this period is one of hard work and little festivity, for December is the month of the Christmas fast. After Christmas, by contrast, the pace of social and festive life increases greatly. There are major holidays for parishes dedicated to Mary and Michael, holidays generally attended by people from other parishes as well. The religious climax of this period is Epiphany, when the ark of each church is taken in solemn procession to the nearest river, where it is watched throughout the night by joyful, singing clergy.

The harvest is mostly in, the weather is clear, the trails are dry. This is a season for visiting friends and relatives and for horse racing and jousting (*gugs*) among the young men. It is also a time of early weddings. Most weddings, however, take place later, after Lent.

The round of feasts and festivities comes to a dramatic halt with the beginning of the fifty-seven day Lenten fast sometime in February or early March, depending on the year.

The Lenten fast is the longest and most strictly adhered to of all the fasts. It is kept by virtually all persons above the age of eight or ten and, like all fasts, prohibits the consumption of meat, milk, eggs, or any other animal product and also prohibits eating anything before noon.

With Easter and the end of the Lenten fast there begins a second period of intense social activity. There are no fast days, not even the Wednesday and Friday fasts which occur throughout the rest of the year. Eating and drinking are heavy, quarrels are common, and wedding feasts frequent. Until the rains begin, agricultural work is relatively light. Fully as much time is spent on house-building as on all forms of agriculture; old houses must be replaced, all houses must be readied for the coming rains, and married sons who have been living with their fathers for two years now move out and establish their own homesteads. With the renewal of the rains the tempo of social life dwindles and the work load increases. The agricultural cycle has begun once again.

Each year the seasonal activities of the household are repeated. Gradually, however, with the passage of the years, the structure of the household changes; for its composition and completeness as a farming unit are a function of the domestic cycle that begins with the marriage and ends with the death or senility of its head as well as a function of his success as an elder in the community.

The first marriage of a boy and girl is expected, if successful, to lead to the founding of a new household. This expectation as well as the bilateral character and comparative flexibility of kinship ties in Damotian social organization is reflected in the way first marriages are arranged and celebrated. Boys first marry in their late teens or early twenties; girls at twelve or thirteen, ideally just before menarche. Usually the bride and groom are not acquainted prior to their wedding; though there is no formal rule of hamlet or parish exogamy, marriages between households of the same community are not favored.[10] In any case first marriages are always arranged.

10. In part this is so that disputes following divorce will not disrupt the community and in part, as will become clear in chapter 8, it is so that the bride and groom and their children will have access to a more widely dispersed set of rist rights.

There are three phases in the arrangement of a first marriage. The first is the matching of the bride and groom. Here the main concerns of those responsible for the arrangements, in addition to observing church rules of exogamy (discussed in chapter 8 below), are that their child's mate should be from a household of good character, should be untainted by leprosy or the suspicion of witchcraft, and should have rist land or at least potentially useful rist rights. Once tentative agreement upon the match has been reached, negotiations enter the second phase, the property agreement. The object here is to make certain that equal amounts of moveable property will be given to the bride and groom to enable them to start their new household. Cattle are the most important form of property, but horses, donkeys, mules, sheep, and small sums of money (and, in the past, slaves) may also be given.[11] After the property agreement has been reached, two men are chosen to represent the interests of the bride and groom respectively in future marital disputes or divorce proceedings, and the banns are read after mass in the churchyard. There remains only the final phase, the wedding.

The wedding is an occasion for feasting on a scale surpassed only at memorial feasts for the dead. Simultaneous but separate feasts must be given at the homesteads of the bride and groom. To each are invited friends, kinsmen, and, above all, neighbors. Most of the guests contribute food and drink to the feast, and these contributions are carefully recorded against the day when they must be reciprocated. Guests who do not expect to reciprocate the invitation, especially high-status guests, help defray the expenses of the wedding with gifts of money.

The primary responsibility for arranging the marriage, providing the dowry of cattle, and sponsoring the wedding feast falls upon the heads of the households in which the bride and groom have been raised since the age of six or seven. Ideally, of course, these heads are the respective fathers. The

11. The formal agreement concerning property is made outdoors on neutral ground and is witnessed by a number of elders. At a later date, after the wedding, the elders must gather again to view the livestock in question and make adjustments for minor discrepancies in their apparent worth.

mothers, if still married to the fathers, are also very actively involved in decisions concerning the marriage of their children. Indeed half of the cattle endowment given the marrying child is considered to come from the mother's half interest in the household herd.

A parent with whom the prospective bride or groom is not living when the marriage is arranged should be consulted, but he (or she) cannot override the guardian's decisions unless he is prepared to assume a share of the marriage costs. I do not have sufficient data on this point but it is my impression that mothers are more apt than fathers to exercise their option to take an active part in arranging and sponsoring the marriage of a child who has not lived with them very much since the age of six or seven. Men generally say that they expect to sponsor the marriages of only those children who have "served" them in their households, regardless of whether they are their own children.[12]

The bilateral character of Amhara kinship is reflected in the equal and nearly symmetrical roles played by the parental households of the bride and groom.[13] At the same time the

12. Service in this sense is something a man's own children also owe him and something a man owes his lord in expectation of eventual reward rather than salary. Well-to-do households sometimes hire a poor boy or girl to do menial tasks in return for board and keep and in some instances a yearly sum of money. Such servants, unlike children fully incorporated into household work roles, cannot expect the household head to marry them off.

13. The bilateral nature of Amhara kinship is reflected in Amhara kinship terminology. In referential terminology for consanguineal kinsmen (given below), for example, generation and lineality are always distinguished, sex is distinguished only in ego's own and the first ascending generation, and no distinction is ever made between ego's mother's and father's kinsmen. The consanguineal kin terms of reference are:

lij	(ego's son or daughter)
wendim	(brother)
ihit	(sister)
abbat	(father)
innat	(mother)
aggot	(father's or mother's brother)
akist	(father's or mother's sister)
ayat	(father's or mother's father or mother)
qedmayat	(any of the eight great-grandparents)

For an extended discussion of Amhara kin terms and their use, see S. Hoben (1972).

degree to which rules of kinship govern marriage arrangements is low in comparison with most other African societies. The fathers or guardians of the bride and groom are not expected to consult their kinsmen about the prospective marriage except to ascertain that it does not violate rules of exogamy. Furthermore, kinsmen are not concerned with the transfer of marriage cattle, nor do they play any special role in the actual celebration of the wedding that distinguishes them from close friends and neighbors.

Though marriage in Dega Damot is certainly of interest to kinsmen it is not primarily the concern of kin groups. It does not, as in many other African societies, celebrate the transfer of reproductive rights in and jural control of the bride from her kin group to that of the groom.

In a limited sense, the right to discipline a woman for misconduct is transferred from her father or guardian to her husband at marriage, but with regard to the ownership of land and moveable property and the right to institute divorce the wife is very much the equal of her husband. In fact the type of marriage arrangement I have described, which is always used for first marriages, is termed *balikkul* or "equal masters" marriage. Nor does marriage greatly affect the status of children born to a union. Children born out of wedlock are bastards (*diqala*) but they suffer no disability with regard to inheritance. Even in cases of admitted adultery the adulterine child inherits land rights from his genitor and not from his pater, and this fact cannot be altered by any process of adoption.

If first marriage does not celebrate a major rearrangement of relations between kin groups, it is nonetheless a major celebration. Most immediately it marks the transition to social adulthood for the bride and groom. It also anticipates the formation of a new household, at first as a budding domestic group within the groom's parental household, and then, if it endures, in a new homestead of its own.

During the first year and one-half or two and one-half years of marriage the newlyweds live in the groom's parental homestead. They do not yet constitute an independent household with its own economic interests. The groom farms along with his father or guardian, and the crops they produce, at least in the first season, are put in the father's storage bins. The bride helps her female affines with the household work much as would any female child her age, except that she is expected to be more shy and reserved, at first, towards the master and mistress of the house. At the end of the second or third agricultural season the young couple take their livestock, their share of the grain they have helped to produce, and move away into a new homestead where they establish an independent if impecunious household.

Not every young married man moves out of the parental household and establishes a new homestead in this way. A youth whose father or guardian is no longer living may stay on with the widow, gradually replacing her in the management of the household and perhaps raising and marrying off his younger siblings as well. A youngest son, if his father is old, may also stay on in the household, assuming authority with his father's senescence or death.

In the years that follow marriage it is hoped that the livestock will multiply, children will be born, and the household will obtain control over an increasing amount of rist land. If all goes well, the household will come to approximate the ideal of the complete farming household. Sooner or later, however, because of ill luck, death, divorce, or the marriage of his sons, a household head with ample resources in land and cattle is likely to find himself without children to fill the positions in his household. It is then that he seeks to bring in children from other households, particularly households of his or his wife's kinsmen, to fill these positions. The most important position of all is that of the plowboy, for unless a man has time to attend moots and courts frequently, as a spectator and a participant, he cannot hope to defend and expand his interest in rist land. The following cases illustrate some of the ways men recruit additional members to their households:

> Molla, a middle-aged man of modest means, lives with his wife and his brother's ten-year-old son. Molla presently

plows jointly with his own son, who has married and established his homestead in a neighboring parish; but anticipating the day when the son will seek greater autonomy, Molla has taken in a son from his brother, who is poor and has many children.

Walé is twenty-five years old and is living with his sixth wife and her twelve-year-old brother. The boy helps Walé with the farmwork. Walé, who has been unusually successful in land litigation for a man of his age, says that, should the boy remain with him, he will sponsor his marriage. Walé's own children, who are young, are living with his fifth wife elsewhere.

Debtera Gété, a man of considerable influence and property, is fifty-five years old and lives with his third wife, two daughters aged seven and ten by his second wife, his father's brother's deceased son's wife, her seventeen-year-old son and his wife, and his mother's father's brother's thirteen-year-old illegitimate son. Debtera Gété sponsored the wedding of the seventeen-year-old boy and expects to marry off the thirteen-year-old as well if he remains in the household.

Old age inevitably brings the household head greater respect in terms of eating and seating precedence and greeting forms, but it does not bring him increased affluence or authority. On the contrary, it is normally a period when his household either declines as a farming establishment or is gradually taken over by the growing domestic group headed by a younger man. An old man too feeble to effectively manage the farming activities of his household may allocate to his children the rent-free use of some of his fields in anticipation of his death. However, he does not legally relinquish his rights until he dies. If he has no plowman living in his household, he must give even the fields he retains to his sons or tenants in return for a share of the crop. Under these circumstances, living as a pensioner, he no longer need trouble himself with keeping many livestock or maintaining a large household. If the old household head has a young married man, perhaps a youngest son, staying on with him, the household may continue to prosper as a farming unit but the young man will gradually assume more authority and the household will gradually change from one identified with the old man to one identified with the young.

The ritual status felt to be most appropriate to an old man (or woman) no longer master of his own affairs or interested in conjugal life is monkhood. The old man who becomes a monk ends his life preparing for death. He must learn what is required of him from the book of monkhood and he must give up his worldly interests. Once more he is allowed to take communion at church, for post-pubescent men and women, excepting only the clergy, are by custom noncommunicants for fear they will violate rules of sexual purity. An old man turned monk may also give up his life in the household and wander from parish to parish, sleeping in the funerary huts found in churchyards. Most old men who become monks, however, continue to live with one of their children or a younger sibling.

The final dissolution of a man's household may be more or less dramatic depending on his position in it at the time of his death. In some cases the passing of a senile old man may be for the most part a ritual occasion with little immediate consequence for the distribution of property or authority. In other cases the sudden death of an elder may bring about the complete breakup of his household, even to the destruction of his homestead so that its timbers may be divided among his heirs. In any case, a man's death signals the final dissolution of the estate of rist land which he has succeeded in bringing together during his lifetime.

The domestic cycle in some form, of course, plays an important part in every peasant society's social organization. What is most distinctive, though by no means unique, about the Damotian domestic cycle I have described is its comparatively low degree of transgenerational continuity. I have tried to make it clear that neither the household, nor the homestead, nor the estate of rist land upon which they depend, are enduring units of social organization in Damot. Equally striking is the weak sense of transgenerational continuity between the kinsmen who make up a household. As I noted previously, the Amharic term *béteseb* (literally, "house people"), which I am glossing as "household," has no direct reference to kinship or to an enduring transgenerational kinship unit.

The weak sense of identity and transgenerational continuity between the kinsmen in a household is also reflected in the absence of any enduring "family name." Children of either sex are addressed by their given name and are distinguished from other people of the same name by the addition of their father's given name.[14] To address someone by his father's name alone is a great insult, implying that the person has no social existence in his own right. Since a household is referred to by the given name of its head and there are a rather limited number of popular names, household names tell little about transgenerational kinship ties between households or their heads.

The Damotian domestic group or household is not primarily a kinship group with a sense of identity and continuity serving as a transgenerational repository of status-honor and economic assets for the members of the community. Nor is it a "natural" familial unit whose size and fortunes are determined primarily by the facts of marriage, birth, death, and inheritance, for neither the members of which it consists nor the land on which it subsists are bound together by invariant rules. It must rather be regarded as an enterprise based in a group of people predominantly linked by ties of kinship, who live together in a single homestead under the authority of a head and work together under his and his wife's direction to exploit the land and livestock under his control.

14. A child initially takes as his father's name the name of his presumed genitor, even if he is an acknowledged adulterine child. He may, however, subsequently become identified with the name of his guardian, often a stepfather, an uncle, or a grandfather, if he is raised in his house from an early age.

4. The Community

The interest a man has in acquiring rist land for the use of his household conflicts with the interests of other household heads. Indeed, with regard to property rights, relations between the household heads in a community are, to a marked degree, characterized by competitiveness, suspicion, and a strong sense of privacy. There are, however, several institutions through which the community's household heads are tied to one another, institutions which thus serve to limit the divisive forces generated by each household's quest for land. The most important of these are the parish and the neighborhood (the former estate of gwilt). Together they define the territorial community and are the subject of this chapter.

In a sense it is misleading to speak of the local community as a bounded unit in Amhara society, for, in the absence of nucleated villages, the diverse types of ties through which household heads are related to one another are not circumscribed very clearly by any single physical or social boundary. In this sense the "local community" could be defined differently from the perspectives of different household heads. Nevertheless, parish and neighborhood give some territorial focus to local Damotian social organization; the parish by providing a focus for religious affairs, and the neighborhood by providing a focus for secular administration.

Parish and church

For most men in most contexts, the parish, a named, bounded territory under the ecclesiastical jurisdiction of a church, is the most important territorial unit of affiliation and identification. Fellow parishioners have a sense of common identity in opposition to people from other parishes; they have a sense of unity among themselves based on their common dependence on their church's ark, and they are mutually interdependent in their differentiated positions as laymen and clerics.

Physically, parishes vary in size from under two to over five square miles, and, though they also vary considerably in shape and topography, it is seldom more than an hour's walk from the farthest homestead to the church; usually it is much less. Parish boundaries, which consist of ravines, streams, and paths, are usually clearly defined, and boundary disputes are uncommon. The average population of the fourteen parishes I crudely censused was 450 persons with variations from under 150 to over 1,600. Today the partitioning of the land and population of Dega Damot into parishes is complete.

The religious and social center of a parish is its church, a circular stone and wood building consisting of three concentric rooms. The building is surrounded by a wooded churchyard which, in turn, is encircled by a low stone wall. Usually there is also a small building on the eastern side of the churchyard for the storage of church properties and another small building or shelter over the gateway to the churchyard, which is always on the west.

Parishioners attribute the sacredness and uniqueness of their church to the fact that, hidden away in the innermost of its three rooms where only the ordained clergy may see it, is the holy ark or *tabot*, a wooden tablet symbolizing the religious figure to whom the church is dedicated. In its most general aspect an ark represents the ark of the covenant and the unity of all Ethiopian Christians. In a more particular aspect it symbolizes the saint, angel, or aspect of divinity to which the parish, along with many other parishes, is dedicated. Finally, in its most particular aspect, the ark represents a refraction of that religious figure which is uniquely associated with the parish. It is in this aspect that it symbolizes the identity of a particular parish against all other parishes, and it is this aspect that is represented in the parish name. This name is compounded of a place name and the ark name, for example, "Horse Country Mikael." Parish names, carrying with them the implication of the ark's uniqueness, are frequently used. In replying to a question about his birthplace, his residence, or his destination, a man is likely to give the name of a parish.

In its unique aspect the ark is personified; it is spoken of as having a personality, moods, and prerogatives. To some extent the nature of its personality is determined by the religious figure of which it is a refraction; thus arks of Mikael are vengeful while arks of Mary are compassionate, but even arks dedicated to the same saint differ from one another in their ability to hear men's prayers and in their willingness to answer them.

Parishioners attach great importance to the mood or temper of their ark, for they believe it affects the fertility of the soil, the abundance of the harvest, and the fecundity and health of man and beast. If the mood of the ark is to be beneficent, its buildings and its properties must be kept in good repair and its masses must be celebrated regularly according to the exacting rite of the Ethiopic church.

In this respect the ark is a perpetual property-holding corporation whose trustees, at any given time, are the parishioners. The ark is spoken of as owning the church and its books, vestments, umbrellas, sistra, censers, crosses, and many other ritual objects. It also has monies which it receives from the occasional sale of trees from the churchyard, from grateful supplicants, and from wealthy patrons. It is owed a number of services and fees by all parishioners, it has the equivalent of gwilt rights over some of the parish's lands, and it has the right to receive ritual ministrations from qualified clergymen.

The organization and management of the ark's affairs is in the hands of two representative officials: the lay *gebez*, and the priest *gebez*. The lay *gebez*, who may be a layman or a cleric, is chosen annually from among the holders of the parish's "priest land" (see below). It is his responsibility to oversee the secular and fiscal management of church affairs and properties. It is often held that one of his main tasks is to suppress peculation by the clergy. The priest *gebez* is chosen from among the church's clergy by the lay *gebez*. He is responsible for the ordering and organization of the church's ritual activities, and he may be sued in church court by parishioners or higher church officials if he is found remiss in carrying out his duties.

The obligation to support the ark and its church falls on parishioners in several ways. All household heads resident in the parish are obligated to help with the maintenance and construction of church buildings. Those who fail to do their part may be fined. Each household head must also provide a basket or two of wheat annually for the preparation of the eucharist and a few baskets of barley for the preparation of a soggy, coarse bread eaten by all who attend church, communicant and noncommunicant alike, after the conclusion of the mass. Finally, all resident household heads must baptize their babies and bury their dead at the parish church and pay for the masses that these ritual services require.

The obligation to support the regular celebration of mass, in contrast to the obligations already mentioned, rests on land rather than residence in the parish. In most parishes the land tracts of one or more descent groups are classified as "priest land" (*qés merét*) and the individuals who hold fields in these tracts are obligated to support the celebration of mass in proportion to the amount of the parish's priest land which they control.[1] Fields of priest land are acquired like any other rist land and may be held by parish residents and nonresidents, laymen and clerics alike. If the holder is a cleric he may fulfill the land's service obligation himself; if not, he may have a member of his household who is a cleric celebrate the requisite masses in his stead. Failing this, he must arrange to have another clergyman perform the service for him as a favor, for pay, or, more commonly, in return for the rent-free use of a part of the field upon which the obligation rests. Despite its service obligation, priest land is much desired, for it is free of the largest part of the government land

1. A detailed description of the way the obligation to support the celebration of mass is divided among the holders of priest land is found in Hoben (1963: chap. 4).

tax, the *gibir*, a tax which represents a commutation to cash of the payment in grain formerly paid to the gwilt-holder.

The religious status of household heads affects the roles they take in parish affairs and towards one another in many ways. The most fundamental distinction in religious status is between laymen (*c̣hewa*)[2] who have little or no church-school education and clerics (*kahinat*)[3] who have attained at least the educational level of the diaconate. In Damot approximately one man in ten is a cleric. The clerics, in turn, in accordance with their educational level, their ordination, and their ritual purity, are divided into deacons (*dīyaqon*), priests (*qés*), and chorister-scribes called *debtera*.

A boy who hopes to become a deacon joins one of the numerous church schools in Dega Damot between the ages of seven and ten. He lives near the church with his teacher (a priest or *debtera* who has attained the educational level of *merīgéta* or *memhir*) and fellow students, begging food for his sustenance and following an arduous course of day and night studies. If he is successful in memorizing the more than two hundred characters of the Ethiopian syllabary and in learning to sing and chant parts of the scriptures and mass, all in Ge'ez (*Gi'iz*), a church language he does not understand, he will be ready to go before the provincial bishop at the end of about four years' study for ordination as a deacon. After another three years or so of additional study and service as a deacon he may go before the bishop again to seek ordination as a priest. Sometime before his ordination as a priest he should be married according to the rite of the church, for either marriage with one woman until his death or celibacy is required of him if he is to maintain his ritual purity; celibacy, though an ideal, is thought rather improbable for a young man. Lastly, a deacon or priest who loses his ritual purity through adultery, remarriage, or permanently

2. The term *c̣hewa* has several other meanings in other contexts. It is used, for example, to refer to nobles as opposed to commoners, affluent farmers as opposed to poor farmers, and men of excellent character as opposed to men of poor character.

3. When contrasting laymen and clerics in casual conversation, most Damotians refer to any cleric as a priest or *qés* even though he may, at a lower taxonomic level, be a deacon or *debtera*.

disfiguring disease loses his ordination and becomes a *debtera*. Priests and deacons, then, have learning, ritual purity, and ordination and are internally ranked by the degree of their education. *Debteras* have learning, but have lost their ritual purity or ordination. Aged laymen who have taken vows as monks and nuns (*menewksé*) have ritual purity but lack education and ordination.[4] They should be accorded honor because of their holiness but they are not fully members of the clergy.

Most deacons and priests are affiliated with particular churches where they partake of the many baptismal, funerary, and holiday feasts provided by laymen, and celebrate mass for a set number of weeks or months annually.[5] The amount of their service obligation is determined by the proportion of the church's priest land for which they are doing service. A cleric may be affiliated with more than one church, provided he can meet the service obligations this entails, and he can celebrate mass as a substitute as often as he pleases, so long as he maintains the usual rules of ritual purity. In addition to serving in the parish church, many priests are tied to individual laymen on a more personal basis, for each household must have a priest to act as a confessor for its members.

Debteras are also affiliated with particular churches where they participate in the long hours of dancing and singing that precede the mass on each major holiday and join in the feasting that follows it. Many of them also act as scribes for illiterate laymen, and some of them turn their reputed arcane knowledge to personal advantage as astrologers, fortune-tellers, herbalists, and wizards.

Differences between laymen and clerics go beyond those I have described in their formal ritual roles and are evident in their life-styles in many ways. The cleric's religious status is symbolized in the distinctive head covering he often wears,

4. Essentially, uneducated laymen who take vows as monks in their old age must be distinguished from the highly educated celibate monks who are found in great monastic centers.

5. The Ethiopic mass is celebrated by five ordained clerics of whom at least two must be priests and three may be deacons.

and he is honored, even on entirely secular occasions, with special greeting forms and seating arrangements, and with precedence in eating. There are also differences in the type of personality thought ideal for the layman and the cleric. In a layman aggressiveness, even violence, in defense of property or honor is a much admired quality, and sexual exploits, if carried out discreetly, are more of a complement to the complete male personality than a vice. In a cleric, by contrast, aggression is lamentable and illicit sex is unforgivable.[6]

Sometimes the priestly life is ridiculed by bantering laymen, as when one of my informants consistently contrasted the status of a priest with that of a man. In the past, secular and religious ideals have occasionally come into open conflict, as when a military lord violated the church's right to give asylum, and when an emperor put to death a group of recalcitrant monks. Most of the time, however, the ideals of layman and priest are seen as complementary and necessary to one another. Laymen may criticize their priests for failing to exemplify the priestly ideal and the priests, in turn, may criticize the laymen for failing to support the church, but all are in essential agreement on the importance of their interdependence.[7]

Because they create a sense of interdependence, the ties between parishioners and their ark and between laymen and the clergy are among the most important that bind men to one another in Dega Damot and help to contain the divisive tendencies generated by their ongoing competition for rist land and political office. The parish as a bounded territory centering on its church gives a geographical focus to these ties and hence to local Damotian social organization. The church and churchyard are the setting for a variety of religious and secular activities. Here men come to worship their

6. For an excellent discussion of personality ideals in Amhara culture, see Levine (1965: chaps. 6 and 7).

7. These contrasting but complementary personality ideals of the active farmer-warrior and the more passive and contemplative priest are consistent with and a reflection of the relationship that is found more generally throughout Amhara society between the ideals of the military and those of the Ethiopic church.

God; they come together collectively or individually with their troubled prayers and, when their prayers are answered, with their gifts of gratitude. Within the sacred precincts of the grass-carpeted, shady churchyard, parishioners also gather to discuss their public affairs and common problems, to settle their minor disputes, to baptize their babies, publish their banns, and bury their dead.

Despite the importance of the legal, moral, and ritual ties that bind a man to his church, the parish does not command the degree of primordial attachment, of deeply rooted sentiment, that is described as characteristic of the local village community in many other peasant societies.[8] In part this is because, except for personal ritual services, men are not bound to attend their own parish's church. Due to the dispersed settlement pattern characteristic of Damot, for many men the closest church to their homestead lies in a neighboring parish. In part, too, the solidarity of the household heads in a parish is lowered by the fact that over 50 percent of them are not living in their natal parish. Finally, the cohesiveness of parishioners is weakened by the many other types of institutional ties and individual interests men have that are not based on parish membership. Prominent among these are the ties men have as residents of a neighborhood.

The neighborhood or estate of gwilt

Just as the parish provides a territorial framework for religious organization, the neighborhood, corresponding to the traditional estate of gwilt land, provides a territorial framework for secular administration. Affiliation with the neighborhood system defines men's jural relationship with government and affects their material interests in many ways. It does not, however, give the household heads resident in a neighborhood a well-developed sense of common identity in opposition to men from other neighborhoods or strong sentiments of solidarity amongst themselves, for the obligations men have in virtue of their affiliation with the neighborhood

8. An excellent description of such villages is found in Pitt-Rivers (1961).

have been defined primarily by their individual relationship with its gwilt-holder and only secondarily by a sense of collective responsibility. For formal obligations this relationship between the household heads and the gwilt-holder has been greatly altered and weakened by the administrative changes of the past four decades described below in chapter 10. For informal expectations and respect the relationship has changed much more slowly. For this reason I will describe both the older and more fully developed relationship between gwilt-holder and household head and the more limited ties that now bind the gwilt-holder, as neighborhood judge, to the men under his jurisdiction.

As a territorial unit, a neighborhood consists of a parish or a part of a parish, but it is always composed of an integral number of descent-group estates.[9] Contiguous neighborhoods may be under the control of the same gwilt-holder, but administratively they remain distinct.

The limited extent to which men identify with the territorial unit I am calling an estate of gwilt, or a neighborhood, is reflected in nomenclature. The unit can be referred to as the gwilt of a particular person or institution, but there is no single generic term in Amharic for the land unit held as gwilt. If it is coterminous with a parish, or if it consists of a part of a parish including the parish church, it bears the same proper name as the parish. If it includes only a part of the parish but does not include the church, it can be referred to by the generic term *goṭ* and has a proper name which is different from that of the parish as a whole. The terms *aṭbīya*, which I am translating as "neighborhood," was not applied to administrative units in Dega Damot prior to the promulgation of Proclamation 90 of 1947 which established neighborhood judges throughout Ethiopia. Even today it is not semantically correct, in Dega Damot, to say that someone holds a neighborhood (*aṭbīya*) as his gwilt. For the sake of

9. In a survey of 66 parishes composing one of Dega Damot's subdistricts, it was found that 40 parishes were coextensive with a single neighborhood, 16 included 2 neighborhoods, 4 included 3 neighborhoods, 2 included 4 neighborhoods, 3 included 5 neighborhoods, none included 6 neighborhoods, 1 had 7 neighborhoods. There were no parishes with more than 7 neighborhoods.

simplicity and clarity, however, I will refer to any territory held as an estate of gwilt, regardless of its relationship to a parish, as an estate of gwilt or a neighborhood.

Traditionally, estates of gwilt were classified according to the status of the grantee who held them and according to the terms of the grant. The broadest distinction was between gwilt granted in perpetuity to a religious institution, which was called *bétekahinat* or "house of the clergy," and gwilt held by a secular official, which was called *bétemengist* or "house of the government." Gwilt held by secular officials was subdivided into gwilt held directly by the provincial ruler, or *ganageb*, and gwilt held by lesser officials, which in the context of this contrast was simply called gwilt. Finally, gwilt held by lesser officials was again subdivided into rist-gwilt, which was in principle hereditary,[10] and *maderīya*-gwilt, which was given on a temporary basis or for life. In Dega Damot approximately one-third of all arable land was classified as the gwilt of religious institutions, and two-thirds as the gwilt of secular officials. Of the gwilt held by secular officials, only a small portion, probably less than 5 percent, was held directly by the ruler.

The church official in charge of a religious institution was responsible for the overall management of its widely scattered gwilt lands,[11] but he delegated his authority over each estate to a locally resident bailiff or *wekīl.* The ruler delegated his

10. "Hereditary" in this context did not mean that there was a fixed rule of succession. It meant rather that a close kinsman, usually a son, a brother, or a brother's or sister's son, who distinguished himself in the ruler's court, would probably be confirmed in the deceased holder's position.

11. There are two kinds of major religious institutions in Dega Damot, as elsewhere in Ethiopia: the monastery or *gedam* and the endowed church center or *debir*. The monastery is ideally a perpetual community of monks living and working together under the direction of their teacher and leader, the *memhir*. The endowed church center is a large and well-built church with daily services and a number of specially endowed ecclesiastical positions not found in ordinary churches. The official in charge of the endowed church center is, in generic terms, known as an *aleqa*, and also has a specific title which is unique to each church center. Both monasteries and endowed churches are centers of advanced learning, calligraphy, and the illumination of manuscripts. There is also much specialization in excellence, and aspiring churchmen travel hundreds of miles to attend a particular religious center. The best-known monastery in Dega Damot,

administrative and judicial responsibilities as gwilt-holder to a local representative with the special title of *bilaténgéta*. The remaining secularly held estates of gwilt were either administered directly by the gwilt-holder, who was titled the gwilt *gež*, or by his appointed bailiff.[12]

Men who lived on estates of gwilt held by religious institutions were often exempted from certain military and labor services (they owed special services instead), but in most other respects all peasants' obligations to their gwilt-holder were essentially similar. Indeed, the classification of the gwilt land on which a man lived was usually of less consequence to him than the character and disposition of the official who exercised the authority entailed in the gwilt rights, for a household head's bond with the gwilt-holder or his steward tended to be personal in nature and diffuse in content.

Prior to the Second World War, the gwilt-holders of Dega Damot and their bailiffs were almost the sole intermediaries between the feudal provincial government and the peasants with regard to the administration of justice, the maintenance of civil order, the organization of statute labor, and the collection of tax and tribute. In his judicial capacity the acting gwilt-holder had the right and the obligation to investigate and arbitrate minor disputes in which persons resident on his estate of gwilt stood accused. In return for this service he received a pledge in currency or kind forfeited by the losing party regardless of whether he was the plaintiff or the accused. If a crime was committed on his estate, the gwilt-holder was bound to investigate it and, if necessary, to convene a public inquest, or *iwis*, to apprehend the criminal; or, failing that, to levy a collective fine to be paid by all household heads under his jurisdiction.

Washera Maryam, for example, is nationally known for studies in *qiné*, an abstruse form of religious poetry (see Levine 1965).

12. The gwilt *gež*(s) of Daga Damot were primarily soldiers and military leaders. Most of them enjoyed grants of rist-gwilt in return for which they were required to perform annual guard service in the "Damot guard" at the ruler's court and to accompany him on military campaigns. The gwilt *gež* expected to provision himself and his entourage when in his lord's service.

If there were a proclamation to be made, the gwilt-holder was responsible for its reaching his peasants. Often these proclamations concerned government works, for the household heads from each estate of gwilt were ordered up by turn to help maintain major trails, to work on the construction of fortifications, buildings, and storage bins anywhere in Dega Damot, and to help with the cultivation of fields known as *hudad*, which were worked for the personal benefit of the provincial ruler or his regional governor.[13] The gwilt-holder was also responsible for his peasants providing government officials and guests passing through his gwilt with such food, drink, and lodging as might be required.

The most important benefit accruing to the gwilt-holder was the land tax or *gibir*.[14] In most estates of gwilt the land tax consisted of one-fifth of all the crops grown. On some estates, however, the land tax was commuted to a single type of produce such as white *ṭéff* or horses, for which the region was renowned. Still other estates had their land tax commuted to *gemeta c̣hew*, a fixed annual payment in salt bars. Finally, as has been remarked, estates classified as "priest land" bore the obligation to support church service in lieu of land tax.

The land tax was paid to the gwilt-holder of the estate in which a field was located, regardless of where the rist-holder, or the cultivator if he were different from the rist-holder, might happen to reside. It was thus common for a single farmer to pay land tax to two or three different gwilt-holders.

The gwilt-holder was assisted in carrying out his work by a minor official known as the *c̣hiqa shum* or, literally, the "mud chief." This official was nominated for a one-year term from amongst the household heads who held rist land in the

13. *Hudad* is no longer found in Dega Damot though there are still numerous hamlets that bear this name. Apparently in Dega Damot *hudad* was land that by government decree was temporarily set aside by the rist-holders in a descent group as a whole. After a few seasons it reverted to the rist-holders and a new *hudad* was created elsewhere. Not every parish had a *hudad* in a particular year but all men were within working distance of a *hudad* in a nearby parish.

14. This tax was of such importance that peasants are still often referred to in Ethiopia by the derivative term *gebar*. In parts of southern Ethiopia the term has the pejorative connotation of serf. In Damot it simply means a taxpaying peasant farmer.

estate, and he was confirmed in his office by the gwilt-holder. Usually the position rotated to all elder rist-holders before any of them had a second term. The *c̣hiqa shum*'s main tasks were to act as messenger and to help supervise the assessment of the land tax in the fields at harvest time. For his services the *c̣hiqa shum* usually received no remuneration other than tax relief, but in some estates there were special fields set aside for the incumbent *c̣hiqa*'s personal use. It is also said that many men did not scruple to use their limited authority in ways that brought them extra rewards. The office of *c̣hiqa shum* still exists today but it is regarded as onerous since it has been largely stripped of its former emoluments.

For some administrative purposes, such as the recruitment of statute labor, a large estate of gwilt land was divided into a number of hamlets, and a representative (*mender fej*) was designated for each. This representative, a leading elder, took orders from the *c̣hiqa shum* and was responsible for seeing that the residents in his hamlet carried them out.

The gwilt-holder, and to a lesser extent the bailiff he might appoint, was a symbol of secular authority in much the same way that the church, or its ark, is a symbol of religious authority. An elaborate etiquette of deference governed all public relations between the gwilt-holder and his peasants. This was evident in the way they had to drape their cotton capes, in the way they had to bow to him, and in the linguistic forms with which they addressed him. A special place was reserved for him in the parish church, if there was one in the estate, and at feasts he had to be served first.

Assessing the gwilt-holder's actual influence and control over his subjects is more difficult than describing formal obligations and rules of etiquette. His power was in some respects greater and in some respects less than the formal rules would suggest. In part it depended on the size and importance of his estate of gwilt, in part on his position in the church or military ruling group, and in part on his personal abilities and inclinations. It is clear, however, that despite the wide scope of his authority, the gwilt-holder was not typically a tyrant, for his freedom of action was limited by the expectations and reactions of his subjects. He might violate the traditional expectations of some of his peasants occasionally, but he could not afford to consistently antagonize a majority of them. A universally unpopular gwilt-holder soon found that his peasants or their oxen were "ill" when he needed them most, and that even the simplest task requiring organization seemed never to get done. The ultimate sanction held by the peasants, however, was their right and ability to move away and establish their homesteads in other estates.

At the time of my fieldwork a centralized bureaucracy had begun to take over many of the responsibilities that had formerly been carried out by the gwilt-holder (see below, chapter 10). Gwilt-holding religious institutions, in particular, have lost almost all of their former secular authority, though they still receive a portion of the land tax from their estates of gwilt. Secular gwilt-holders, by contrast, have been able to retain more of their traditional authority as incumbents by fiat of the office of neighborhood judge.

Officially the neighborhood judge (*aṭbīya dañña*) is empowered to hear civil disputes involving claims of under $10 U.S. ($25 Eth.) and criminal disputes in which the damages are less than $6 U.S. ($15 Eth.). He may conduct hearings at any convenient time and place—usually outdoors—and he must be accompanied by two elders who are to assist and advise him. Instead of the pledges or wagers he formerly received from litigants, the neighborhood judge receives only small, fixed fees. In Dega Damot, however, neighborhood judges are still in an important intermediary position between the peasantry and the administration, for the handful of government workers who represent their respective ministries in the district capital of Feres Bét cannot function without their assistance. In recognition of this, neighborhood judges who occupy their office in virtue of their possession of gwilt rights are given a rebate of about 10 percent of the land taxes collected on their estate.

Other types of community ties

Household heads are related to one another by many types of institutional ties in addition to those that are based on membership in parish and neighborhood. Characteristically, however, these other ties are voluntarily entered into or activated and are maintained only so long as all parties concerned deem them advantageous. Ties based on kinship, vicinage, and friendship, for example, are all utilized on a reciprocal basis to organize such cooperative ventures as getting in the harvest, building a house, and staging a wedding feast.[15] Such ties link men together in unbounded networks, for each household mobilizes a unique constellation of friends, neighbors, and kinsmen to help it with its major tasks. There are also several types of voluntary groups such as the religious sodalities or *mahibers* that bring a dozen or so members together for a feast each month on a particular saint's day; the *senbeté* or Sunday feasting society, and, among the salaried officials of Feres Bét and a few well-to-do peasants, there is the recently introduced rotating credit association or *ikub*. Finally, there are the type of hierarchically structured networks of patron-client ties that Adrian Mayer calls quasi-groups (Mayer 1966), linking government officials and other influential men with their supporters.

Though all of these institutional ties affect the ways in which and the extent to which household heads compete for rist land, the parish and the neighborhood provide the most enduring and legally binding territorial framework of local Damotian social organization. This organizational importance of parish and neighborhood is, of course, a reflection of the fact that they are the local institutions through which the elite groups of traditional Amhara society, the church and the military, exercised administrative control over their subjects.

15. There are comparatively few ties based on kinship in Amhara society that are jurally or morally binding. Aside from the rights and obligations already mentioned in connection with household and marriage, the most important tie is the obligation of sons, brothers, and, some say, uncles to avenge murder. Parents and children have a moral obligation to assist one another in time of trouble, and siblings will often help one another if they are on good terms, though there are no sanctions that can be brought to bear on them if they fail to do so and cases of sibling enmity are numerous.

Together the parish and neighborhood defined the political, economic, and cultural incompleteness of the local community, its relationship of dependence on other segments of society that makes it appropriate to speak of Amhara farmers as peasants.[16] Politically the local community was incomplete because the authority with which its members dominate one another was largely derived from political office granted by members of the elite. Economically it was incomplete because a portion of the tax and tribute paid by its members was used to support the elites. Culturally the community was incomplete because the sanctity of its priests and, more generally, many of the standards by which its members judged one another had reference to the ideas and ideals of the monastic and courtly life.

Damotian peasants have been well aware of the incompleteness of their communities, of their dependence on the elites, and, for the most part, have accepted these conditions. Occasionally they have resented particular impositions of their feudal masters, but they have never questioned their right to rule. Similarly, they have taken pride in their distinctive local customs and in the uniqueness of each locality's history, but they have always recognized the validity and superiority of the high cultural tradition borne in purest form by their elites.

The peasants' acceptance of their lowly position in the social order as natural and inevitable has been fostered by a particular view of history, land, and polity, a view which relates the institutions of Damotian social organization to the historical traditions of Amhara civilization.[17]

16. Thus Alfred Kroeber, whose description of peasants is widely cited, remarks that "[peasants] form a class segment of a larger population. . . . They constitute part-societies with part-cultures (Kroeber 1948: 284)." Fallers (1961) has discussed the use of the word "peasants" in sub-Saharan African kingdoms, and Gamst (1970) has commented on the applicability of the term in Ethiopia.

17. Brief accounts of these historical traditions are to be found in Levine (1965), Perham (1948), and Trimingham (1952). Some of the traditions are myths and legends, others are well documented. My concern here is not with their historicity but only with their impact on the consciousness and social organization of Dega Damot.

5. Local Legend and National Tradition

The territorially based institutions described in the previous chapter and the landholding descent corporations described in the following chapters cannot be understood in terms of rights, duties, and constellations of interest alone, for each of them has a conceptual or ideological dimension as well. This conceptual dimension is encapsulated in a cycle of legends which at once account for the origins and interrelations of parish, neighborhood, and descent group and infuse them with an aura of legitimacy by linking them with the Amhara great tradition.

History to the ordinary folk of Dega Damot is not a continuous process. It consists of a number of isolated and essentially unrelated events thought somewhat vaguely to have occurred in "ancient times," a period stretching back from just beyond the memory of the oldest living men, which presently means beyond the reign of Emperor Yohannis (1872–89).

The events of this hazy past are related to the most important places, periods, and personages of Ethiopian tradition: the ancient city of Axum, center of the old empire and home of the first Ethiopian emperor, Menilek, son of King Solomon, who had the ark of the covenant brought from Jerusalem; the golden age of Amhara civilization following the restoration of the Solomonic line by Emperor Yekuno Amlak and Abuna Tekle Haymanot in the latter part of the thirteenth century, a time when a series of emperors led their victorious armies on seasonal campaigns against the Muslim states to the southeast, pushing back the infidels, building churches, and endowing monasteries; the destruction of the land and its churches by a Muslim jihad under Mohamed Grañ in the second quarter of the sixteenth century; and the glorious days of the court at Gondar in the seventeenth century.

Most Amhara are little concerned with the past as such. What is important to them about these major events of traditional history is their representation on the present-day landscape and their projection into current administrative and social relationships. Contemporary relationships are justified with reference to these historical representations, and changes in these relationships, particularly changes having to do with land rights, usually involve changes in the interpretation of "history."

According to legend, the founding ancestor of Dega Damot as a whole was King Tekle Haymanot who came with his wife, Gennet, from Jerusalem.[1] Informants are unclear as to whether there were already people living in Dega Damot when King Tekle Haymanot arrived, but it is not a matter of great importance to them, for legends of this type are used primarily to account for the origins of land units and rights vested in them, not for the origins of people. King Tekle Haymanot had three sons and four daughters, one of whom is said to have married the mayor (*kentība*) of Gondar. Two of the sons settled in the district to the east of Dega Damot. Each of the other children are associated in legend with the founding of one or more of the regional subdivisions of Dega Damot which today have become subdistricts.

At a more parochial level each parish also has a founding ancestor and a legend that relates how he established its church.[2] Many of these parish founders are considered to be descendents of King Tekle Haymanot. Founders not of this

1. Informants are adamant that this was not the King Tekle Haymanot who ruled Gojjam at the turn of the present century, of whom they are well aware. Nor, they insist, with less vehemence, could it be one of the Gondarine emperors who bore the name; their Tekle Haymanot, they insist, came from Jerusalem.

2. This founding ancestor, who may be a man or a woman, is sometimes spoken of as the first father or principal ancestor of the parish (*wanna abbat*) and sometimes as the ark planter (*ye tabot tekay*).

royal lineage are identified in many instances as friends and followers of those who were. There are no benefits other than nostalgic pride associated with the parishes founded by descendents of Tekle Haymanot, but the legends associated with these parishes provide a genealogical and geographical skeleton for Dega Damot as a whole.

The founding legend of a parish accounts for the origin of descent-group land tracts, the basic land units of the rist system. It recounts the circumstances under which the parish founder first settled, founded a church, and apportioned rist rights over large tracts of land to himself, his major retainers, and to the priests and deacons who were to celebrate mass in the church. Each of these tracts is identified with one of the present-day descent-group land tracts, and the individual to whom it was first granted is regarded as the first holder or "first father" (*wanna abbat*) of the corporation holding it as rist.

Most descent-group land tracts are thought to have originated at the time when the parish in which they are located was founded. Some, however, are said to be of more recent origin. They are thought to represent tracts of initially uncleared land granted to a forceful military leader or simply settled by him some generations after the founding of the parish, into which they were incorporated for purposes of ecclesiastical administration.

The founding legend and subsequent "history" of a parish also account for its relationship to estates of gwilt, the modern neighborhoods. In most cases the parish founder himself is considered to have been the first gwilt-holder. The parish as he founded it, then, is coterminous with a single estate of gwilt or neighborhood. The additional estates of gwilt found today within some large parishes are usually identified as land tracts incorporated into the parish subsequent to its founding. Again, the first grantee of such land tracts is considered to have been its first gwilt-holder.

The same legends that account for the origin of parish, land tract, and neighborhood as territorial units also account for the association of particular rights and obligations with each of them. The founding legend of a parish is thus, in an important sense, a charter for present-day social relationships. Ideally, for example, the obligation to support the celebration of mass in the parish church rests on those who hold rist land in the land tracts initially granted to its first clergymen. The obligation to support the gwilt-holder rests on those who hold rist land in the land tracts granted to the first gwilt-holder. Similarly, eligibility for the office of lay *gebez* rests on the possession of rist land in the land tract held by the first lay *gebez,* and eligibility for the office of *ç̣hiqa shum*, the peasant assistant to the gwilt-holder, rests on the possession of rist land in the land tract held by the first *ç̣hiqa shum.*

The foregoing account is idealized in that it presents an oversimplified picture of parish organization. There are many deviations from this idealized picture and hence much organizational variation between parishes. In some parishes today, the obligation to support the celebration of the mass rests in part on land tracts which are not believed to have been first held by clergy, while in other parishes land tracts first held by clergy have been absolved of their service obligations. In still other parishes there are today no land tracts that are considered to be church land and the obligation to support the celebration of the mass falls equally on all the parish's land tracts. Estates of gwilt believed to have been distinct initially have, in some instances, been merged under the jurisdiction of a single gwilt-holder, while other estates of gwilt first held by secular lords have been transferred to the control of monasteries. Finally, the offices of *gebez* and *ç̣hiqa shum* are in many cases associated with land tracts other than those of their first holders.

Such deviations from the ideal order do not strike the elders of Dega Damot as anomalous, for they are viewed simply as perturbations in the original order of the parish that have been brought about by the great men and great events of the intervening years. If a parish has no designated church land, the explanation may be that the land was lost in the hardship and confusion that followed the burning of the church by the Muslim invader Mohamed Grañ. If a land tract has lost its pre-emptory right to an administrative office, this may be attributed to the scurrilous performance of one of its former incumbents. If gwilt rights over a parish have been transferred from the original holder's line to a monastery, this may be accounted for by a miracle performed for some great military lord by the patron saint of the parish.

In an important sense, then, it is not meaningful to speak of any type of parish as typical, for it is typical of the parish that the exact interrelations of its component institutions are unique. For the sake of clarity in presentation, however, I have tried to draw most of the necessarily detailed and complex illustrative material in this book from two parishes located near the administrative center of Feres Bét and from one descent group's land tract within each. The parishes, though adjacent to one another, are very different. One of them, Feres Bét Mikael, is large, populous, politically central, and administratively complex. The other, Dereqé Maryam, is small in area and population, has never been the seat of government, and is administratively simple.

Feres Bét Mikael (map 2) is located on the high plateau at an altitude of about 11,000 feet above sea level. On the south it is bounded by a ridge-top trail that marks the central Gojjam watershed. On the northeast it is bounded by a small all-year creek, and most of its northwestern boundary is a steep cliff that drops away to the Gumara River valley. With a population of 1,374 people (exclusive of the town of Feres Bét) living in 372 households, Feres Bét was the most populous parish censused.

According to legend, Feres Bét was founded by the son of King Tekle Haymanot, Dejazmach Asibo, who camped near the present location of the church one night on his way to battle. The next morning, the virgin monk who, as was customary, always carried the dejazmach's ark was overcome with a mysterious drowsiness. Sensing a miracle, the dejazmach burnt incense, prayed, and remained in Feres Bét another night. On the following morning the monk awoke without difficulty and set off carrying the ark. Suddenly he was swept off his feet by a whirlwind and set down again unharmed on the site where the parish church of Feres Bét

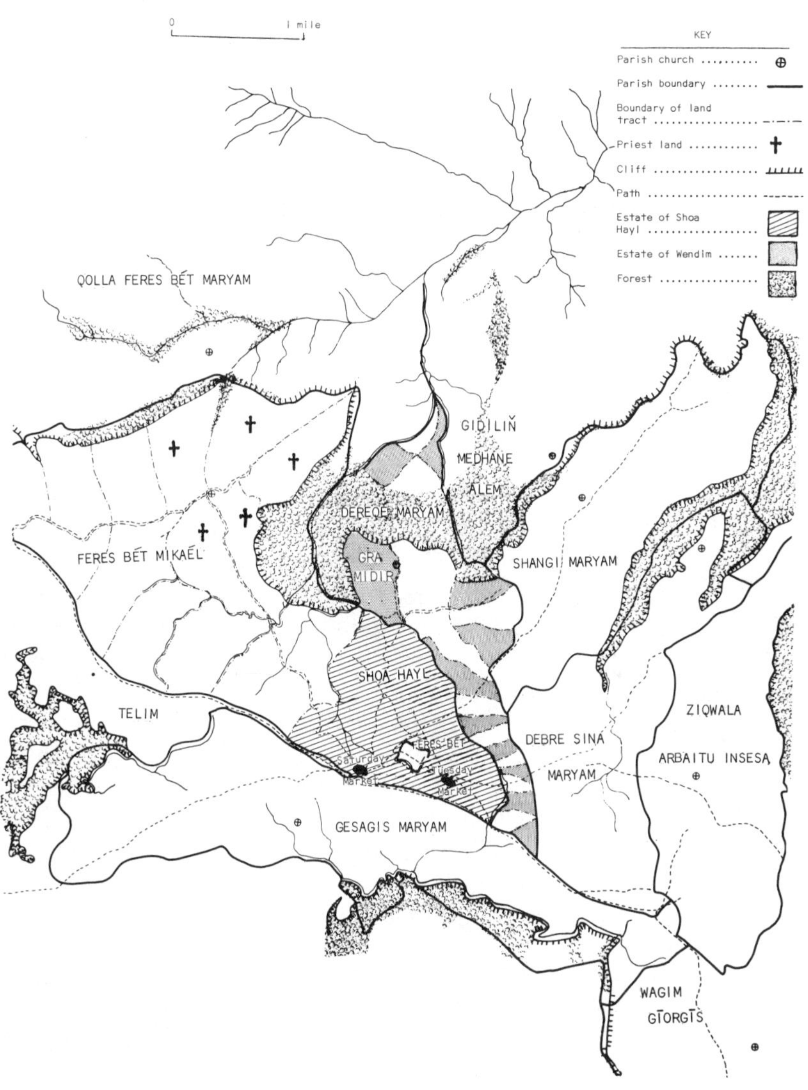

Map 2. Parishes in area of intensive study

now stands. The dejazmach understood the meaning of the miracle and built a hut to house the ark temporarily until a proper church could be built. And thus the parish of Feres Bét Mikael was founded.

The dejazmach appointed five clergymen to serve the newly "planted" ark. For their service he is said to have given each of them a tract of land. Today, of course, these five clergymen are considered ancestral first settlers and the land tract each of them was given is the tract of rist land shared by his descendents. The clergy in Feres Bét are well endowed. Today they include twenty priests, ten deacons, and one teacher. The church itself is well built and well decorated with wall paintings.

The rest of the land around the place where the ark was placed was allegedly given as rist and gwilt to the dejazmach's sister, Qeñazmach Kolét, who eventually gave it to her daughter, Qusqwamawīt. Dejazmach Asibo, Qeñazmach Kolét, or Qusqwamawīt are all, at different times, referred to as the "chief ancestor" of the parish as a whole, depending on whether it is the speaker's intention to stress the closeness of Feres Bét to the ancient founding king or to differentiate it from all or some of the other parishes said to have been founded by Dejazmach Asibo and his sister.

It is said that gwilt rights over Feres Bét were retained for some generations by descendents of Qusqwamawīt. Eventually, however, the gwilt-holder, or gwilt *gež*, of Feres Bét attempted to withhold from the king at Gondar a part of the tribute of horses paid annually at that time. As a result of the ensuing court intrigue, the gwilt rights over Feres Bét were taken away from the line of Qusqwamawīt and kept by the ruler—first by the ruler at Gondar and later by the ruler of Gojjam. These events are said to account for the fact that in recent times Feres Bét has been the *ganageb* or personal gwilt of the ruler of Gojjam. Legend also recounts that at the time when gwilt rights were taken away from the descendents of Qusqwamawīt these descendents were given the exclusive privilege of holding the office of *c̣hiqa shum*. Today only a descendent or, more accurately, a descendent who holds rist land in Qusqwamawīt's land tract, is eligible for the dubious honor of being appointed to this office.

At one time the parish is said to have included a portion of the adjacent lowlands in the Gumara valley to the north. It is said, however, that the lowlanders found the steep climb to the church on the plateau tiresome, and that when their population had increased sufficiently they built another church, received an ark from the bishop, and founded their present parish, Qolla Feres Bét Maryam.

Today, in addition to the five land tracts initially granted to the clergy and the land tract retained by Qusqwamawīt, there are, in Feres Bét, nine other first settlers' land tracts said to have been granted as uncleared land to great men and warriors in later years. Such land tracts are often referred to as *gashsha meréts*, an appellation which refers to the grantee's military service and is not, as in Shoa, a unit of land measurement. In all, there are fifteen first settlers' estates in the parish of Feres Bét Mikael, five of which bear the obligation to support the celebration of mass (see map 2). Detailed illustrations of land division and land disputes will be drawn from one of these estates, that of a settler named Shoa Hayl.

Though it is generally assumed from his name that Shoa Hayl came from the province of Shoa, no one is certain just when or from whence he came. What is believed to be important about him is that he settled in the vicinity of Feres Bét and had children. The estate of Shoa Hayl covers an area of one and a half square miles at the extreme eastern end of Feres Bét Mikael and includes the town of Feres Bét, the administrative center of all Dega Damot. Perched atop the highest knoll in Shoa Hayl on the Dega Damot divide, the walled town has a commanding view of the surrounding countryside. Ridges running out from the town divide the estate of Shoa Hayl into three watersheds. Excellent all-year springs, believed to be the abodes of evil spirits, are located in each of these watersheds. Lowlands along the streams that bound Shoa Hayl to the north and west and depressions running from springs to the streams provide pasturage during the dry season and are too wet for cultivation during the rains. Most of the remaining land in Shoa Hayl is cultivated, though the land to the south of *bahir mesk* swamp is of such low quality that it is tilled but one year in three. Because of its altitude and exposure, common barley, *mesno* barley, and potatoes are the only important staple crops grown in Shoa Hayl.

Exclusive of the townsmen, few of whom directly engage in agriculture, Shoa Hayl had a population of under three hundred people living in seventy homesteads in 1962 (map 3). Collectively, these homesteads are commonly referred to as the *mender*, or hamlet, of Shoa Hayl. The term *mender*, however, is a relative one and may be used for any grouping of homesteads within a parish; in the limiting case, a man's homestead may even be referred to as his *mender*. When a greater degree of specificity is desired, the *mender* of Shoa Hayl is often broken down into *lay mender* ("upper hamlet") and *tay mender* ("lower hamlet"). It is also characteristic of Amhara social organization that the area included in the hamlet of Shoa Hayl does not correspond exactly to the estate of the first-settler Shoa Hayl. As a hamlet, represented in parish affairs upon occasion by a single man, Shoa Hayl includes a small group of homesteads in its northwest corner which are on the neighboring estate of Dīmo; at the same time, the southwestern corner of the estate of Shoa Hayl is said to be a part of the neighboring hamlet of Sew Argif, a community largely made up of weavers. It is the estate of Shoa Hayl, rather than the hamlet, that is of prime concern here.

In 1962 fifty-four of the seventy-one household heads living on Shoa Hayl's estate were farmers. Six of these were also priests. One household head was a weaver, one was a smith, and one was a tanner. All of these men engaged in agriculture as well. Ten homesteads were headed by women. Four household heads were titled. One of them, a *grazmach*, was the *aṭbīya dañña* of the entire parish of Feres Bét. Another was an old man who was in charge of guarding prisoners under Ras Hailu, the last independent ruler of Gojjam before the Second World War. The third was an old man who attained

Map 3. Homesteads and fields in Shoa Hayl

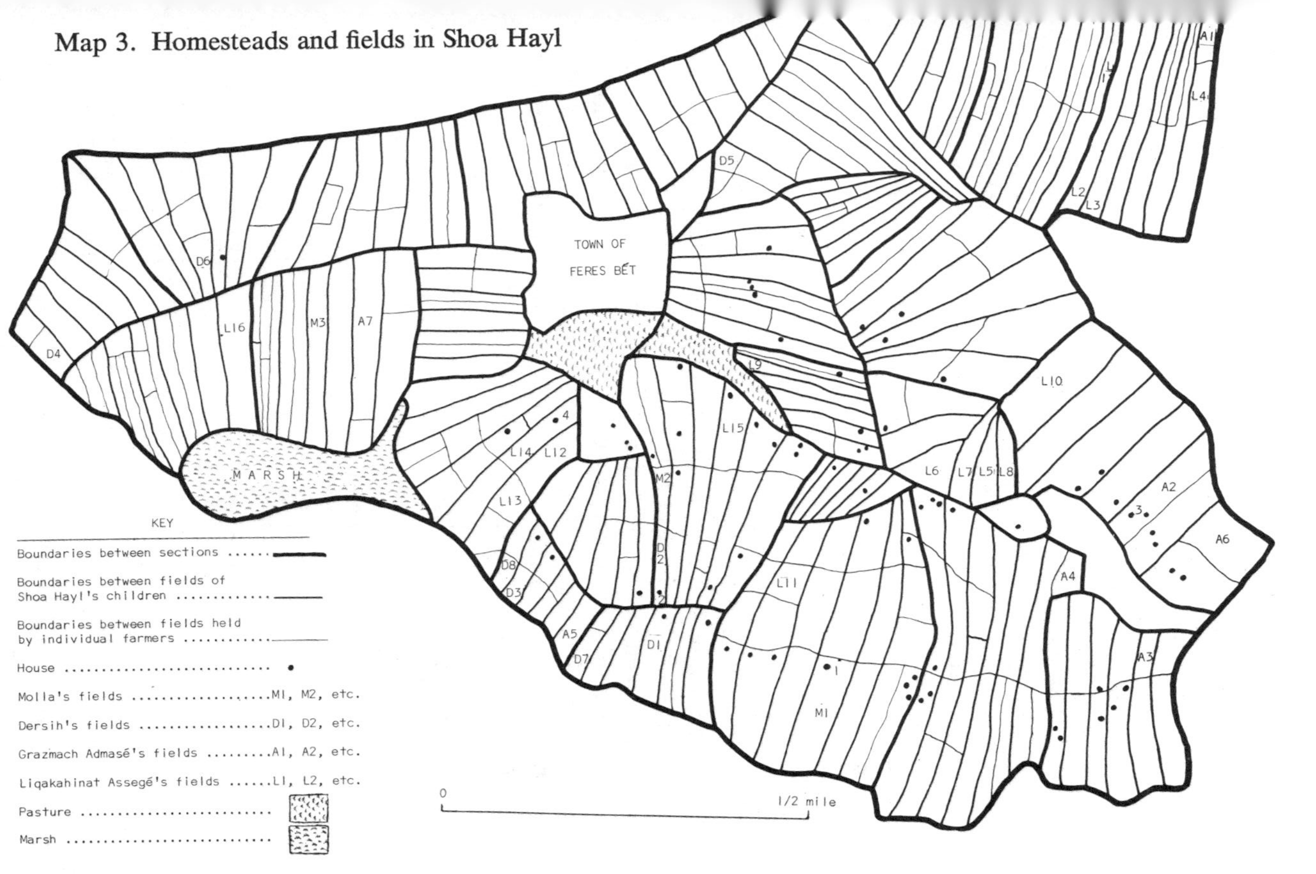

the ecclesiastic title of *līqekahinat* and the secular rank of *grazmach.* He served as chief clerk of Dega Damot under Ras Hailu and under the present regime, until he was succeeded in office by his son. The old man was a large landholder, possessing more fields in Shoa Hayl than anyone else. At the time of the study there were 329 fields in the estate of Shoa Hayl (map 3).

The pattern of landholding in Shoa Hayl has undoubtedly been influenced by its proximity to the political and administrative center of Dega Damot. Men of political importance, who are often titled, have sought to obtain rist land in Shoa Hayl in order to provide a convenient supply of grain for the "town" residence they maintain in Feres Bét. Consequently, the proportion of land held by titled men and the proportion of land worked in tenancy are above average, probably as high as anywhere in Dega Damot.

Despite this concentration of land in the hands of titled men, there were, at the time of the study, 153 people who had a direct interest in the land of Shoa Hayl, of whom not less than 119 held at least one field rent-free. Not less than seventeen people held land in tenancy only. Sufficient data concerning the other seventeen people's claims were not obtained. The distribution of fields among the 119 known holders is shown in table 1. In all, about one-fourth of the fields in Shoa Hayl's estate were worked by tenants.

TABLE 1 DISTRIBUTION OF SHOA HAYL'S FIELDS

Fields held	No. of holders	Fields held	No. of holders
1	62	11	0
2	25	12	0
3	11	13	0
4	4	14	0
5	3	15	0
6	6	16	0
7	3	17	0
8	2	18	0
9	1	19	1
10	1	19+	0
		Total holders 119	
		Total fields 287*	

*There is insufficient data for the other 42 fields.

Available data concerning the relationship between social status and land holding in Shoa Hayl are summarized in table 2a. It is evident that titled men as a group are 14 percent over-represented in landholding, ordinary farmers are 11 percent under-represented, and clerics as a group are represented in proportion to their numbers. The residence of the 119 people known to hold land in Shoa Hayl is shown by status in table 2b.

TABLE 2a SOCIAL STATUS AND LANDHOLDING IN SHOA HAYL

Status	Holders of this status		Fields held by them	
	Number	*% of Total*	*Number*	*% of Total*
Titled	13	11	75	25
Cleric	9	8	24	8
Farmer	84	71	179	60
Other*	13	11	18	6
Totals	119	101	296†	99

*Includes merchants, nontitled government officials, and others resident in the town of Feres Bét.

†There were 33 fields for which this data was not available.

TABLE 2b RESIDENCE OF LANDHOLDERS IN SHOA HAYL

Status	*Resident in Shoa Hayl*	*Resident in Town*	*Resident outside Shoa Hayl or town*
Titled	3	1	9
Cleric	5	0	4
Farmer	38	0	46
Other	0	13	0

Across the creek, to the northeast of Feres Bét Mikael, lies the parish of Dereqé Maryam (map 2). The arable lands of Dereqé are divided into a highland and a lowland section, separated by a belt of cliff and forest. The larger section, where most of the homesteads and the church are located, lies on the plateau. Bounded by the creek on the southwest and by trails and a rocky outcropping on the northeast, this section runs from the watershed, at its southern tip, to a jutting promontory in the north where its walled churchyard commands a broad view of the Gumara valley. The more recently settled and not yet fully cleared lowland section to the north lies at the foot of the steep slopes more than a thousand feet below. At the time of a census taken in 1962, Dereqé had a total population of only 177 people living in under sixty homesteads.

In keeping with its small size and relative political unimportance, the founding legend of Dereqé is more humble than that of its neighbor, Feres Bét Mikael. The legend recounts how a nontitled man named Ze Sellasé founded Dereqé some generations after Dejazmach Asibo "planted the ark" in Feres Bét. Soon after founding the parish, Ze Sellasé is said to have given some land west of the church to a certain Wendim. In public, Wendim is said to have been Ze Sellasé's brother; in private, influential men whose interests are strongly identified with Ze Sellasé's estate say that Wendim was only Ze Sellasé's servant. This disagreement, and a certain amount of associated rancor, is the residue of a prolonged and bitter land dispute which took place a few generations ago.

The dispute was opened by a gwilt *gež* of Dereqé who claimed descent from Ze Sellasé. He claimed that, as Wendim had been only a servant of Ze Sellasé, the former's descendents had no legal right to the land to the west of the church which they held and claimed as their rist land. The major landholders in Wendim's estate countered that Wendim was not Ze Sellasé's servant or even his loyal follower but his brother. As his descendents, they contended, they were entitled to a full half of all the parish lands, not just the meager portion they then held. The case dragged on for years and was finally decided in favor of Wendim after the death of the gwilt gež who had first raised the issue. The cultivated lands of the parish were then divided equally into a number of sections for Wendim and Ze Sellasé. As additional lands were brought under cultivation, the process of division continued, producing the pattern of division shown on map 2.

Dereqé constitutes a single estate of gwilt. Gwilt rights over the estate are associated with Ze Sellasé's line. Indeed, all remembered former gwilt gež are said to have been descendents of Ze Sellasé. The current gwilt gež, a powerful old man who was chief clerk of Dega Damot for many years, claims descent from Wendim. Given the degree to which bilaterally traced pedigrees ramify in more than ten generations, it would appear, however, that the wily gwilt gež found it politically expedient to identify his interests with those of men who held most of their land through Wendim.

As neither Wendim nor Ze Sellasé is said to have been a priest, all the lands of the parish must bear the obligation to support celebration of mass equally. The clergy includes only seven priests and five deacons. Similarly, the offices of *çhiqa shum* and *çhewa gebez* rotate annually between men holding rist land in the two first settlers' estates.

The estate of Wendim is divided into eleven sections of land. Only one of these sections will be used for illustrative purposes. It is the section which lies to the west of the parish church in the area where Wendim is said to have first settled (map 2). It is bounded on the north and west by forested bluffs. Its southern and eastern boundaries are largely made up of streams. The low land along these streams and a meadow just outside the church gate provide the principal permanent pasturage in the section. The church characteristically occupies the highest ground in the parish. The lands of Wendim's section fall gently away from it in all directions.

The fifteen homesteads located in the section (map 4) make up the hamlet of Gra Midir. The hamlet of Gra Midir cannot, however, be identified with the estate of Wendim as a whole, for there are a number of homesteads located on the other sections of Wendim's estate which fall within the hamlets in Dereqé. The social composition of Gra Midir, like the founding legend of Dereqé, is commonplace. Eight of its household heads are ordinary farmers, five are clerics, three are single women, and one is a weaver. There are no titled men resident in Gra Midir.

The Gra Midir section of Wendim's estate was divided at the time of study into fifty-six fields. Altogether twenty-eight men have an active interest in the land as landholders, tenants, or both. All of these hold at least one field rent-free. The most striking differences between the landholding pattern of Gra Midir and Shoa Hayl concern the status of landholders, the proportion of nonresident holders, and the rate of ten-

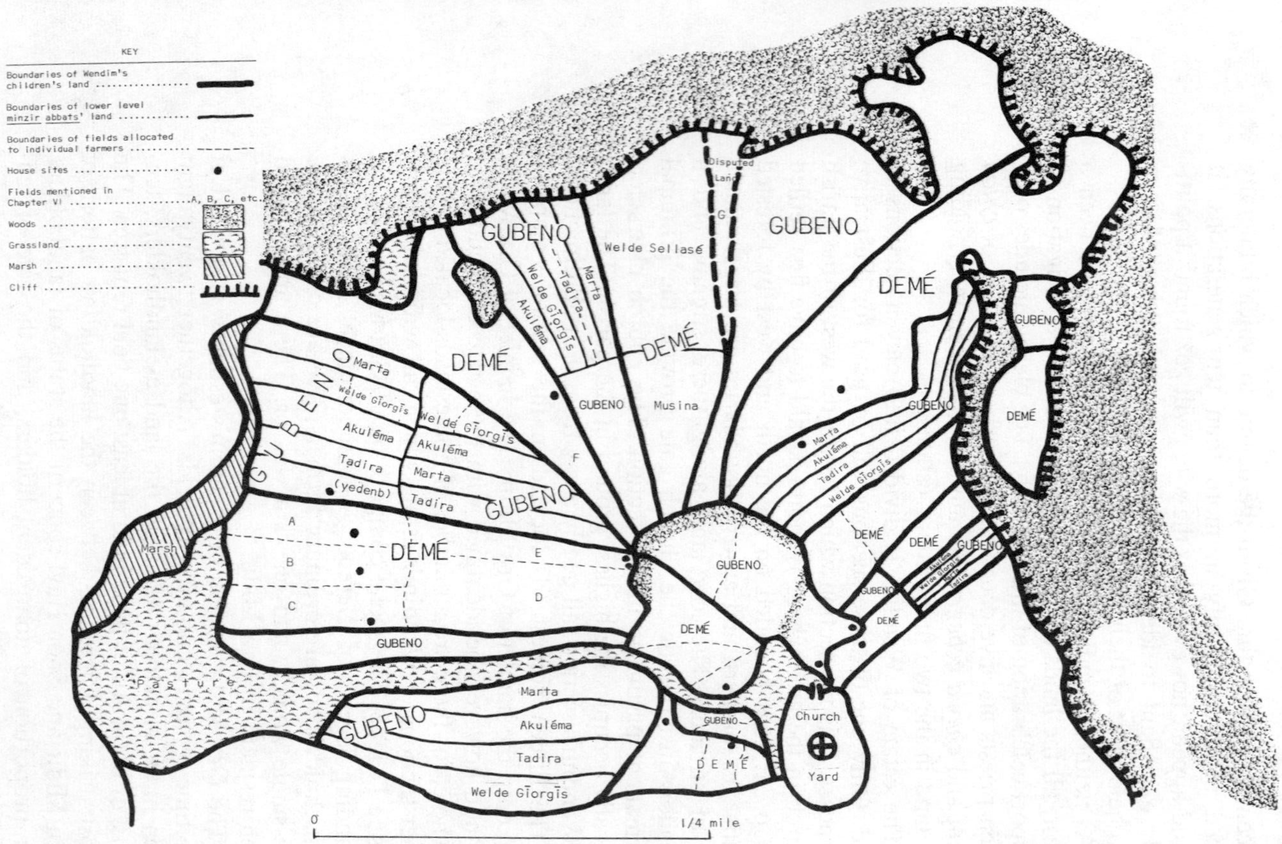
KEY
Boundaries of Wendim's children's land
Boundaries of lower level minzir abbats' land
Boundaries of fields allocated to individual farmers
House sites
Fields mentioned in Chapter VI ....A, B, C, etc.
Woods
Grassland
Marsh
Cliff
GUBENO
DEMÉ
Marta
Tadira
Welde Gīorgīs
Akuléma
Welde Sellasé
Disputed Land
G
Musina
F
E
D
A
B
C
(yedenb)
Marsh
Pasture
Church
Yard
0
1/4 mile

Map 4. Division of Wendim's Gra Midir land section

ancy. Only two out of the fifty-six fields are held by a titled man. Fifteen of the fields, or 27 percent of the total, are held by nonresidents, and only four of the fields are worked in tenancy. In part, these differences are due to the political unimportance of Dereqé, as compared with Feres Bét. In part they reflect the fact that Gra Midir is the most densely settled section in Wendim's estate. Nonresident landholders, a group which always includes a relatively high proportion of titled men, hold a somewhat higher proportion of the land in the other sections of Wendim's estate.

Though the pattern of landholding found in Wendim's Gra Midir tract is more frequently encountered than that of Shoa Hayl, it is misleading to consider any specific pattern of landholding "typical" in Dega Damot. As has already been noted, what is constant from parish to parish is the set of processes, such as inheritance, litigation, clearing, and church service, through which people acquire, defend, and lose control of land. The relative importance of these processes changes over time and varies with such factors as population density, available land for clearing, political prominence, and the curative reputation of the local church or its associated spring of holy water. The pattern of holding found in a particular parish at a particular time thus represents the cumulative effect of the processes that are currently operative and have been operative in the past in that parish.

6. The Descent Corporation and Its Estate

The Amhara cultural paradigm or theory of land tenure with which I am concerned here is important, not because it directly determines the decisions of living men or produces the observed pattern of landholding, but because it serves to define and limit people's choices, to shape their strategies, and to rally others to support their positions. It provides them with the sole idiom in terms of which they can legally justify their claims to rist land. It would be a mistake to think that these cultural principles of land tenure completely account for the process of land allocation in Dega Damot, but it would be an equally great mistake to consider them unreal, irrelevant, or less important than the needs and interests which motivate men to manipulate them to their own advantage.

The scope of this chapter, then, is limited in two respects: first, it takes as the unit for analysis the descent corporation and its estate rather than the individual and his rights; and second, it is primarily concerned with the pattern of land division and with its meaning for Damotians but not with the ongoing processes which create or change this pattern.

The division of the first settler's estate and the genealogical charter

The Damotian theory of land tenure is a theory of descent. In it, as in many other theories of descent, genealogical relationships play a crucial role in the structuring of people's relations to property and to one another. Their fundamental importance in the Amhara case derives from the basic cultural postulate that a person's land rights should be divided *per stirpes* among all of his or her descendents. Remembered genealogical relations among a first settler's descendents serve as a charter for the division of his or her land tract (the descent corporation's estate) and hence for the internal structure of the group of men and women who share it (the members of the descent corporation).

Amhara genealogical charters are in part a record of past events, of marriage and birth, fragments of history, and in part they are the product of men's attempts to manipulate the institutional relationships these charters are believed to govern. What I am concerned with here, however, is not their historicity but their relationship to the pattern of land division in first settlers' land tracts. This relationship, as will be seen, is more complex than is suggested by the simple postulate of *per stirpes* land division; for the observed pattern of division cannot be accounted for by reference to the charter alone, and not all of the remembered genealogical relationships in the charter are represented in the division of the land. This lack of correspondence, this partial independence beween the pattern of land division and the genealogical charters the pattern is thought to represent, plays a vitally important role in the functioning of the rist system and will be illustrated in detail.

The principles of division by father and division by allotment

There are two culturally recognized modes of land division through which the first settler's land tract, the estate of the descent corporation, is subdivided and allocated to living men: division "by father" (*beabbat*) and division by "allotment" (*bemeṭen*). Understanding the ways these two types of division are implemented and how they differ from one another is of the utmost importance.

Division by father is a way of dividing land bearing the name of a remote ancestor (including the first settler himself) into equal shares in the names of his remembered children. Division by allotment is a way of assigning the smallest shares of land produced through division by father directly to the living descendents of the ancestral share holder without regard for the exact structure of the intermediate genealogical ties.

Division by father is used to divide a first settler's land tract into smaller sections in accordance with the *per stirpes* rule of division. The land tract (or sections of it) is thus divided into equal shares in the names of his putative children, or, more precisely, in the names of all those of his children through whom living landholders trace their descent. The children's shares (or, as will become clear, sections of them) in turn are each subdivided into equal shares in the name of those of their respective children through whom living landholders trace their descent. This process of division by father may be carried downward any number of generations, but in Dega Damot it is not usually carried in most lines beyond the third or fourth descending generation from the first settler; that is, it is not usually carried out beyond the generational level of his great-great-grandchildren. Living landholders usually place themselves somewhere between the seventh and eleventh generation.

Through division by father the names of the first settler's descendents in the first few descending generations come to be associated with particular pieces of land; the higher generational levels of the descent corporation's genealogical charter are, in this way, written on the land.

Division by father is also of crucial importance to the structural differentiation of the descent corporation that holds the land tract as its estate; for the land that has been divided by father in the name of a particular ancestor becomes the focus of interest to those of his descendents who hold it and the ancestor himself becomes a symbol of their corporate identity. The ancestor is thus a point of structural segmentation in the genealogical charter and those who hold his land constitute a segment of the larger descent corporation.

The structural significance of ancestors in whose name land has been divided by father is reflected in linguistic usage.

The elders of Dega Damot refer to a first settler, in the context of land division, as a chief father or ancestor (*wanna abbat*).[1] Any of the chief ancestor's descendents in whose name land has been divided by father are termed divisional ancestors or *minzir abbat* (sing.) while all his other descendents are simply called ancestors or *abbat* (sing.). This point is of great importance and bears repeating. An ancestor is termed a minzir abbat if, and only if, land has been assigned to him through division by father. If no land has been divided in his name, an ancestor is not considered to be a minzir abbat even if he is a link in the chain of ancestors—the descent line—through which people validate their right to rist land. The distinction is critical, for only the minzir abbat (and of course the first settler or chief ancestor) has land bearing his name, a group of people who use that land as rist, and a representative, or *fej*, to look after the group's collective interests.

It is essential to remember that division by father is an ongoing process and not an account of historical events. It is a principle of Amhara land law used by living men to divide, subdivide, and redivide the estates of first settlers in response to changing political and demographic pressures. The observable pattern of division among the minzir abbats in a land tract results from the way this principle has been applied, through time and under such pressures, to decisions concerning land disputes; the pattern does not result from an actual division of land carried out long ago between the heirs of remote ancestors at the time of their deaths. Moreover, as is explained in the following section, there are variations in the way division of land by father is implemented.

The fields of a minzir abbat that have not been further subdivided (or, as is explained below, assigned) by father are referred to as the *yedenb* or undivided portion of that minzir abbat. It is these fields, or parts of them, that are assigned directly to living people through the other basic process of division, that of allotment.

1. There is considerable variation in the terminology used to describe ancestors in other Amhara areas I visited.

In division by allotment the exact nature of the intervening genealogical links is ignored (though they must be lineal), and fields are alloted to the minzir abbat's accepted descendents by his representative or *fej* in accordance with a number of less formal and more pragmatic considerations, such as how much of the minzir abbat's land the recipient already holds as rist, the location of his homestead in relation to the land in question, his standing in the local community, and his regional political influence.

Division by father and division by allotment contrast in several important respects. Division by father potentially involves the redivision of a large portion of a first settler's estate and is therefore a matter of political concern to many people. Division by allotment does not require major changes in the pattern of land division and is hence a more private matter, concerning only a few landholders. Moreover, division by father represents a rigorous application of the ideal cultural postulate that a person's rist should be divided equally among all his children. Division by allotment, on the other hand, follows only the spirit but not the letter of this postulate; for, though it allocates land only to descendents of the appropriate ancestor, it does not do so *per stirpes*. For this reason division by father is considered by Damotians to be legally binding and permanent, while division by allotment is considered to be less formal and more subject to change. Division by father is also considered less amicable because it almost always represents the result of a prolonged conflict over land that could not be settled through further adjustments in the less formal process of division by allotment.

To the outside observer there appears to be much variation in the way in which first settlers' land tracts have been divided and parcelled out to corporation members. To Damotian elders, however, the pattern of division is everywhere essentially the same, since it represents to them the application, in some combination, of the principles of division by father and division by allotment.

At one extreme are land tracts in long-settled parishes in which division by father (subject to certain limitations that will be explained presently) has been carried down to the generation of living men.[2] At the other extreme are land tracts in which division by father has not yet begun and where land is allocated entirely by allotment. In these tracts, which invariably occupy partly uncleared mountainous forest land, even the requirement of descent from the first settler may be suspended and all comers given land to clear so long as their request has been approved by a committee of resident elders known as *yewenz daññа*. It is universally held, however, that when uncleared land is no longer available in these tracts they will be divided by father in the name of the first settler's children, who are indeed remembered, and that only persons who are able to trace descent from them will be allowed to retain their land.

The vast majority of land tracts, however, are "mixed" types in which the pattern of division is the result of both division by father and division by allotment. The two cases with which I will now illustrate land division in greater detail are of this mixed type. Even in this type of land tract there is considerable variation in the pattern of division, variation that reflects flexibility in the way the principles of land division are implemented.

The implementation of land division

The land tracts, or descent corporation estates, I have chosen for illustrative purposes are, once again, those of Shoa Hayl in the parish of Feres Bét Mikael, and Wendim in the parish of Dereqé Maryam (map 2). The way Shoa Hayl's land tract has been divided by father is shown on map 5. The upper generational levels of the genealogical charter this pattern of division by father is thought to represent are shown in figure 2. The way the portion of Wendim's land tract (discussed above, in chapter 5) has been divided by father is shown on

2. In some other parts of Ethiopia, such as the Gera Midir district of the subprovince of Menz in Shoa province, which I had the opportunity to study in 1968–70, the process of division by father is usually carried down to the present generation. Beyond the first few descending generations, however, fields are not actually subdivided but assigned in their entirety to one or another of the ancestor's children. This type of division also is found in Dega Damot and is discussed below.

map 4, and the upper generational levels of the charter it is thought to represent are shown in figure 3. Only those ancestors in figures 2 and 3 who are shaded are minzir abbats, while all other ancestors are of only potential significance to division by father since land may be divided in their names at some time in the future.

At first glance the correspondence between land division and genealogical charter is not obvious for either Shoa Hayl or Wendim. Indeed, the actual pattern of division is in some ways more complex and in some ways less complex than the general rule of *per stirpes* division and the structure of the charter alone would suggest. The most important reason for the greater complexity is that in these land tracts, as in most first-settlers' land tracts, the share of each minzir abbat consists of a number of dispersed fields rather than a single large one.

As is usually the case, the land tracts of both Shoa Hayl and Wendim are composed of a number of smaller sections (*maṭefiya*, sing.), and it is these sections which are individually divided in the names of their respective first settlers' children. Shoa Hayl's land tract's thirty-two sections (map 6) are massed together, while Wendim's eleven sections (map 2) are separated from one another by sections of another first settler's tract. This difference is not regarded by the elders as significant.

The size and shape of these land tract sections are influenced by the distribution of the natural features, such as trails, stream beds, and rocks, that mark the sections' boundaries,[3] by historical factors, and by the elders' desire for truly equal division. Most sections are said to represent land that was divided by father on a particular occasion after having been brought under cultivation on an ad hoc basis by those men who had the energy and the need to clear it. At the same time, each section tends to have a unique agricultural potential, one producing a fine crop of potatoes in a wet year,

3. Such features are visible on aerial photographs, but ascertaining which of them constitute boundaries required much time-consuming and suspicion-provoking investigation on the ground.

Map 5. Division by father in Shoa Hayl

another a good stand of barley in a year when the rains begin early but abate for a few weeks before commencing again in earnest. Assigning the first settler's children land in each section thus assures them an equal share of each type of soil in the entire land tract.[4]

The division of the first settler's land tract into sections and the consequent dispersal of each minzir abbat's share of the tract indirectly introduces yet another variation and complexity into the pattern of land division. This is that each section of the tract and each field of a minzir abbat may be treated as a separate unit with respect to division. Consequently, some of a land tract's sections may be divided in the name of the first settlers' children while others are not, and some of a minzir abbat's fields may be divided by father in the name of his children while others are not. So long as even one field has been divided in an ancestor's name, however, he is considered to be a minzir abbat; his segment of the descent corporation has corporate existence and a representative to look after its affairs.

The extent to which and the way in which the thirty-two sections that make up Shoa Hayl's land tract (map 6) have been divided by father in the name of his six children (fig. 2) can be seen on map 5. Two sections, Q and R on Map 6, are still in permanent pasture, though I was told that the way they will be divided has already been agreed upon. Two other small sections, V and X on Map 6, are the house sites of old people who maintain that their land is still the undivided portion or *yedenb* of Shoa Hayl. The twenty-seven other sections for which I was able to obtain sufficient data have each been divided into six equal shares in the name of Shoa Hayl's six children: Gebré, Teklé, Nudé, Qusqo, Senbeta, and Kokeba.[5] A child's share is referred to as his lot land (*ịta merét*) because it is assigned to him by casting lots.

4. The farmers' understandable desire to have land in many sections in order to minimize the risk of total crop failure is a factor that must be taken into account in any land reform program that attempts to consolidate holdings.

5. Section Y has been divided by father, but I did not succeed in mapping it. I do not know the status of section GG.

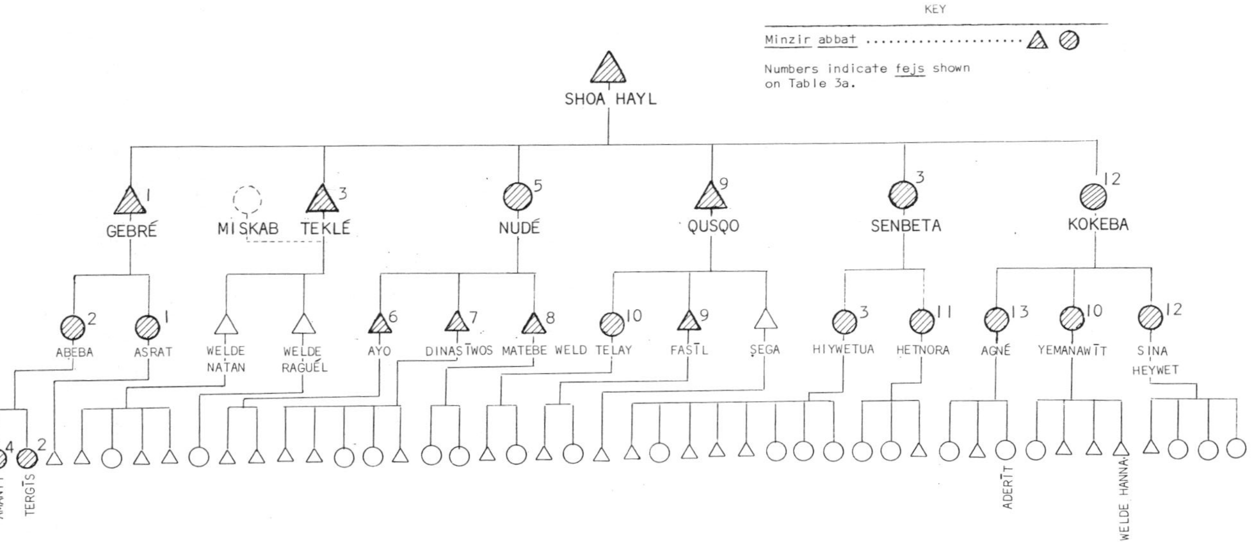

Fig. 2. The genealogical charter of Shoa Hayl

The shares of Shoa Hayl's children in each section are in the form of long narrow strips of land which invariably run from the high ground to the low ground, once again to ensure that the division of each type of soil will be as equal as possible. The six strips of section K (map 6) shown on map 5, for example, run from the ridge-top trail that separates sections A, B, and C from sections J, K, and L, down to the marsh. Most fields are divided in this way. The unusual pattern of division in section T (map 6) is due to the fact that it is a basin sloping down from all sides to the point where it intersects the boundary of sections O and U.

The order of the children's strips in each section was established by casting lots at the time when the section was divided by father. It therefore varies from section to section. In section J, for example, from left to right the order is Senbeta, Kokeba, Gebré, Qusqo, Nudé, and Teklé, while in the adjacent section K it is Kokeba, Nudé, Senbeta, Gebré, Qusqo, and Teklé.

The boundaries between the strips are poorly marked. Occasionally they are separated by a dead furrow or a narrow strip of untilled land. Usually, however, their borders are remembered with reference to but a few rocky outcroppings, boulders, and the odd boundary stone. It is difficult or impossible for anyone who does not know the section well to discern these boundaries, and, even among those who do, disputes are not unknown. Indeed, charges of "pushing" these minimal boundaries are frequently heard in moot and court, and occasionally the disputes result in violence. The absence of clearer, more indelible boundaries between Shoa Hayl's children's strips is also consonant with their impermanence; for, as will be explained later, they have been redrawn three times since 1920.

The division of Wendim's Gra Midir land section (one of his eleven sections) between his two children, Demé and Gubeno (fig. 3), is shown on map 4. Probably because the section is larger, the pattern of division in it is more complex than in any of Shoa Hayl's sections. The pasture to the south of the church near the marsh has not yet been divided by father and is therefore considered the portion or *yedenb* of

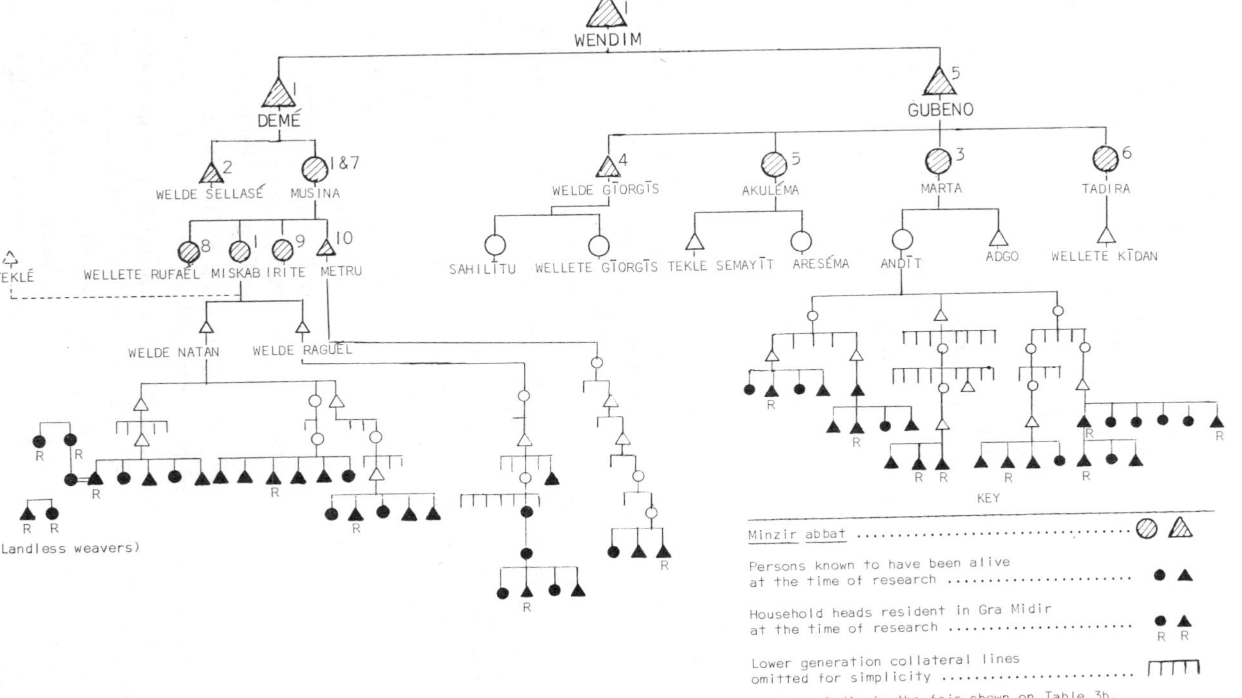

Fig. 3. The genealogical charter of Wendim

Wendim himself or, rather, since it is uncultivated, the *shī belo*. The grassy meadow in front of the churchyard is used for staging church processionals on major holidays and for public ceremonies mourning the dead. The churchyard itself lies between the land of Wendim and the land of Dereqé Maryam's other first settler, Ze Sellasé. It is not considered to belong to either of them.

The remainder of the section has been divided into sixteen fields, eight for each of Wendim's two sons, Demé and Gubeno. The object of this elaborate pattern of subdivision is again to make certain that the minzir abbats receive truly equal shares. The fields, which are more irregularly shaped than those of Shoa Hayl because of land form, run from the church-topped knoll down to a steep bluff in the north, a deep ravine in the west, and a marshy creek bottom in the south.

As map 5 indicates, only a few of Shoa Hayl's children's fields have been subdivided into even narrower but equally long strip fields in the name of his grandchildren. The field of Shoa Hayl's daughter Kokeba in section K (maps 5 and 6), for example, has been divided into three strips in the name of her three children Agné, Yemanawīt, and Sina Heywet (fig. 2); and the field of Shoa Hayl's son Gebré in section H has been divided into two strips in the name of his daughters Abeba and Asrat. Most of Shoa Hayl's children's fields, however, have not been subdivided despite the fact that, as figure 2 indicates, almost all of his grandchildren and two of his great-grandchildren are minzir abbats. In part this is an accurate reflection of the fact that division by father and hence the structural differentiation of the descent corporation and its members' interests has not proceeded very far at the generational level of Shoa Hayl's grandchildren.

The absence of further subdivision of the fields of Shoa Hayl's children is in part misleading, however; for some of these fields have been assigned in their entirety to Shoa Hayl's children's children. Through this process, for example, equal numbers of Kokeba's fields, and presumably equal amounts of land, are assigned undivided to Agné, Yemanawīt, and Sina Heywet. Assigning fields in this manner is not felt to be fully in keeping with the rule of equal division, and it is re-

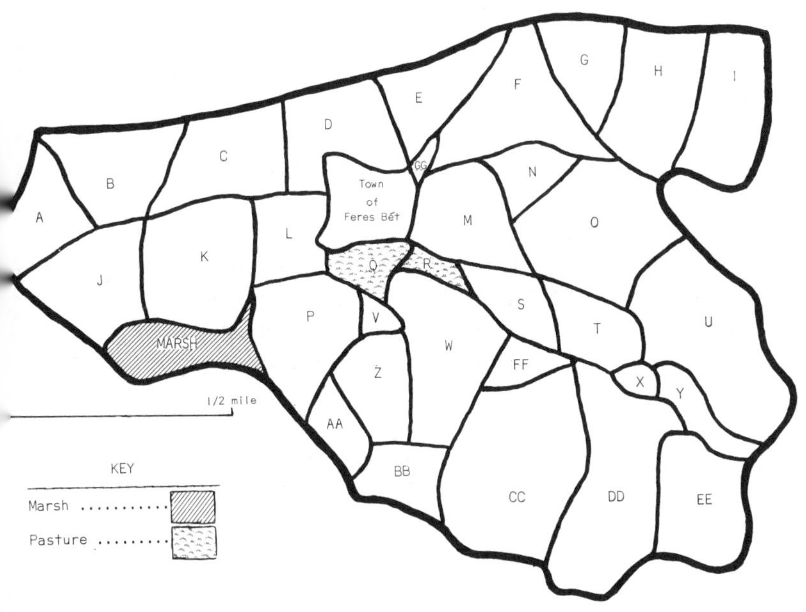

Map 6. Land sections in Shoa Hayl

garded as temporary, but it is frequently employed at the lower generational levels of division by father to avoid further reduction in the size of fields that are already none too large for efficient cultivation. Because no new boundaries are drawn to memorialize the arrangements made in division by father when fields are assigned in their entirety to an ancestor's children, the practice often leads to later ambiguity and conflict. This is illustrated in case 4, chapter 8.

One of the eight fields of Wendim's son Demé, shown on map 4, has been subdivided in the name of his children, Welde Sellasé and Musina; they have also had land divided in their names in other sections of Wendim's land tract and are, as figure 3 indicates, minzir abbats. Division by father has proceeded farther in the fields of Wendim's other son,

Gubeno. Five of his fields have been divided into strips in the name of his four children: Marta, Akuléma, Tadira, and Welde Gīorgīs. The greater extent of division among Gubeno's children is the result of a land case some years ago in which a priest moving into Dereqé successfully claimed land in the name of Welde Gīorgīs, who had not previously been considered a minzir abbat.

In principle, the lower generational limits to which division by father has been carried in a land tract and hence the degree of segmentation of the corporation should be quite clearly defined. A field, it would seem, has either been subdivided (or assigned in its entirety) or it has not, and an ancestor is either a minzir abbat with a representative or he is not. Yet in reality, because this generational level—this cutting edge of division by father—is also the generational level of maximal dispute over land it is often unclear, ambiguous, and unstable. Small narrow fields such as those that have been divided in the name of Shoa Hayl's grandchildren are sometimes merged again gradually to lose their separate identity. Often this happens when the individual who holds the field of one of the minzir abbats (for example, a field of Kokeba's child Agné, in figure 2) obtains control over the adjacent fields of that minzir abbat's siblings (in this instance the fields of Yemanawīt and Sina Heywet) through one of the arrangements described in the next chapter. It is to this individual's advantage to maintain that the land never was divided by father, that it is really the portion of the sibling's parent (in this case the portion of Kokeba), for if it is undivided he has a rist right to all of it, whereas if it was divided he may have a rist right in only one child's share. With the passage of time the status of the land becomes hazy and, unless tested in a land dispute, remains indeterminate. When division by father is carried out by assigning fields in their entirety instead of by subdivision, ambiguity can arise even more quickly, for there are no boundaries to be erased or forgotten.

Another source of ambiguity about the lower limits of division by father is that a long time may pass, sometimes years, between the formal agreement to divide land, the casting of lots, and the actual measurement or assignation of fields. In such a situation one informant may say the land has been divided because the lots have been cast, while another may say it has not because he has not yet received his share of the land.

Finally, there is a degree of relativity about the way ancestors' names are applied to fields that contributes to the hazy definition of the lower limits of division by father. A field of Asrat (fig. 2), for example, may be referred to as the land of Asrat, of Gebré, or of Shoa Hayl, depending on whether the contrast intended is with Abeba, Teklé, or one of the other first settlers in the parish in Feres Bét. The choice of names is determined in usage by the generational level at which there is actual or potential conflict and by the self-interest of the speaker.

The smallest fields produced through division by father, or pieces of them, are the fields held by living individuals. It is said that there are a few land tracts in Dega Damot where these fields are held entirely through division by father; that is, as I noted previously, where division by father has been carried down to the generation of living men. In most land tracts, however, including those of Shoa Hayl and Wendim, they are held on the basis of division by allotment rather than division by father. In other words they are held by descendents of the minzir abbat whose portion they represent, subject to the regulatory jurisdiction of that minzir abbat's representative but without regard to the exact structure of intermediate genealogical relationships.

The relationship between the pattern of land division produced by division by father and the pattern of individual holding in the land tract of Shoa Hayl can be seen by comparing map 5 with map 3. Note that some minimal minzir abbats' fields are held undivided by living persons while others are subdivided into from two to six smaller fields. For example, the field of Kokeba (fig. 2) in section O (map 6) is held by one person, while Kokeba's field in section W has been divided into four separate plots. Characteristically, these smaller plots are cross sections of Kokeba's field rather than even narrower strips running its full length; for in division by allotment equal division is no longer an overriding concern. The horizontal boundaries separating the plots in a minzir abbat's field are usually pathways, and it is because of this that they tend to crosscut several fields.

Since neither of Kokeba's fields in this example have been divided by father—that is, they are both considered his portion or *yedenb*—their disposition among living descendents is by allotment. This means that descent from Kokeba in any line is sufficient to justify possession of either Kokeba's field in O or any of the plots in W. It does not matter whether this descent is traced through Agné, Yemanawīt, or Sina Heywet. Kokeba's field in section K, by contrast, has been divided by father. To assert a rist right in the strip of this field assigned to Kokeba's child Agné, an individual must trace his descent from Kokeba through Agné. It does not matter, however, through which of Agné's three children he traces his pedigree, for the structure of the intermediate charter is not relevant to division by allotment.

The relationship between division by father and the pattern of individual holding in the Gra Midir land section of Wendim is shown by map 4. Once again, some of the minimal minzir abbats' fields, for example, Demé's field labelled F on map 4, are held in their entirety by a single person, while others, such as Demé's field including plots A through E on map 4, are divided into many plots.

This completes the illustrative description of the pattern of land division in the estates of Shoa Hayl and Wendim, and of the way it is thought to represent the application of the principles of division by father and division by allotment to the estates' respective genealogical charters. The discussion began with the first settler's land tract, the corporation's estate, and ended with the small fields held and cultivated by living individuals. It should be clearer now why, in Amhara land theory, these individually held fields are not the basic or immutable units of the rist system, but only shares in the estate of a descent-chartered landholding corporation.

It is also evident from the foregoing description that the rule of equal inheritance on which the elders insist that their land tenure system is based, does not, in itself, account for the pattern of land division in a first settler's estate. It is not a description of the way land is actually divided but a cultural principle embodied in specific norms relevant to specific contexts. The way in which the principle of equal inheritance is institutionalized in the contexts of land divison with which I have been concerned in this section deserves a final comment.

First, it should be noted that, since the rule is *per stirpes* and not *per capita*, it is not even ideally directed towards creating an equal division of land among descendents of any generational level below that of the first settler's children. For example, Demé's daughter Musina has the right, according to the *per stirpes* rule, to one-fourth of all Wendim's land tract, while Gubeno's daughter Marta has the right to only one-eighth (fig. 3). Similarly, Kokeba's daughter Agné has the right to one-eighteenth of Shoa Hayl's land tract, but Gebré's daughter Abeba has the right to one-twelfth.

Second, while the equal division of land is a matter of meticulous concern in division by father it is a matter of comparative indifference in division by allotment. To put it another way, in the context of dividing land between the segments of a descent corporation (the minzir abbats) equality is crucial; in the context of allocating the *yedenb* land of the segment to living individuals it is not.

Finally, since division by father, with its intense concern for equality, may be applied to each of an ancestor's fields individually, the resulting pattern of division sometimes appears to be far from equal. An example of this is found in Wendim. Only a few of Demé's fields have been divided in the name of his children Welde Sellasé and Musina. Due to circumstances that will be explained in the next chapter, all of Demé's other fields are held by persons tracing their descent through Musina. The descendents of Welde Sellasé, therefore, tend to regard Demé's fields as fields that have in fact, if not formally, been unfairly assigned to Musina.

The genealogical charter

In the previous sections of this chapter I took the pattern of land division in the descent corporation's estate as a given and showed how it is thought by the elders to represent the application of the two principles of division to the corporation's genealogical charter. In doing so, I inevitably, like the elders, stressed the correspondence between the pattern of land division and the structure of the charter, and I ignored discrepancies between them. Yet there are many discrepancies, and they play a major part in conflict over land and hence in the dynamics of the rist system. In this section I shall examine these discrepancies. I take the charter as a starting point and focus attention on those parts of it which, for one reason or another, are not represented in the pattern of land division and therefore are not the basis of structural segmentation in the descent corporation; I then examine the closely related problem of the extent to which knowledge about the charter is widely held and agreed upon.

Discrepancies between the charter and land division

In most descent corporation estates, as in those of Shoa Hayl and Wendim, division by father has not even begun below the third or fourth generation of the corporation's genealogical charter. The ambilaterally traced pedigrees through which living people claim rist land are usually from eight to ten generations deep or at least five to seven generations below the lowest minzir abbats. There are thus a great many remembered genealogical relationships which have not yet been "written" on the first settler's land tract through division by father. Most of these relationships are of little public concern, since they are of no immediate relevance to the division of land or the segmentation of the corporation. Normally it is the ancestors in the generation just below the lowest minzir abbats who are the subject of controversy and who play a part in litigation over land.

There are also, however, in most descent corporation charters at the generational level of the minzir abbats ancestors in whose name no land has been divided; for though ideally division by father, insofar as it is carried out, and hence the segmentation of the descent corporation, should correspond to the structure of the genealogical charter, in practice it seldom does. There are, in fact, many discrepancies between remembered genealogy and the way in which land is divided by father; most of them are related to the fact that an ancestor is not given his share of land in division by father unless a living person tracing a pedigree through him successfully presses a claim to his share of the land. Discrepancies at these higher generational levels of the charter are usually at the heart of major land disputes, for they involve a correspondingly higher proportion of the descent corporation's estate.

Not infrequently a child or grandchild of the first settler is remembered for whom no land has been divided, even though the process of division by father has been carried out completely amongst the other siblings at that generational level. The Amhara explanation of this, of course, is that none of his descendents have asked for, or, literally, sued for his share of the land. It is said of such landless ancestor that he has not been "brought in yet." Until recently, for example, Demé's son Welde Sellasé had not been brought in, that is, he had no land and had not become a minzir abbat. Since according to the *per stirpes* rule Welde Sellasé is entitled to one-fourth of all Wendim's land tract, attempts to bring him in have been the focus of intense legal and political activity.

When an ancestor such as Welde Sellasé is brought in, he can change the structural significance of his sibling. Thus before Welde Sellasé was a minzir abbat, Musina had no structural significance because she was not a point of segmentation. She was not usually cited as an ancestor, and those of Demé's fields which were divided were divided directly in the name of Musina's children Miskab, Welette Rufaél, Irite, and Metru.

In this way ancestors who had no siblings, or at least no siblings for whom land has been divided, are often telescoped out of the charter for most purposes. It was only after I had been investigating the charter of Wendim for some months that I learned from the elders that Wendim is in a genealogical but not structural sense believed to be the grandfather, not the father, of Demé and Gubeno. Wendim, according to this account, had only one child, a son named Yohannis, who, in turn, was the father of Demé and Gubeno. The idea of a Yohannis is, however, regarded with some ambivalence. On the one hand, the shadowy Yohannis may have had siblings, and should even one descendent of one of them press his suit, he would have a formal right to one-half of Wendim's land tract! On the other hand, Yohannis, if he existed, must have had a wife through whom all of the descendents of Demé and Gubeno have potential claims to land in other parishes.

Knowledge of the genealogical charter

The genealogical structure of a descent corporation's charter is a matter of great concern because it greatly affects men's interests in land. Knowledge about the charter is a matter of crucial importance. There is much variation in the extent to which this knowledge is widely disseminated and agreed upon, variation which is related to the generational level concerned and the degree to which land has been divided by father at that level.

Despite their importance in land disputes, or perhaps because of this importance, genealogical charters are not written down in any official or systematic fashion. Many men have notebooks containing their pedigrees, lists of lineal ancestors reaching back to the first settlers of several estates in which they hold or hope to hold rist land. Often these lists include the siblings of ancestors, particularly in higher generations, but there is no attempt by the corporation fejs and their influential friends to write down an authoritative and binding version of even the higher generational levels of the charter. My attempts to record charters frequently aroused suspicion. As one elder remarked, only half in jest, "Today you write down all our ancestors, in ten years you'll have all our rist."

The names of first settlers are widely known and generally agreed upon; indeed, sometimes, as with Shoa Hayl, his name is incorporated into the name of the hamlet most closely associated with the land tract. The names and genealogical relationships of well-established minzir abbats, that is, minzir abbats who have received a large portion of the land to which they are entitled, are known and agreed upon by most household heads who hold rist land in the land tract, and by many other people who have rist rights in the estate through which they hope to claim land in the future.

Below the level of well-established minzir abbats, the charter is less widely known and less well agreed upon, for it has not yet been clearly written on the land through division by father. Knowledge about a particular ancestor in this intermediate generational level is held, for the most part, by those men who hold or hope to hold rist land by a pedigree traced through him or one of his siblings. Often the right to speak about him (or her) and his offspring, at least in public, is considered the prerogative of the more influential of these men. For example, on one occasion I asked a group of elders who had assembled to arbitrate a boundary dispute to tell me about the descendents of Shoa Hayl. One of them obligingly told me the names of Shoa Hayl's six children and was well into his fifteen grandchildren when he was stopped by a growing murmur from the other elders, who objected that it was all very well to talk about Shoa Hayl's children, but that discussing their descendents was a delicate matter. On another occasion I recited the names of a certain ancestor's children to a wily old man who had professed to know nothing about them though he himself was the ancestor's fej. He drew himself up angrily and thundered, "Who has been telling you about my ancestors?" He then, with a vengeance, gave me the genealogical information I sought, presumably to make certain that I would not give credence to some jealous rival's version of the charter.

As this sense of secrecy, anxiety, and possessiveness suggests, genealogical relationships in this region of the charter, where division by father is just beginning or is just about to begin, are subject to manipulation. Indeed, attempts to manipulate the charter play a central role in the politics of Amhara land tenure.

Altering a descent corporation's charter at this generational level, however, while possible, is not as easy as it might seem to be in light of the secrecy with which it is discussed;

most of the ancestors and genealogical relationships of which it consists are duplicated in the charters of other descent corporations. This is because ancestors, like living men and women, can be "affiliated" with more than one descent corporation.

While most first settlers, or "chief fathers" as they are called in a genealogical context, are uniquely associated with a single descent corporation's charter, most of their descendents are associated with more than one charter.[6] For example, Shoa Hayl's son Teklé (fig. 2) is said to have married Miskab, great-granddaughter of Wendim (fig. 3), and to have had two children by her, Welde Natan and Welde Raguél. These children are remembered in both Shoa Hayl's and Wendim's charters.

Some ancestors have had land divided in their names in more than one land tract and hence have attained the status of minzir abbats, with corporate segments in more than one corporation. When this occurs, the ancestor must be regarded as the apical ancestor or symbolic head of a distinct corporate segment in each of the descent corporations in which he has had land divided in his name by father. Each of these corporate segments, in principle, has its own land, its own membership, and its own representative or fej. The fact that a man holds rist land by virtue of a pedigree traced through the ancestor in one descent corporation may be used in court as presumptive evidence of descent when he claims rist land through the same ancestor in another descent corporation; it does not, in theory or in practice, assure him that his claim will be recognized or that he will be given the land. At the same time there is no formal rule to prevent an individual from holding rist land in more than one of the ancestor's corporate segments, or, if he is influential, from representing more than one of these segments as their fej. The degree to

6. The main exceptions to this generalization are the children and grandchildren of the legendary King Tekle Haymanot, some of whom are said to have founded many parishes and are hence spoken of as first settlers of many corporations. In the context of rist rights, however, each of the descent corporations founded by one of these illustrious ancestors is usually treated as a separate entity.

which the membership and leadership of an ancestor's corporate segment in different corporations are in fact distinct or overlapping is thus an empirical question; analytically, however, since the segments are parts of different corporations with different estates they are distinct from one another.

Men who trace their rist rights through the same ancestor but in different descent corporations frequently disagree on crucial genealogical issues—a major reason why such issues are avoided in polite conversation. The extent of their disagreement is generally related to whether there are also influential men who hold rist land through the ancestor in both corporations; and the emotion it arouses is related to the imminence and magnitude of the land dispute it threatens to trigger. Of particular importance in this last respect is whether the ancestor is a minzir abbat in the corporations concerned. Three cases will help to illustrate these points.

The remembered descendents of the marriage between Teklé and Miskab cited above are identical, at least in the first few generations. This is consistent with the fact that several influential men hold land in the land tracts of both Shoa Hayl and Wendim (the land tracts are adjacent) through descent from the children of this marriage. The children, Welde Natan and Welde Raguél, have not yet attained the status of minzir abbats in the corporation of either Shoa Hayl or Wendim; should they do so in the near future, however, it appears that the same man, an old nobleman, will become the fej of both the corporate segments of Welde Raguél.

The situation is somewhat different with respect to the multiple affiliation of the children of Shoa Hayl's daughter, Kokeba, who is said to have married Priest Sergu Mesqel, the first settler or chief father of a descent corporation in the parish of Shangi Maryam some two miles away (map 2). There are few men who presently hold rist land through Kokeba's children in both Shoa Hayl and Sergu Mesqel. There are significant differences in the way the descendents of this marriage are remembered by the elders of Feres Bét and Shangi Maryam. In the Sergu Mesqel version, held by the elders of Shangi Maryam, Agné, Sina Heywet, and

Yemanawīt are the great-grandchildren of Sergu Mesqel and Kokeba, while in the Shoa Hayl version, held by the elders of Feres Bét, the three are their children. This difference does not affect land division unless it is asserted in the future that the intermediate ancestors in the Shangi version had siblings, a possibility the Shoa Hayl version of the charter would preclude. There is also a difference in the sex of Agné and Sina Heywet which is of no structural significance. The most striking contradiction between the charters, however, is in the children of Sina Heywet, who are not the same in name or number. This contradiction is still latent in a sense, because, though Sina Heywet's children are minzir abbats in Sergu Mesqel, they are not yet minzir abbats in Shoa Hayl; in fact, division between Kokeba's children has only been partly carried out. The elders are well aware of these discrepancies and of their potentially disturbing effect on land distribution. Consequently, each side took great pains to assure me of the authenticity of their version of the charter.

Disagreement with regard to the genealogical status of Ṣega, the son of Qusqo (himself the son of Shoa Hayl), is even greater. Up to the time of my fieldwork, this son, Ṣega (fig. 2), had not been brought in as a minzir abbat, and no one had been able to claim rist land in Shoa Hayl by virtue of a descent line traced through him. In a parish beyond Shangi Maryam, in the lowlands to the north, Sega is a minzir abbat by virtue of descent from his mother, Qusqo's wife. In hopes of protecting themselves against future claims, the interested elders of Shoa Hayl have gone further than in the case of Kokeba and now maintain that Sega was his mother's child by another man and hence was not really entitled to share Qusqo's land with his siblings Fasīl and Telay (fig. 2).

Below the crucially important genealogical region, where division by father is beginning or about to begin, is a vast morass of ambilaterally traced genealogical ties. Knowledge of this low-level genealogy is of little public concern most of the time. Men know only the fragments, or rather strands, of genealogical information that is pertinent to their pedigrees and hence to their personal interest in land. Many ancestors are undoubtedly forgotten in this lower region, though not as many as would be convenient for the anthropologist. I was able to collect the names of nearly two thousand living persons who were considered descendents of one first settler (less than one hundred of them actually held land in the first settler's land tract) before I began to appreciate how useless it was to gather such data.

The central role of the descent corporation's genealogical charter in land division and land disputes raises questions about the relationship between genealogical knowledge and power. Genealogical knowledge is undoubtedly an asset for the man who seeks to become an influential elder. A man with an unusually rich fund of genealogical information is termed a "father counter" (*abbat qotari*) or a "rist counter" (*rist qotari*). He is called frequently to testify as a witness in land disputes, which may bring him profit as well as prestige, and he is able to watch carefully over his own interests in land. Extensive genealogical knowledge about a particular descent corporation's charter, or a part of it, also improves a man's chances of being selected as fej for the corporation or one of its corporate segments.

It would be a mistake, however, to exaggerate the role of genealogical information in the politics of Amhara land tenure and to suggest that knowledge is power. Many men with genealogical expertise are without political influence because they lack the other attributes of leadership, and many men with influence have attained the office of fej, though their knowledge of the ancestors is limited. In the last analysis, particularly in major land disputes involving claims through division by father, it is not so much that knowledge of the genealogical charter is power, as it is that power enables those who wield it to enunciate an authoritative version of the charter.

The organization of the descent corporation's landholders

Earlier I pointed out that the individuals who hold rist land in a descent corporation's estate do not constitute a cohesive, multipurpose kinship group. In this section I first clarify this point in light of the picture of descent corporation structure presented in this chapter, and then I describe the organizational role of descent corporation representatives or fejs.

The landholders

The 50 to 150 or more men and women who hold fields in a first settler's land tract as their rist are, in a sense, shareholders in a genealogically chartered, internally segmented landholding corporation. Like the shareholders of a joint stock company, they may have little to do with one another except in relation to the property in which they share rights. It is for this reason that I began this discussion by describing the corporation's estate and the principles according to which it is subdivided, rather than by describing the corporation's landholders and their interrelations.

Despite their belief in common descent from the first settler, the corporation's landholders do not have an ideology of kinship solidarity; in fact, in the pedigrees through which they validate their rights to rist land, most of them are not related to one another by the type of close ties to which the Amhara concept of kinship or *zimdinna* has primary reference. This is because close kinsmen find it advantageous to move apart from one another and to establish their homesteads and rist landholdings in different estates through different lines of descent, or, at least, to press their claims to rist land through different minzir abbats of the same corporation. Figure 3 shows the pedigrees through which those of Wendim's landholders who were resident in the village of Gra Midir in 1962 validated their right to share his estate.

If a corporation's landholders are not, for the most part, close kinsmen, neither are they necessarily neighbors or friends. Only 46 of the 119 people who hold rist land in Shoa Hayl's estate, for example, are resident on it; another 14 land holders dwell in the town of Feres Bét while the remaining 59 are resident elsewhere. Nor are the landholders brought together by common rituals or social obligations. In fact, it is only for purposes of land division and taxation that they must assemble, and even on these occasions many of them delegate a kinsman to represent their interests. Many of a corporation's landholders, usually a majority, are at least acquainted with one another, for the social world of the Amhara peasant is not, after all, unbounded; but some of them, particularly those who are nonresident landlords, have never met.

Finally, fellow landholders have little sense of common identity through their common descent. They have no cult of ancestral worship, no insignia, songs, or other symbols of unity. They do not identify themselves by the name of their common ancestor, as Wendims or Shoa Haylans, for example, but rather as that ancestor's descendents (*tewella-joch*, pl.) or rist-holders (*risteñoch*, pl.). This lack of identification with a particular ancestor, except occasionally in the heat of a land dispute, is, of course, a reflection of the fact that most men have rist rights in many estates and rist land in several. Similarly, many men hold land through more than one corporate segment within a particular descent corporation. Of the ninety-two landholders in Shoa Hayl for whom sufficient data is available, fifty-five hold rist land in only one of Shoa Hayl's six children's corporate segments, twenty-two hold rist land in two of these segments, seven hold rist land in three segments, eight hold rist land in four segments, one holds rist land in five segments, and none hold rist land in all six segments. It is clear that many of these landholders will not find their interests unambiguously identified with one minzir abbat or another in intersegmental land disputes.

Occasionally it happens that landholders whose interests are strongly identified with a particular corporation or one of its corporate segments find themselves united by the common need to protect their land against the claims of others. In the absence of "outside" threats to their land, however, any sense of solidarity generated upon these occasions of conflict is quickly lost, and men's relations as landholding codescendents are overridden in social interaction by numerous other types of relationships.

The role of the fej

The real proprietors of a descent corporation's affairs are the influential elders, the titled men and the officeholders who are elected from amongst its landholders to represent the corporation and each of its corporate segments as fejs. The fej has both external representative and internal administrative responsibilities. As representative, he must defend his ancestor's estate against encroachment on its boundaries and, if the corporation he represents is that of a minzir abbat, he must make certain that it is equal to those of the ancestor's siblings. At the time of my first fieldwork, for example, there was a dispute between the landholders of Demé and Gubeno as to whether the land of Wendim had been divided equally between them (the immediate issue was whether field G on map 4 belonged to Demé or Gubeno). In this dispute Demé and Gubeno were represented by their respective fejs.

It is also the fej's responsibility as representative of his ancestor to receive all new claims for rist land in the ancestor's estate, both through division by father and division by allotment. If he rejects the validity of the claimant's pedigree, the fej can be sued by the claimant. If he accepts the validity of the new claim, the fej must assume his responsibilities as the estate's administrator, for he must either reallocate to the claimant land held by someone else, or, if the claim requires division by father, he must supervise the division or redivision of his ancestor's estate by lot. Here I am concerned primarily with the fej's official responsibilities; a more detailed description of how the fej makes decisions is found in chapter 8.

The fej must be a landholder or the husband of a landholder in the corporation or corporate segment he is to represent. Ideally, he is supposed to be chosen by the other landholders and confirmed in his office by the explicit and public recognition of all of them. In the past, I was told, each landholder was required to step forward in front of the gwiltholder and two elders and to swear that he would accept the new fej as his representative and arbitrator. Since the Second World War, the landholders usually indicate their assent by signing or marking a paper in front of witnesses. The paper is then kept by the fej. At the time of his appointment the fej should choose another respected elder to be his guarantor (*was*), a procedure followed in all traditional contractual arrangements. Should the fej default in his fiscal or legal responsibilities, the guarantor is held fully responsible.

In practice the process through which a man is selected to be fej is not always so formal. Following the death of a fej, his responsibilities may devolve onto a capable and respected son or may be taken up without formalities by an elder who is obviously the only qualified candidate. It is only when a major dispute occurs, particularly one that goes to government court, that the ad hoc fej is required to formalize his position by proving that he has the consent and support of the other landholders.

The fej's position gives him a degree of discretionary power to influence the outcome of land disputes, and other landholders often suspect that he uses this power to his and his friends' advantage. So long as his decisions are not grossly unreasonable, however—that is, out of keeping with political reality—the other landholders are unlikely to actively oppose his decisions. In part, this reflects the low cohesion of the landholders, but it is also related to the fact that the fej is usually a man of influence and authority in his own right. Individual holders are not anxious to antagonize him, for his support, or at least the absence of his opposition, may someday be essential to their interests.

The above average political status of many fejs, particularly those who represent minzir abbats in the higher generational levels of the genealogical charter, is no coincidence, nor is it primarily attributable to their control of descent corporation affairs. Men are asked to become fejs precisely because they already are influential and respected elders or titled men and because they hold positions of authority in secular administration. It is felt that within the descent corporation, as in any Amhara secular grouping, only a "big man" can successfully arbitrate the quarrels of others. It is also recognized that a powerful fej can best defend the estate of the corporation in major land disputes. In fact, a corporation's landholders sometimes choose a new and more influential fej in the midst of a serious land dispute, as occurred, for example, in the case of Musina vs. Welde Sellasé discussed in chapter 8.

The structure of a descent corporation's fejships corresponds, by definition, to the structure of its corporate segmentation. There is one fejship for each minzir abbat and one for the first settler. The number of fejships in a corporation, however, always exceeds the number of men who occupy them, since some men act as fej for more than one ancestor. The relationship between fejships and their incumbents in Shoa Hayl and Wendim can be seen in tables 3a and 3b. In Shoa Hayl both Gebré and his daughter Asrat are represented by Bilata Ṭiruneh, while Asrat's sister Abeba and one of her daughters are represented by priest Asris. Similarly, in Wendim one man, Wibé, represents Wendim, Demé, Musina, and Miskab. Altogether, Shoa Hayl's twenty minzir abbats are represented by fourteen men, and Wendim's fourteen minzir abbats are represented by ten men. There is thus an even greater concentration of decision-making power in the

TABLE 3a THE FEJSHIPS OF SHOA HAYL

Fejship	Fej	No.*	Title	Residence
Gebré	Bilata Ṭiruneh	1	yes	Feres Bét
Abeba	Priest Asris	2	no	Feres Bét
Amanīt	Adegeh	4	no	Feres Bét
Tergīs	Priest Asris	2	no	Feres Bét
Asrat	Bilata Ṭiruneh	1	yes	Feres Bét
Teklé	Līqekahinat Assegé	3	yes	Feres Bét
Nudé	Grazmach Anniley	5	yes	Feres Bét
Ayo	Mengisté	6	no	Feres Bét
Dinasīwos	Gété	7	no	Feres Bét
Matebe Weld	Negusé	8	no	Feres Bét
Qusqo	Ayalew	9	no	distant parish
Telay	Yigzaw	10	no	Dereqé
Fasīl	Ayalew	9	no	distant parish
Senbeta	Līqekahinat Assegé	3	yes	Feres Bét
Hiywetua	Līqekahinat Assegé	3	yes	Feres Bét
Hetnora	Aleqa Desta	11	no†	Ziqwalla
Kokeba	Grazmach Fenta	12	yes	Dereqé
Agné	Balambiras Anteneh	13	yes	Feres Bét
Yemanawīt	Yigzaw	10	no	Dereqé
Sina Heywet	Grazmach Fenta	12	yes	Dereqé

NOTE: At the time of fieldwork Shoa Hayl did not have a fej because his corporation had not been involved in a dispute with another corporation for many years.

*Numbers are coded to figure 2 to indicate the ancestors these individuals represent.

†The term *aleqa* is a title given to minor officeholders such as the *c̣hiqa shum* in the present case. The same term is used for the official in charge of a major religious institution (see Appendix).

TABLE 3b THE FEJSHIPS OF WENDIM

Fejship	Fej	No.*	Title	Residence
Wendim	Wibé	1	no	Dereqé
Demé	Wibé	1	no	Dereqé
Welde Sellasé	Wibishet	2	no	Feres Bét
Musina†	Wibé and	1	no	Dereqé
	Līqekahinat Assegé	7	yes	Feres Bét
Wellete Rufaél	Priest Berhané	8	no	Dereqé
Miskab	Wibé	1	no	Dereqé
Irite	Taddese	9	no	Shangi (Maryam)
Metru	Mengistu	10	no	Gidiliñ
Gubeno	Yigzaw	5	no	Dereqé
Welde Gīorgīs	Priest Alemu	4	no	Dereqé
Akuléma	Yigzaw	5	no	Dereqé
Marta	Priest Asris	3	no	Feres Bét
Tadira	Desta	6	no	Feres Bét

*Numbers are coded to figure 3 to indicate the ancestors these individuals represent.

†The second fej listed, Līqekahinat Assegé, represented Musina in the dispute discussed in case 5, chapter 8.

descent corporation than the number of fejships alone would suggest.

Powerful men often hold fejships in more than one corporation. Līqekahinat Assegé, the former church official and chief clerk of Dega Damot under its last great independent ruler, Ras Hailu, holds the fejships of Teklé, Senbeta, and Hiywetua in Shoa Hayl and, during a dispute, for Musina in Wendim. He holds fejships in many other corporations as well and holds two parishes as his gwilt, one of which is Dereqé Maryam. This overrepresentation of powerful men in the fejships, particularly of higher generation minzir abbats, is evident in Shoa Hayl. Four of Shoa Hayl's six children (Teklé, Nudé, Senbeta, and Kokeba) are represented by titled men, while only three of his twelve grandchildren and neither of his two great-grandchildren who are minzir abbats are represented by men with titles. Here, once again, I am concerned only with the structure of descent corporation leadership; the effects of this overrepresentation of powerful men that results in an interlocking directorate of descent corporations is considered at greater length in chapters 8 and 9.

7. Individual Rights in Land

In this chapter the perspective of analysis shifts from the descent corporation and its estate to the living individual and his lands. The central issue is no longer the way in which the estate of a first settler is divided among many household heads; it is rather the way in which a single household head conceptualizes and classifies the rist rights by which he is able to claim rist land in many estates, and the ways in which he is able to obtain the use of lands in which he has no rist rights.

Rist rights

In its most general sense *rist* refers not only to the rights an individual believes he has through known descent lines but also those he feels vaguely he must have through yet other lines known to his "relatives." Rist, in this general sense, is a basic value for the free man of Damot. In addition to its economic significance it contributes to his sense of individualism and liberty. When asked where his rist is, a man in an expansive mood may reply, "everywhere in Dega Damot." If pressed further, he may tell of his rist in the parish where he lives, in nearby parishes, and perhaps even in other subdistricts or districts.

In this most general sense, rist usually has as much psychological as economic significance. Nevertheless, when an individual finds it expedient to take up residence in a new parish for political or personal reasons, he may be able to obtain rist land by investigating and pursuing his rist rights.

Similarly, a man who attains office may expand his holdings by claiming land through previously latent rist rights.

The term rist may be used in a somewhat more restricted sense to refer to descent corporation estates where any of an individual's lineal ancestors in recent generations are known to have held land as rist. In this sense a person is likely to say, "I have rist in Wendim but I don't plow it," or "I have rist in Wendim but my relatives are plowing it." The most restricted and immediate reference of rist, of course, is to land over which an individual has effective control by virtue of his recognized claim to descent from the appropriate minzir abbat.

The various meanings of *rist* may be distinguished by the context in which the term is used, but it is often necessary to ask the speaker for further clarification if the details of the situation under discussion are not already known. The tendency of men of authority and office to use *rist* in its most general sense when speaking of their personal rights has given more than one casual visitor to Gojjam the incorrect impression that land is concentrated in the hands of the "ruling class."

There is a striking contradiction between the Amhara postulate that rist rights are inherited equally through men and women and the way in which people conceptualize the pedigrees through which they validate their claims to rist. According to the *per stirpes* rule of inheritance, rist rights pass to a child from his mother and father, through them from his four grandparents, and through them, in turn, from his eight great-grandparents. Significantly, however, people never think of their pedigrees or ascent lines as bifurcating in each ascending generation. Even elders who pride themselves on their genealogical expertise almost never trace pedigrees through all of their great-grandparents. Indeed, few men can say how many grandparents they have without counting them, and only one elder questioned was aware of the fact that he had eight great-grandparents. Discussions on the subject usually lead to considerable confusion; a confusion which is compounded by the fact that most men do not know the names of all their great-grandparents.

This cultural blindspot prevents most men from realizing that almost everyone in Damot must have rist rights in almost every descent corporation. Such a realization, by exposing the flexibility and arbitrariness of the rist system, would undoubtedly reduce the elders' commitment to it; for, at present, they firmly believe it to be logically consistent and legally based.

Pedigrees and their classification

The crucial point is not that Damotians fail to understand the full implications of bilateral descent. It is that they consider such issues irrelevant to their personal interests. What an elder is concerned with is a series of pedigrees, or lines of descent, through each of which he holds rist land or hopes to claim it. Each pedigree consists of a chain of lineal ancestors of either sex which links a man (or his children, through his wife) to a minzir abbat and, through him, to a first settler. Usually an elder who takes pride in his genealogical expertise also knows the names of at least the number of his ancestors' siblings as well; for they are actual or potential points of segmentation in the corporation and may have a crucial bearing on land disputes. Pedigrees may be recited either from the speaker "upward" or from the ancestor "downward"; however, they tend to be longer (generationally deeper) in the former case than in the latter. This difference is related to the context in which the pedigree is being recited. When an elder recites a pedigree upward he tends to include as many lineal ancestors as possible, since each is a potential branching point where he may be able to trace out another line to validate further rist rights. When he recites a pedigree downward it is usually in the context of validating a claim to land in a particular corporation, and ancestors who are structurally irrelevant to the existing pattern of land division are often omitted.

The pedigrees through which two important elders validate their claims to rist land are shown in figures 4 and 5. Pedigrees through which they claim to have rist rights but through

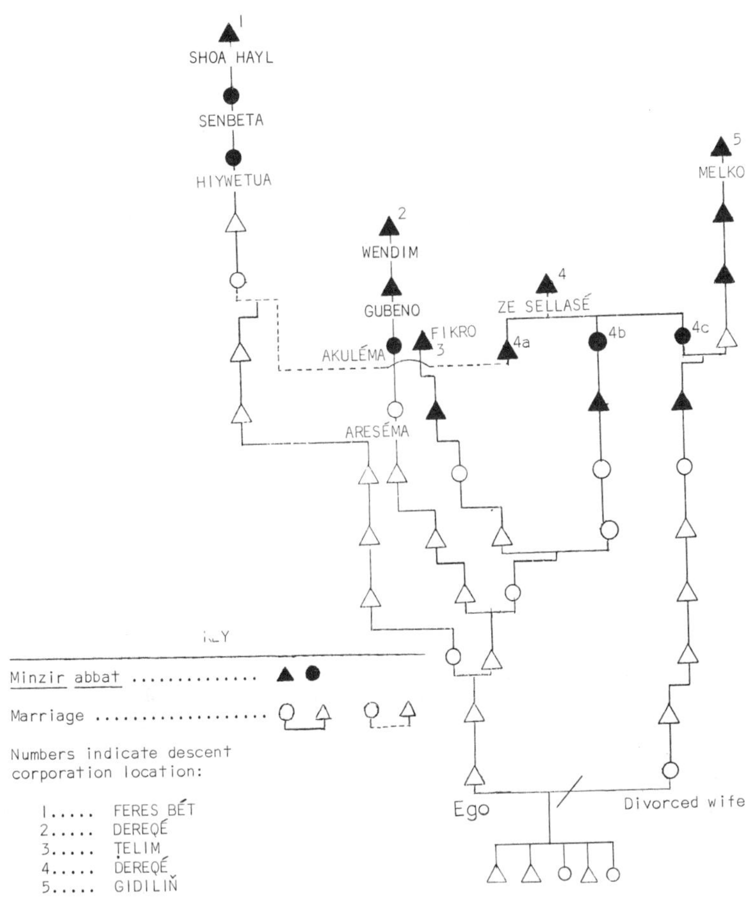

Fig. 4. The pedigrees of an elder from Dereqé Maryam

which they do not presently hold rist land are not shown. The elder whose pedigrees are shown in figure 4, Yigzaw, presently lives in a homestead of three huts to the east of the church in the parish of Dereqé Maryam. In 1962 his household included in addition to himself: his present wife; his

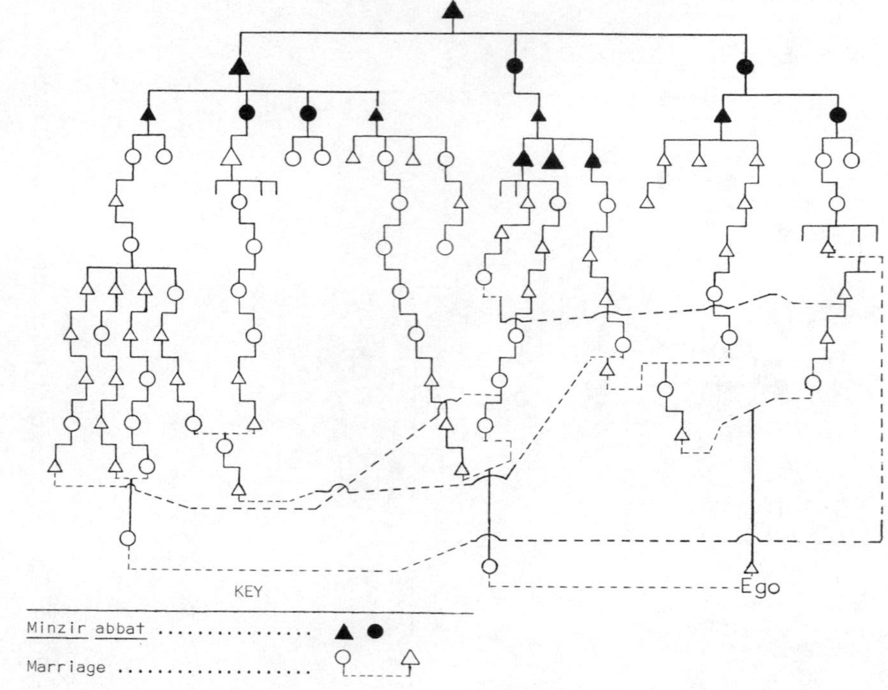

Fig. 5. The pedigree of an elder

wife's sister's daughter's two daughters; his wife's sister's son; his wife's brother's son; his son's son (by a former marriage); and a female servant (of slave origin) who receives food and annual presents of clothes for her service.

Yigzaw's unusually large household is commensurate with his unusually large holding of rist land. Altogether, in 1962, he held twenty fields in four parishes. Three of these fields, including his homestead site, are rist land he holds through his pedigree to Ze Sellasé's son 4A (fig. 4). He holds another four fields in another segment of the same corporation through Ze Sellasé's daughter 4B, and he has yet another field in another segment of the corporation through 4C. Yigzaw has three more fields in the nearby parish of Gidiliñ Medhane Alem in the corporation of Melko. It should be noted that the field held through 4C and those held through Melko are validated by a pedigree traced through Yigzaw's former (now divorced) wife. Yigzaw claims custodial rights in these fields because they are traced through his son's son (by the former wife) who is still living with him. Yigzaw has another five fields in Dereqé Maryam in the corporation of Wendim, two in Ṭelim Mikael in the corporation of Fikro, and two in the parish of Feres Bét Mikael in the corporation of Shoa Hayl.

The elder whose pedigrees are shown in figure 5, Negusé, lives in Mesk Kīdane Mihiret, a parish some fifteen miles to the northeast of Feres Bét. Negusé has been prominent in the local administration of his parish and has held minor administrative office every few years. As figure 5 indicates, he holds rist land in eight different minimal segments of a single descent corporation. Since the parish has only one descent corporation, there is a sense in which its segments are structurally analogous to the distinct corporations that make up a parish like Feres Bét.

Not all men are equally proficient at recounting their lines of descent. Young men and unambitious men are often content to indicate a pedigree by listing a few immediate lineal forebears and then asserting that the most remote of these is an accepted descendent of the appropriate minzir abbat. Should such men become embroiled in land litigation, they must call in and consult elders who know more about the pedigrees in question. Today it is increasingly common for men who do not consider themselves to be experts on rist to have their pedigrees written in a notebook which they guard jealously against the day when it may be of some use.

A man classifies his rist land and his potential rist rights into three types in accordance with the way he traces the validating pedigree. Thus he refers to all the rist land and rist rights he validates with pedigrees traced through his father as "father's rist"; he refers to all the rist land and rist rights he validates with pedigrees traced through his mother as "mother's rist"; and he refers to all the rist land and rist rights he validates with pedigrees traced through his wife as "wife's rist." It is important to note that this schema classifies rist land in accordance with the way the person in question traces his pedigree and not in accordance with his relationship to the person from whom he acquired the land. Thus, a man classifies a field as "mother's rist" even though he received it from his father, provided, of course, that the man traces his validating pedigree to the land through his mother (in other words, provided that the man's father held the land as his "wife's rist").

The emphasis placed on the proximate genealogical link in the pedigree by this system of classification reflects the fact that there are significant differences in the customary rules governing the acquisition of "father's," "mother's," and "wife's" rist. The most important difference between "father's rist" and "mother's rist" in this regard is that the former cannot by custom be claimed from the widowed mother so long as she continues to head her deceased husband's household, while the latter can be claimed from the father once the mother is dead. On the other hand, a man can claim "wife's rist" only after his wife has given him a child and can keep it only so long as he continues to support that child. In other words, a man does not have any rights to rist in virtue of his marriage to his wife but only as trustee or custodian for the children he has with her. For this reason, wife's rist is also referred to as "children's rist." These differences between the three types of rist and their structural implications for interpersonal conflicts of interest are discussed at greater length in the following chapter.

Secondary land rights

Secondary land rights are those through which a person can defend his right to hold or cultivate land even though it is not acknowledged to be his by rist right. Secondary rights include those of tenancy and various types of loan and exchange. There is no one Amharic term which covers all of these types of right. They have been grouped here for heuristic purposes and because, in the context of litigation, they are similar in an important respect: the holder of secondary rights in a field cannot defend his right to the field himself but must call a person with rist rights in the field to defend it for him. The person called is termed the *wabī*, or "giver," of the secondary rightholder. Unless the *wabī* comes to court, defends his rist right and agrees that he has transferred it to the secondary rightholder, the latter will lose the case and the land in question.

Tenancy. Tenancy is considered a joint agricultural venture in which a shared crop is produced by combining in various ways the land, oxen, labor, and seed of the two or more persons concerned. Though the status of the landholder and the tenant (*teṭemaj*) are not necessarily equal, the tenancy arrangement is regarded as a mutually advantageous, voluntarily entered contractual relationship.

It must be stressed that tenancy in Dega Damot does not involve the type of subordination, dependence, and one-sided control that it does in many other traditional agrarian societies. Tenants, as was noted previously, do not constitute a distinct class of landless people. Only a few men (with the exception of artisans) are totally dependent on land they cultivate in tenancy. Moreover, even these men are seldom dependent for all their land on a single landlord. A "big man" may have many tenants working his scattered fields, but they do not form a residentially, socially, economically, or politically integrated unit. Each of them has a bond with the large landholder, but they have little relationship and no obligations to one another by virtue of their individual ties to him.

Several types of tenancy arrangements can be distinguished according to the type of contribution made by each of the contracting parties. In the commonest form of tenancy the landholder contributes the land and half of the seed; the tenant contributes the rest of the seed, his own oxen, and his labor. The crops are divided in the field at harvest time. The tenant's share varies from three-quarters of the crop for common barley to one-half for *mesno* barley. If the tenant has only one ox and the landlord supplies the other, the tenant's share drops somewhat—from one-half to one-third, for example, in several cases recorded. Such ox-sharing arrangements are often made after the death of oxen, neither the tenant nor the landholder having enough animals to plow by himself.

Tenancy arrangements between an ordinary man and a man of power and authority may have a "political" as well as an economic dimension. The tenant may become the landlord's "follower," visiting him often with small gifts of liquor, beer, or livestock, escorting him on journeys, and attending church festivals in his retinue. In this, as in any patron-client tie in Dega Damot, the landlord gains honor and support while the tenant expects help in court, or protection and an occasional gift. The share of the crop paid to the landlord is sometimes less than the customary amount when the "political" aspect of the relationship is paramount. This is particularly true when the field held by the tenant is at a great distance from the landlord's residential parish. In yet another arrangement, a great man may give land rent-free to artisans in return for their skilled labor.

Loan. The right to cultivate rist land may be loaned or given in a kind of rent-free tenancy to fulfill political, economic, or social obligations. A powerful leader may loan land to a supporter. There are many circumstances under which land is loaned to less fortunate kin or, under some circumstances, nonkin as a contribution towards their support. A well-to-do man often allocates the use of a field or two to a divorced wife if she has children by him and has not married again. She, in turn, gives the land out in tenancy. Several cases were recorded in which a man had loaned a field he held as "mother's rist" to his paternal half-brother, who, of course, had no rist right in the field himself, since he had a different set of rist rights through his own mother.

A man who raises and marries off a boy who is not his own son normally loans the young man a few fields when he establishes his own homestead. Since rist rights cannot be passed to him, the young man will only be secure in his tenure so long as the man who raised him is alive, unless he can contrive to trace an appropriate pedigree to himself or his wife.

Land may be loaned for any number of years. When it is loaned to the aged it is usually held until the death of the recipient. When it is loaned to the young it is usually held until the death of the donor, at which time the recipient usually tries to retain the land as rist, if challenged. If land has been held for many years by loan and perhaps has even passed to the son of the first recipient, the claim by which it is held may be indeterminate until there is a dispute.

Exchange. A man may also obtain the use of a field not considered to be his rist by exchanging for it a field of his rist land which he holds in a less convenient location. He may find such an exchange advantageous because he has inherited a field in a parish distant from his residence and wishes to consolidate his lands into larger tracts that are closer to his homestead.

Alternatively, he may formally agree to an exchange in order to retain a conveniently located field which is already in his possession. This occurs after a major land dispute when the lands held by the segments of a corporation are relocated. Though the individual in question has been alloted a field in his segment's new land he prefers to "exchange" it for the conveniently located field he has held all along which has now been assigned to someone from another segment.

An exchange is a private agreement between two parties. It does not concern the other landholders or the fej, since in principle it is only the use rights and not the rist rights which are being exchanged. In fact, however, if the exchange endures for many years it is not unlikely that the men or their heirs will manage to trace a pedigree to the minzir abbats in whose estates the fields are located.

Temporary rights established through clearing land. A parish resident may, with the tacit permission of his neighbors and of the gwilt-holder, clear and bring into cultivation available forest lands. One who obtains land in this way has the right as the "clearing farmer" (*mentro arash*) to use the land for a fixed period of time. The exact number of years varies from parish to parish, but three is most common. After the temporary rights of the farmer who has cleared the land expire, the land is incorporated into the parish rist system. If it lies within a descent corporation's estate, it is simply absorbed into that estate. If it is located outside the boundaries of existing corporations' estates, it may be incorporated into one of them or it may be divided up and apportioned to several estates, as was the case with the recently cleared lowlands of Dereqé Maryam which were eventually divided between the parish's two corporations, Wendim and Ze Sellasé.

Subsequent to its incorporation into the parish's rist system, the newly cleared land is subject to division by father and to allotment by the fej, like any other land. The individual who cleared it has no stronger rights in it than any other recognized rist right-holder but, unless he cannot establish a pedigree to the ancestor to whom it has been assigned, he is usually able to retain possession of at least some part of it.

Possession without right

Over 15 percent of the 282 fields in Shoa Hayl's estate for which sufficient data were gathered were held by people who had in them no recognized right of any type. Such fields are said to be held by possession, or *beyažish.* A person may come to have possession of a field in which he has no right in several ways. He may have first obtained the field through tenancy or loan and subsequently retained it free of obligation after the donor's death. He may have acquired the field as "wife's rist" and retained it after the death or divorce of his wife, even though he does not support any of the children he has had by her. He may have brought the land into cultivation and retained it beyond the recognized period of time. Alternatively, fields held *beyažish* are often fields in which the holder formerly had a rist right but which have been "left behind" in a reallocation of minzir abbats' land following a major land dispute. This is most likely to occur if the holder is an elderly and respected parishioner and the field in question has been fertilized over the years with ashes and dung from his homestead. Upon his death, however, his heirs may be asked to give up the field.

Regardless of how he has come to have a field *beyažish*, a man's chances of retaining it are much better if it is the site of his homestead than if it is not. For this reason men often build their homesteads on wife's land, exchanged land, loaned land, or other land in which they have a tenuous claim in order to "hold it down."

Significant as it is in terms of frequency and strategy, the holding of land *beyažish*, or mere possession, does not constitute a legally recognized type of land right by which a field can be defended.

To summarize, the rights through which a man is able to obtain and defend the use of farm land in Dega Damot include rist rights which, in principle, are hereditary, inalienable, and inextinguishable, and other rights to land which are, in principle, nonhereditary, alienable, and temporary. In a sense, these other rights are derivative of rist rights; for they are invariably rights in land which is either someone else's rist or land over which no individual, only a descent corporation, presently has rist rights.

Rist rights and rist land

Important as they are in establishing a legal claim to land, rist rights do not, in themselves, ensure their holder possession of a particular field of rist land, or, indeed, of any land at all. In fact, while the nature of land rights and of the land tenure system in general are considered patently clear and unambiguous by all interested elders, the right that a particular person has to a particular field is often subject to much doubt and disagreement. This is not surprising in light of the great number of persons who are eligible, according to customary law, to claim and hold the fields of each minzir abbat.

Under these circumstances, possession is of the utmost importance. Until there is a dispute over a field, the right by which it is held is of little interest to the community as a whole; in fact, there is often considerable disagreement between the holder and other persons about just what kind of a right, if any, he has.

It is only when disputes arise over the possession of a field that land rights are of crucial importance, but then they are formally treated as the only relevant issue. Many other factors may determine whether there will be a dispute over a particular field and who will support the litigants when a dispute does arise, but in the context of litigation the rights described in this chapter constitute the only legally binding idiom of discourse.

An interesting and important consequence of the "periodic relevance" of land rights to the possession of a field is that, as I remarked in the first chapter, a man may acquire a field through one type of right and yet defend it at some later date through another type of right. Regardless of whether he initially gained control over a field through inheritance, gift, loan, clearing, tenancy, or simply plowing up the common pasture, the field will remain his until someone asks him to give it up or share it.

Another consequence of the relationship between rist rights and possession is that the type of right by which a person claims or defends a field does not indicate from whom he acquired it or by what process. In a survey of 93 fields stated by the holder to be "father's rist," 49 had been acquired from the father or a guardian by inheritance or as a gift in anticipation of inheritance. Another 39 fields had been acquired from people not considered significant kinsmen through action brought against the descent corporation fej.

In a survey of thirty-eight fields held as "mother's rist," it was found that eighteen had been inherited or received as a gift from the mother, her kinsmen, or a guardian; thirteen had been acquired from people not considered significant kin through action against the descent corporation fej; three had been acquired as gifts from affinal kinsmen; and four had been acquired by other means from nonkin. In a survey of forty-two fields held as "wife's rist," it was found that eleven had been received from wife's kinsmen through inheritance or gift; twenty-two had been acquired from people not considered to be significant kin by action against the descent corporation fej; three had been inherited from the person's own mother or father; and six had been obtained in other ways.

In view of the wide range of rist rights traced by most men and the evident ambiguity encountered in determining whether one of these rights validates a claim to a particular piece of land, it is essential to investigate not only how men obtain rist rights, as has been done in this chapter, but also to ask how men can actually obtain and hold rist land in respect of some of their rights. This question informs the discussion of the following chapter.

8. The Acquisition of Rist Land

The lands on which each household depends for its livelihood do not constitute a clearly delimited estate which passes intact from the household head to a principal heir. They rather represent a collection of fields brought together under the management of the household head through diverse processes and strategies and validated through diverse types of land rights.

The most important ways in which men acquire rist land are by inheritance or by gift in anticipation of inheritance, and by presenting claims to the representatives of descent corporations. In the former case the land is actually received from a close kinsman, in the latter it is usually, though not always, received from someone who is not considered to be a significant kinsman. Less important ways of acquiring rist land include claiming it from wife's kinsmen, taking it in tenancy in anticipation of establishing a rist claim after the death of the landlord, clearing forest land, plowing up pasture land, and taking over land abandoned by someone who has left the area.

In a survey of 206 fields held as rist by twenty-six household heads resident in Shoa Hayl, it was found that 44 percent of the fields had been acquired by inheritance or by gift in anticipation of inheritance, 43 percent by claims presented to the descent corporation; 5 percent were acquired from wife's kin, 2 percent had been taken first in tenancy, and 4 percent had been taken as forest, pasture, or abandoned land.

The relative importance to an individual of these various ways of acquiring land depends on his position in the domestic cycle, his standing in his local community, and his status in the wider sphere of regional politics. A young married man usually obtains most of his land through inheritance or through gift in anticipation of inheritance. The social setting in which such land transfers occur is largely defined by the norms, interests, and sentiments of household and kinship relations. Somewhat older men whose fathers are dead or who live in a different community from their fathers try to obtain additional fields from the representatives of descent corporations by pressing claims for land through division by allotment. Such claims are formally argued in terms of descent rules, but their success or failure is strongly influenced by interests relating to community organization and leadership. Finally, those elders and officeholders who attain prominence in the wider political community of Dega Damot try to claim additional land by demanding a further division of land by father; that is, by "bringing in a new minzir abbat." Such claims are formally argued in terms of descent corporation ideology and rules, but their success depends heavily on the plaintiff's ability to mobilize support for his cause through his personal political ties.

Inheritance, gift, and the domestic cycle

This section is about the processes of inheritance and of gift in anticipation of inheritance through which rist land passes from the people of one generation to their offspring in the next. It is thus concerned with the domestic cycle, discussed in relation to the household in chapter 3; with the way in which the children of a household marry, move out, establish their own households, and have their own children; and with the way they obtain rist land through the dissolution of the parental household.

The rules of inheritance

The rules governing the inheritance of rist lands can be stated quite briefly. The most basic rule, and the one invariably cited, is that a person's rist land must be divided equally among all his (male and female) children. To this general rule must be added the following provisos: (1) children may not inherit their father's rist lands at his death so long as their mother is alive and continues to reside in the parental homestead as the household head; (2) rist land inherited by children who are minors may be used by the kinsman who acts as guardian until they marry and establish their own households.

These rules define enforceable rights through which persons can demand their rist land. They do not, however, in themselves determine the actual disposition of a parent's rist land; for a person need not insist on obtaining or retaining his rightful rist land. A father, for example, may give rist land to his children before his death. A widow may give her late husband's rist land to her children, though she continues to reside as the head of his household. A child need not insist on receiving his or her share of the parent's rist even after the death of both parents.

The way in which these rules are implemented and the extent to which they are followed are affected by variations in the domestic cycle, particularly by the children's age, marital status, and residence at the time of their parents' deaths. The effects of such variations require somewhat more extended comment. For the sake of exposition it is convenient to first consider a household in which the children all grew up before the household head's death, and then to consider various alternative types of development. There is no sense, however, in which the completed domestic cycle is more typical or normal than the others.

A well-to-do peasant may give his unmarried teen-age son the responsibility of cultivating a field or two with the expectation that the fields will eventually be the son's, but most youths are not seriously concerned with obtaining or managing land before they marry and, a year or two later, establish their own homesteads. From then on, gaining and retaining control over rist land is a dominant concern of the young household head.

A father with ample rist land for his own household's needs may give the use of a field or two to his newly independent married son or, less frequently, to his son-in-law. Most fathers, however, are unable to afford such generosity and must retain partial control over any land they give to their sons, either working it with the sons jointly and dividing the crops or asking them to pay the normal tenant's share of the crop. If the father has little rist land and many children, the contribution of inherited land to the children's households' estates will never be great, and unless they are successful in obtaining land in other ways it may be years before they are self-sufficient. In the meantime they may have to depend on land worked in tenancy and send some of their children off to live with a more fortunate kinsman, usually the children's grandparent, aunt, or uncle.

Rist land that has been given to sons and sons-in-law during the father's lifetime is usually retained by them at his death. The disposition of the rest of his rist lands depends on the status of his widow and the type of right by which he held them. If the widow is the mother of her late husband's children and continues to reside in his homestead as the head of his household, she is entitled to retain control over all of his land. Normally she gives the land to her grown sons who, in return, pay her a share of the crop as rent. If she wishes, she may, of course, give some of the land to her sons and sons-in-law rent-free in anticipation of eventual inheritance. If the sons do not want to use the land in tenancy or she does not want to give it to them, the widow may give it to other tenants.

If the widow remarries, her grown sons will almost never permit her to remain in her former husband's homestead; for they say the new husband is trying to steal from them their father's rist. Subsequent to her remarriage and consequent removal to her new husband's homestead the widow cannot retain control over any of her deceased husband's rist land which he held as his "father's" or "mother's" rist; that is, through descent lines traced through his mother or father. It may be claimed in equal shares by all of the dead man's children. Those fields which are her own, fields which her deceased husband held as "wife's" or "children's" rist, cannot be taken from her and are cultivated by her new husband.

Upon her death these fields can be claimed equally by all her children by either husband.

If the widow is an old woman or for any other reason chooses to live with one of her sons as a dependent member of his household, she relinquishes her rights to her late husband's land and it may be claimed in equal shares by all of his children. If the widow is not the mother of a man's children she has no right to stay on in his household or to control his rist land. The children's mother, however, even though she has been divorced for years, has the right to return to the deceased man's homestead to control his rist. She may not, of course, bring a new husband in with her.

Sons and daughters who have not yet married at the time of their father's death usually continue to live with their mother if she maintains the household. It is common for a married son to stay on in his father's household under such circumstances, gradually coming to act as guardian for his younger siblings. He or one of his younger brothers is likely to take over the leadership of the household as the mother grows old.

If the head of a household dies before any of his sons have reached their majority, his widow may remarry and bring her new husband to live in her homestead as her children's stepfather. When her sons by her first marriage reach the age of marriage, however, they may and usually do force their stepfather to leave the homestead and give up the fields he has been cultivating to support the household. The sons' mother may divorce her husband or accompany him, but the former alternative is the more common.

If the widow remarries while her children are small and goes to live with her new husband, her children by the first marriage are likely to go to live with a guardian who may be their father's brother, mother's brother, or grandfather on either side. The guardian takes possession of the fields of the deceased father and cultivates them until the children reach their majority and marry. An older brother who has married can also act as a guardian for his younger siblings. He, too, is responsible for giving them land as they marry.

Guardians of all types are said to be remiss in giving land back to their wards.

Should the mother die before the father, married children have the right to claim equal shares of her rist land; that is, of all the rist land held by their father as his "wife's" rist. This is true whether the father initially obtained the land from the mother's kinsmen, from the descent corporation, or in any other manner. The sons may allow their father to retain all or a part of their mother's rist after her death if they "love" him. There is a tendency, however, to agree with the proverb that where there is rist there is no love.

Due to a comparatively high rate of divorce and remarriage, it is not unusual for a man or a woman to have children by several spouses. In such cases all children retain the right to claim an equal share of the parent's rist land. Legitimacy of birth is irrelevant so long as paternity is recognized. Bastards suffer no disability in the inheritance of land.

As had been remarked, children are not required to claim their share of a parent's rist land. A son who has established his homestead far from his natal area or who has left Dega Damot may choose not to claim his rist. In most instances, though, it is the daughter who does not receive her share of the rist land. Unless there is great need, her husband hesitates to claim her land; for to do so is considered greedy and creates strains between him and his brothers-in-law that the fragile marriage bond can ill afford. If the daughter's husband builds his homestead on his wife's land near her parental homestead, he can obtain her rist land without difficulty, but such dependency on and proximity with the wife's kin is considered highly undesirable.

The division of parental lands

Through the processes of inheritance and gift in anticipation of inheritance the parent's rist lands eventually pass, usually in more or less equal amounts, to those of their children who lay claim to them. Not all of their fields, however, are divided equally among all of the children, as is suggested by the ideal rule of division most often cited. On the contrary, in practice it is usually only large fields located near the parental homestead that are subdivided among the children. Other fields are allocated undivided to one or another child, usually to a child to whose homestead a field is most conveniently located.

This tendency to apportion all or most of the fields in one location to one child and those in another location to another child is of crucial importance; it means that though the parents' rist land and their potential rist rights pass to their children equally, their rist lands and associated interests in specific descent corporations do not. It is through this process of division and the residential separation which accompanies it that the children's rist-holdings and active interests in descent corporations begin to become differentiated from one another.

The dispersal of sons away from the parental homestead is related to the desire on the part of father and son alike to maximize the amount of rist land controlled by their respective households. The father almost invariably holds more rist land in the first settlers' estates of the parish in which he is resident than he does in first settlers' estates located elsewhere. This is in large part because as a local elder he has been able to participate to advantage in the process of "division by allotment." If he has many sons, a man will try to "spread" them out over the rist land which he holds in more distant estates, that is, those in which he has considerably less land than he could obtain if he were a resident. His sons, as residents, can hope in time to expand their holdings substantially without further depleting the land supply available to their father or their siblings. At the same time, in the final division of the father's rist lands each son will try to obtain at least some fields or parts of fields in parishes other than his own. This is not only to meet his immediate economic needs but to enable him, in his turn, to spread his sons away from his own homestead.

The location of the son's homestead is subject to contradictory norms. While it is recognized that, if land is in short supply in relation to the number of sons to be provided for, it is desirable for some sons to move away, it is said that ideally a son should live next to his father so that he can continue to work with him, to honor him, and to help him in his old age.

Residential decisions are thus affected by several factors. Older sons of ordinary farmers often build their new homesteads at some distance from their father's. Younger sons are more likely to be found near the parental homestead. On the average it was found that in long-settled and densely populated parishes one out of every two male household heads was not living in his natal parish.

In parishes which have large amounts of uncleared but potentially utilizable land, there is a notable exception to the dispersal pattern. In these parishes additional land can be cleared in proportion to the amount of labor available. Under such conditions, a man's sons clear new land instead of moving away to compete for land which is already under cultivation. In parishes with much uncleared land, it is not unusual to find a hamlet made up of a half-dozen or more patrilineally related kin, perhaps the offspring of a single grandfather or great-grandfather. These are the parishes mentioned above in which land is divided only by allotment and not by "father." As the available uncleared land diminishes, the more common rist system is instituted and the localized clusters of patri-kin break up.

Acquiring rist through marriage

Whether or not a man's sons remain in their natal parish, each of them acquires a new and distinct set of rist rights and related interests through each woman with whom he has children. That these rights will be largely distinct from those acquired through the parents is ensured by church rules of exogamy which forbid marriage with a woman who shares a common ancestor in any line in six or fewer ascending generations (that is, marriage is permitted with sixth cousins but prohibited with all closer kin). While no one is able to trace all his kinship relations to the "seventh house" as is required by this rule, it is precisely those genealogical links which are associated with land rights that are remembered. If it is known that a prospective bride and groom have rist rights through the same minzir abbat, then it is known that they have common lineal ancestry. It remains only to trace out the exact degree of linkage. Marriages do occasionally occur between persons known to be related in less than seven degrees or "houses," but people "murmur about it."

In most instances the exogamy rule is observed with sufficient rigor that the bride and groom have at least a large part of their rist rights through different minzir abbats. The religiously sanctioned rule of exogamy thus not only gives the sons potential access to new rist lands but it also further differentiates the bundles of rist rights that will eventually be available to their children.

Fathers are keenly aware of the advantages that can be derived from the careful selection of their sons' brides. Indeed the father's concern that the prospective bride have acknowledged rist rights ranks only after his concern that her family background be untainted with the suspicion of leprosy and the evil eye.

Through marriage or, more accurately, through fathering children whom he supports, a man thus gains access to a new set of rist rights. Whether he will be able to obtain rist land in virtue of these rights is another question. From a tactical point of view, the land he may hope to obtain falls into two classes. The first comprises land given to him by his wife's kinsmen. The other, and statistically by far the more important, comprises land which he may claim in his wife's name from the fej of a descent corporation.

Obtaining land through the descent corporation

With the passage of the years and the growth of his household, a man gradually attains the status of elderhood. He acts as arbitrator when his neighbors quarrel with their wives or with each other. He gives council to others at the informal moots held in the churchyard after Sunday mass. He speaks up at meetings convened to discuss the repair of the church or the implementation of a government order to clear a trail. He helps to conduct an inquest held to investigate an unsolved crime in his own or some nearby parish; and he frequents the local *aṭbīya daññа*'s court, listening to the disputes along with the judge and offering the litigants his advice freely on substantive and legal points.

To the extent that he becomes a successful elder a man thus becomes involved in a widening circle of community and interpersonal affairs. Among these are the affairs of descent corporations through which he attempts to acquire additional rist land. For most men these attempts meet with at least some success; for, next to inheritance, the most important way in which men acquire rist land is by claims made through the descent corporation. In all, a little under one-half of the fields surveyed had passed to their present holders as the result of such action. For upwardly mobile men, claims through the descent corporation assume a particularly great importance, usually accounting for more of their fields than all other means combined.

Fields acquired through the descent corporation, unlike fields acquired through inheritance, are almost invariably acquired from men or women who are not reckoned as close kin and who are not moved to give up the land by kinship obligations or personal sentiments. The basic question is no longer, "What right does the claimant have to the land?" for each man's rist rights are very extensive and far exceed his holding. It is rather, "For what reasons and under what conditions does the previous holder or 'defendant' relinquish his land to the claimant?"

The kinds of community interests, legal norms, and political realities that enable one man to take rist land from another must be understood in relation to the two types of claims that can be lodged against the fej of a descent corporation: claims for land through division by allotment; and claims for land through division by father.

Claims for land through division by allotment

A claim for land through division by allotment is a claim for a share of the *yedenb* land of a minzir abbat. It does not require a further subdivision or a redivision of a land section by father. It may be uncontested, it may require the arbitration of elders, or, all else failing, it may be taken to court. In any case, a claim for land through division by allotment involves at most a few fields and is generally a matter that concerns only a few people. It may be brought by an established elder, and its success depends in large part on the support he can muster in the community where the land is located.

A claim for a share of the rist land of a minzir abbat by allotment is first presented to the fej of that minzir abbat. At least some of the minzir abbat's land must still be *yedenb* land, that is, land which is not divided by father. To present his claim, the claimant tells the fej that he is a descendant of the minzir abbat. If requested, he may back up his claim by reciting his descent line back to the minzir abbat or one of his acknowledged descendents.

If the fej denies the request, the claimant may take him to court. If, as is more common in requests for land through division by allotment, the fej recognizes the claim as legitimate, he assigns one or more fields already held by another person to the claimant. The fej is asserting that the person or persons whose land has been designated either have no rist right in the land or that, though they have a rist right, they presently hold "too much" of the land. According to custom only unfertilized land should be designated for reallocation by the fej. While this rule is generally followed, exceptions are sometimes made if all or most of the designated holder's land is fertilized.

The claimant then approaches the designated holder, informs him of the fej's decision and asks him to give up the land either immediately or, if it is under cultivation, after the harvest. The holder has the option of giving up the land, offering to compromise by giving up some fraction of the amount requested, or refusing to give up any land at all. Unless his position is extremely weak, the defendant will not take the first option, for he may fare better and can fare no worse if he submits the issue to arbitration. For similar reasons the claimant seldom will accept a compromise or a refusal without recourse to arbitration.

Any respected elder, including the fej himself, may be asked to arbitrate the dispute. If the initial attempt fails, a yet more respected elder may be sought out or the dispute may be taken before a moot of elders held in the churchyard after mass. If all else fails, the dispute goes to the court of the *aṭbiya dañña* or, if the amount of land involved is known to be too great, to the district court.

Though the desire of the disputants to maximize their holdings of rist land is essentially unchanged whether they are before the elders or in government court, there are significant differences in the formal objectives of the elders and the court and in the normative principles to which they look for guidance. The elders will not award the claimant any land unless they accept the validity of his pedigree, but their primary objective is reconciliation—to find an amicable and reasonable solution which will enable the disputants to live together peaceably as members of the same community.

Because they seek reconciliation and have no means of enforcing their recommendations, other than by rather diffuse community pressure, the elders must take into consideration many aspects of the disputants' status in the community. The most important of these have to do with whether the disputants are resident members of the parish, whether they really "need" the land, whether, as clergy, they perform a religious service to the community, and whether they have the social prestige that accrues to leading elders. The elders' final assessment of a man's community standing in these respects is expressed in terms of whether he has too much rist land in the estate in question.

The significance of residence in the parish where the land being claimed is located is not due to any formal or legal rule but to the fact that the elders are inclined to recognize the claims of their friends and neighbors who share with them the burden of collective service to the gwilt-holder and the local church. Nonresidents deplete the land available to residents but do not contribute to the discharge of these responsibilities. The claims of nonresidents are accordingly looked upon with less favor than those of residents. The distinction between residents and nonresident landholders is recognized in the Amharic distinction between *yedarī arashoch*, or "outside farmers," and *yewist arashoch*, or "inside farmers."

The notion of "need" is less precise than that of residence. Basically, the notion is that it is wrong to deprive a resident member in good standing of land which he needs for the support of his household members. It is less often invoked to aid a claimant who is a new resident, more or less a stranger, than it is to protect a long-time resident defendant whose plight is of greater concern. Often it is tacitly invoked by the fej before a dispute arises, when he passes over the fields of the poor, the weak, and the aged, who could not defend their last lands well in litigation, and designates the fields of those who are better off. Were it not for this notion that it is wrong to take from a fellow parishioner his last few fields, it seems likely, in light of the fierce competition for land and the role of power in this competition, that there would be a much larger landless population in Dega Damot today.

The land claims of a priest or church schoolteacher may be looked upon with special favor if the land section concerned owes services to the parish church which the landholders are unable to meet adequately. Under these circumstances not only are long latent rist rights recognized without objection, but sometimes a priest or teacher is actively sought out and offered land and perhaps a house site.

The notion of what constitutes holding too much land is related to prestige and is even more difficult to define than the notion of need. Inasmuch as social status in the community is in part a product of the amount of land held, the concept of having too much land for one's status is somewhat circular. There are, however, other important factors which affect a man's status and concomitant estimates of the amount of land he should enjoy. Paramount among these are the frequency with which a man is asked to arbitrate the disputes of his fellows and is appointed to unofficial or official posts of parish and neighborhood administration. It is generally accepted as appropriate or at least inevitable that such a man, a leader in his community, should hold more land in local descent corporations' estates than lesser men hold.

The converse of the general tendency for men of standing to obtain and hold land is that it is sometimes difficult for a man of low standing, perhaps a young man who, as an only son, has inherited much land from his father, to retain his land. Particularly if his father had no recognized rights in some of his fields, the son is likely to be singled out as a holder with "too much" land.

In government court, in contrast to arbitration by the elders, the objective of the proceedings is not so much to conciliate through compromise as to reach a legally correct, impersonal judgment through the application of the rules of the rist system. From the point of view of the litigants, however, court proceedings serve primarily as a battleground on which to fight a war of attrition, to wear one another down, each hoping eventually to reach a more advantageous out-of-court settlement. This tactical or political, rather than legal, use of the courts cannot be overstressed; for except in minor disputes, such as disputes over boundaries and cattle paths, land litigation is a form of political activity, and the court system serves as a political arena.

Cases brought against the defendant holder. In cases in which the plaintiff is claiming land from the present holder designated by the fej, rather than from the fej himself, the strict adherence of courts to the ideal rules of the rist system tend to give the plaintiff an initial tactical advantage; he need only establish his descent from the appropriate minzir abbat to validate his right to at least some share of the land. Given the ramifications of all men's rist lines, this is seldom difficult.

Once the claim of the plaintiff is established, the defendant has open to him several lines of defense. First of all, if he is not to lose the fields in question outright, the defendant must prove that he has rist rights or secondary rights in the fields. Rist rights are, once more, established by calling witnesses. Even if the defendant can establish that he has rist rights to the land, however, he may be ordered to share the fields with the claimant, for has not the latter also rist rights?

As an alternative to sharing the land, the defendant can now claim that he does not have too much of the minzir abbat's land and that the fej was unjust or in error in giving his land to the plaintiff in the first place. This maneuver, if successful, turns the case back upon the fej and requires a review of all landholding in the estate. Since this strategy pits the defendant against the fej and perhaps the majority of the more important men holding land in the estate, it is not to be undertaken lightly. Furthermore, the defendant often is in a weak position, if not because of his descent claim at least because of his ability to support protracted litigation and make numerous enemies. After all, it was for this reason that the fej designated his lands to begin with.

If the defendant is not able to establish a rist claim through witnesses who will support his genealogical right, he must call the person who has given him the land or who has rist rights in it as his *wabī*. The latter must assume the place of the defendant if he wishes to help him retain possession of the land.

Several kinds of out-of-court tactics are used by both plaintiffs and defendants. These are aimed at harassing the opponent into a favorable out-of-court settlement. The strategy most often used by the defendant, who, of course, has possession of the field, is simply stalling so as to prolong the proceedings. One way he does this is by calling many witnesses who are sick, far away, or occupied with important business on the day set for the hearing. Alternatively, the defendant himself may be "unable" to attend the proceedings on the appointed day, but he runs the risk of a fine for not appearing. Communications are slow and uncertain in Damot and the successive hearings that usually are required for a single case are often several months apart. Under these conditions it is not unusual for a land case to drag on for a year or more. By this time the plaintiff may be willing to settle for less of the land he claims in order to get on with the business of plowing and planting. The plaintiff, too, may try to prolong the case if he has other men in his household who work his land and if his opponent does not; for the defendant will weary of the inconvenience of going to court.

If the plaintiff is a man of standing and substance, his best strategy is to increase the cost of the case for his less well-off opponent. He does this by prolonging the case, by appealing it to a higher and more distant court, if appropriate, and by trying to have court hearings set for days when he knows the defendant will be unable to come and will hence be fined. Litigants, particularly defendants, frequently claim that their opponents have given bribes (*gubbo*) to the judge not so much to influence his decisions as to affect the timing of the subsequent hearing. A final tactic that may be used by either party but is most often used by defendants is to threaten a counter-suit for fields in another land section through another minzir abbat.

The tactics, principles, and procedures employed in litigation concerning claims for rist land can be best illustrated by examining several cases from the records of the *aṭbīya dañña* of Feres Bét Mikael. In 1966 the *aṭbīya dañña* held his court somewhat irregularly in a wood-and-grass structure which he referred to as his office. The majority of *aṭbīya* courts are still held in the open air. Present with the *aṭbīya dañña* was his clerk, an unpaid and unofficial appointee hoping to gain a government position in the future, and at least two elders, who are required by law.

During the period of about one year the *aṭbīya dañña* heard 176 cases of which 78 concerned rist. Four of these cases are presented here.

Case 1: Gellew vs. Gétahun

August 27

The elders present at the court were Bītew and Grazmach Anniley. The plaintiff, Gellew, made the following plea:

"Priest Gétahun refused to give me my rist from Matebe Weld, Denasīwes, and Ayo [the three children of the minzir abbat Nudé in figure 2], which was designated as mine by the fejs of these three minzir abbats [in whose names the land of Nudé is incompletely divided]. If the accused agrees with me, let him give me the land. If he does not agree with me, let me prove my case. The estimated value of the land is $23." (This last information is supplied because the jurisdiction of the court is limited to cases which do not involve more than Eth. $25).

The accused, Priest Gétahun, made the following reply: "The rist of Matebe Weld and Ayo is my own. I do not know whether the plaintiff is a rist-holder [*risteñña*] or not. Let him count his ancestry and tell me how he is descended from the minzir abbats. Then, if I agree with him, I will share the land with him, but if I do not agree with him, let him prove his case in court. I am not, however, plowing the *iṭa merét* of Denasīwes [that is, the land assigned by lot to Denasīwes in the division of Nudé's land by father]."

The judge ordered that the value of the rist land must be estimated, and the following elders were chosen to do this: Debtera Gété, the judge's brother; Ato Bīresaw, the *chiqa shum* of the parish that year; and Ato Kasa. These elders were ordered to bring a written estimate of the value of the land to the court at the following hearing, which was set for October 3.

October 3

The plaintiff and the accused were not present. The hearing was rescheduled for November 20.

November 20

The elders present at the court were Chekol and Ṭiruneh. The plaintiff and the accused were present. The estimate of the value of the land had not been sent to the court. The court again ordered that the land must be estimated. The next hearing was set for December 2.

December 2

The plaintiff and the accused were absent. The court ordered the plaintiff and the accused to come to the next hearing, which was set for December 20.

December 20

The plaintiff was present but the accused was absent. The court ruled that if the accused did not come for the next hearing on January 8 the case would be concluded anyway.

January 8

The elders present at the court were Grazmach Yenéneh and Teferra. The plaintiff was present, but the accused was absent for unknown reasons.

The court ordered that the accused must pay Eth. $2 *kisara*[1] to the plaintiff. The plaintiff was told to take a note from the court to the accused to make him appear in court at the next hearing, which was set for January 31.

January 31

The elders present at court were Ṭiruneh and Teferra. The plaintiff and the accused were present. The accused was asked by the court if he had had the land estimated. He answered that he had not been aware of the time when the estimate was to take place (he was supposed to accompany the elders who actually make the estimate). The court decided that another date must be set to have the land estimated, and another court hearing was set for February 14.

February 14

The plaintiff was present, but the accused was absent. The court gave the following decision in the case.

"The accused has not complied with the orders of the court. He was told to have the land estimated (requiring its measurement), but he did not. Furthermore, he did not appear in court on the appointed days. Since this is a civil case the accused must give the rist to the plaintiff. In addition, he must pay the plaintiff $5 *kisara.* If the accused wants to open the case again, he can do so by paying the regular $10 fee. This case is hereby concluded and entered into the archives [a wooden box that unfortunately did not prove impervious to the depredations of rats]. Written notice that the case has been thus concluded is to be issued to the plaintiff and to the accused."

1. A small fine the court can impose on the plaintiff or the accused for failing to appear on the appointed day.

The case of Gellew vs. Gétahun illustrates well the tactic of stalling. The defendant did little in his own defense and thwarted the measurement of the land which might have put the case into a higher and more expensive court. He succeeded, however, in postponing what he felt was an inevitable decision for half a year. Furthermore, there is no assurance that the plaintiff actually received the land. In the absence of a stronger civil administration, the court has no direct way of enforcing its decisions. If the defendant refuses to give up the land, the plaintiff may open a criminal case against him. More often, having established his position more soundly, the plaintiff will agree to settle for a share of the land he has claimed; a share which is smaller than the court award but larger than he could have received without going to court.

Case 2: Iwnetu vs. Tegeññe

No date given

The elders present at court were Tesemma and Berhané. The plaintiff, Iwnetu, made the following plea.

"Tegeññe refused to give me my children's Kokeba: Yemanawīt: Welde Hanna [the upper part of his descent line from the minzir abbat Kokeba—see figure 2] and my Sina Heywet [another child of Kokeba] rist. Let him come and speak for himself. If he agrees with me, let him give me the land. If he denies me, let me prove my case."

The accused, Tegeññe, gave the following reply: "I have a *wabī* for the Yemanawīt rist; my *wabī* is Immahoy Shashitu. I can bring her to court. The Sina Heywet rist is mine, however, and I will defend it myself."

The court ordered the accused to bring his *wabī* for the hearing set for June 2.

June 2

The plaintiff and the accused were absent. Another hearing was set for June 26, and it was decided by the court that if the litigants did not appear on that date the case would be closed.

June 26

The elders present at court were Wetadir Nuré and Molla. The plaintiff and the accused were present. The *wabī* of the accused was also present. When the judge asked the *wabī* if she would accept the case from the defendant she said she would (this applies only to the Yemanawīt land). The court ordered that the *wabī* be given a copy of the original complaint and set the next hearing for July 26.

July 26

The plaintiff, the accused, and the judge were all absent. The hearing was rescheduled for August 14.

August 14

The plaintiff and the accused were absent. The judge said that if the litigants did not attend the next hearing the case would be closed, and the next hearing was set for October 9.

October 9

The elders present at court were Minayyehu and Grazmach Yenéneh. The plaintiff was present, but the accused was absent. The court gave the following ruling:

"The accused and his *wabī* did not come to court for the last three hearings. The case is a civil one; the plaintiff has wasted his time attending court. Hence it is hereby ordered that the accused give the land in question to the plaintiff. If the accused objects because the case was closed in his absence, he can reopen it by paying the usual $10. fee. This case is hereby closed and placed in the archives."

Once again the primary objective of the defendant and his *wabī* was to stall. By doing so, they have managed to retain the land long enough to sow it. The harvest is theirs, regardless of the court decision. They have thus extended their control for at least one agricultural season. In fact, the land in question was eventually divided in an out-of-court settlement.

Cases brought against the fej. Cases in which the fej himself is the defendant differ in two important respects from those in which the defendant is the landholder designated by the fej. First, as is illustrated in case 3, the claimant usually has a much harder time obtaining a favorable decision both because the fej is ipso facto a leading elder with influence, and because the fej has the support of other ristholders who fear that they may be asked to give up land. Second, as is illustrated in case 4, cases brought against the fej often lead to new pressures for a further division of the minzir abbat's land by father.

Case 3: Yilma and Weyzero Wuddinesh vs. Priest Asris and Qeñazmach Melaku

No date

The plaintiffs, Qeñazmach Yilma and Weyzero Wuddinesh, made the following plea.

"Qeñazmach Melaku [who is also a church official with a considerable amount of secular power over the clergy of Dega Damot] and Priest Asris [the fej of the descent corporation concerned] refuse to give us our Gebré: Abeba: Amanīt rist [see the genealogy, figure 2]. We accused them in another case [that is, accused them of keeping the land themselves, rather than dividing it for the plaintiffs], and they agreed in court to give us a share of the land. A judge was chosen to help apportion the land and the case was closed. The two men we have mentioned have not yet divided the land for us. Let them come to court now and give their reply."

Copies of the complaint were sent to the defendants and the next hearing was set for April 13.

April 13

The elders present at the court were Aleqa Mersha and Zelleke. The plaintiffs and the defendants were present. The first defendant, Qeñazmach Melaku, seventy-five years old, gave the following reply.

"Priest Asris gave me those three fields of Amanīt—or rather, he showed me where the three fields were [the proper duty of the fej] but I have never plowed them [that is, never prevented the defendants from using them]."

The second defendant, Priest Asris, made the following report.

"I did not plow that land I showed to Qeñazmach Melaku either."

The plaintiffs were then ordered to prove their case (by calling witnesses to testify in their behalf) at the next hearing set for May 12.

May 12

The plaintiffs were absent. The defendants were present. The judge ruled that, since the plaintiffs could not prove their case, the case would be closed. If the plaintiffs can find witnesses, they may open the case again.

It is striking how quickly the case was closed in this instance, considering how many hearings were set in some of the other cases. The implication that the plaintiffs are having difficulty in finding men who would witness in their behalf is also significant. The defendants in this case are men of great influence, one of them in the sphere of parish affairs and of descent corporation affairs. The other, through his office, has influence throughout the district.

Case 4 opens with a simple request by a claimant for land from the fej of the minzir abbat's descent corporation. By the end of the proceedings, however, it appears that the chain of events started here may result in further subdivision of lands by father.

Case 4: Fente vs. Balamberas Anteneh

No date

The plaintiff, Fente, made the following plea.

"Balamberas Anteneh has refused to give me my share of the Kokeba rist [the Balamberas is the fej of the minzir abbat's corporation consisting of holders through one of Kokeba's three children, Agné; for the genealogy relevant to this case, see figure 2]. Let him come to court and speak. If he agrees with me, let him give me the land. If he does not agree with me, let me prove my case."

(The plaintiff was claiming land through a descent line which traces back to Shoa Hayl, Kokeba, and Agné through Aderīt, one of Agné's children. Unbeknown to the plaintiff, the division of Agné's land by father had begun and Aderīt had achieved the status of minzir abbat and had a fej. The plaintiff should have taken his claim to this fej in the first place. He might have done so, except that, as will become evident, there was some confusion about the status of the fej-ship and the degree to which the land had been divided.)

The fej for Agné, Balamberas Anteneh, gave the following defence.

"I am not the fej for Aderīt. Let Qeñazmach Wendim come to tell us about the rist."

The judge ordered Balamberas Anteneh to appear at the next hearing on March 29 with the fej of Aderīt, Qeñazmach Wendim.

March 29

The plaintiff and the defendant were present. Qeñazmach Wendim was also there, as ordered. The defendant said:

"If the fej of Aderīt agrees with the plaintiff, let him give the plaintiff land. If he does not, let him present his case."

Qeñazmach Wendim gave his age as seventy-six, his occupation as farming (he had not held public office since the Second World War), and his home parish as Feres Bét. He said it was true that he was the fej for Aderīt, but that no one (that is, the others using the land) had officially appointed him to the office. He had simply taken the job because nobody else was doing it. Then he gave the names of all the people using land through Aderīt and the location of each field. (There follows a list of eight names in the court record.) He then said that he had not received the rest of Aderīt's lands from the higher fej (*yelay fej*), that is, the fej of Agné, Aderīt's mother, but that he recognized the plaintiff's claim and would try to give him land from Aderīt's share.

The judge ordered the fej of Agné, Balamberas Anteneh, to give the rest of the land, according to the rule of division by father, to the fej of Aderīt (that is, one-third of the total), and he ordered the fej of Aderīt, Wendim, to give the plaintiff land from this additional supply. The allocation of land to the plaintiff by Aderīt's fej was to be carried out in the presence of the fej of Agné. The next hearing was set for May 7.

May 7

The elders present at the court were Adegeh and Alaminih. The plaintiff was present but the defendant was not. The plaintiff reminded the court that the fej had been ordered to divide the land for him but said it had not yet been done.

The court ordered: that the fej give the plaintiff his land; that the fej pay the plaintiff $5 *kisara* for causing him to waste his time; and that the fej pay court costs for the plaintiff upon presentation of his receipts showing these costs.

Part of the difficulty everyone is having in this case arises from the fact that the division of Kokeba's lands among her three children and of Agné's land among hers was carried out by assigning fields in their entirety rather than by subdivision. Instead of all thirty-two of Kokeba's shares being divided into three strips each, some of them have been assigned undivided to one or another of her children. For this reason it is not always clear whether a particular share is the *yedenb* land of Kokeba or has been assigned to Agné or, in turn, to Aderīt.

Claims for land through division by father

A claim for land through division by father, if successful, may eventually require the redivision or subdivision of a first settler's estate or a minzir abbat's land section in the name of an ancestor who has not previously had land or been considered a minzir abbat. This process is aptly termed "bringing in" a (new) minzir abbat.

Since it involves a large amount of land, an attempt to "bring in" a new minzir abbat is always a matter of concern to many people. The exact amount of land is determined by the accepted genealogical relations between the relevant minzir abbats. A claim to the land of a seventh and previously unrecognized child of Shoa Hayl, for example, is a claim to one-seventh of each of Shoa Hayl's sections.

Only a powerful individual or a coalition of influential elders will attempt to bring in a new minzir abbat; for, if the claim is to be successful, it is necessary to overcome the combined efforts of all the men who currently hold the land in question. It is thus almost inevitable that a claim for land through division by father is sooner or later drawn into the wider arena of interparish and district-wide political activity.

A claim for the land of a new minzir abbat is first presented to the fej or fejs whose descent corporations presently control the land from which the new "estate" must be apportioned. The fej approached must represent an ancestor who is either the sibling or the parent of the ancestor in whose name the claim is being made. If the siblings of the ancestor the claimant is trying to bring in have already achieved the status of minzir abbat, then the claim is presented to their fejs. Thus, when a claimant asked for the land of Welde Gīorgīs, child of Gubeno (fig. 3) he approached the fejs of Gubeno's other children, Akuléma, Marta, and Tadira, in whose names many of Gubeno's lands had already been divided.

If none of the siblings of the ancestor the claimant is trying to bring in have become minzir abbats, that is, if their parent's land is still all *yedenb*, then the claim must be presented to the fej of the parent's corporation. In the case of Welde Sellasé vs. Musina (case 5) discussed below, the claimant, a descendant of Welde Sellasé had to approach the fej of Demé since Musina had no fej or estate until after the dispute arose.

A claim for division by father need not be lodged at the lowest generational level at which division has previously been carried out. In general, however, the higher the generational level at which the claim is made, the more land is involved and hence the more people will oppose the action. Only a man of great power would attempt to open such a claim. All of the claimants instrumental in the redivision of Shoa Hayl's land (case 7) were titled men and had the authority of government office.

The fej to whom the claim is presented may deny its validity on genealogical grounds. If he does so, the claimants may take him to court or, if their position is weak, they may drop the matter altogether. Alternatively, the fej may recognize the genealogical validity of the claim but attempt to make a compromise settlement with claimants by offering them a few fields instead of the full share to which they are entitled. The fields offered are once again those of holders who are said by the fej to have no rist right in the land, or to have too much of the land. If the claimants accept the compromise offered by the fej they must approach these holders, reach a settlement with them or take them to court.

By effecting a compromise the fej can, for the time being, shift the burden of land loss away from himself and his influential fellow landholders. The claimants, for their part, by accepting less than their rightful amount of rist land, are able to avoid a long and bitter fight.

A compromise is always regarded as a tentative arrangement, however, for once the validity of the claim has been recognized in principle it is inevitable that sooner or later other claimants tracing their descent from the new minzir abbat will ask for their share of his land and thus force further division. For this reason, a new minzir abbat's corporation is considered to have been created as soon as the claim has been recognized, regardless of how much or little land the claimants are initially given. The leader of the claimants becomes the fej of the new corporation. It is his responsibility to represent the corporation's interests in ensuing disputes and to consider the subsequent claims of other persons for a share of the new minzir abbat's land through division by allotment.

With the passage of time and changes in personal power and interests, compromise settlements prove to be unstable. New claims are made and a new settlement must be found. Sometimes it is found by simply reassigning a few more fields to the new minzir abbat; sometimes, if the position of the defendants is strong, the validity of the claim is denied altogether, as in case 5; sometimes, if the position of the claimants is strong, the land is redivided so that the minzir abbat's corporation at last receives his full share, as in case 7.

The claimant's decision to ask for the land of a new minzir abbat, the fej's decision to recognize the claim, and both parties' willingness or unwillingness to compromise are determined in large part by their respective political positions, by their ability to engage in protracted litigation, and by their willingness to antagonize powerful men or large groups of landholders. The dynamics of this relationship between genealogical charters, land division, and political power can be understood more fully by examining disputes that have taken place during the past few decades in Dereqé Maryam and Feres Bét Mikael.

Case 5: Welde Sellasé vs. Musina

The case of Welde Sellasé vs. Musina concerns two attempts made by descendents of Welde Sellasé to obtain his share of his father's land, a share which had previously been held by people tracing descent through the father's other child, Musina (fig. 3).

Until after the Italian occupation no one held rist land in Demé by virtue of a recognized claim through Demé's child Welde Sellasé. The lands of Demé were mostly *yedenb*, undivided, but in some contexts they were spoken of as belonging to incipient corporations founded by Demé's four "children," Miskab, Wellete Rufaél, Irite, and Meṭru. Since the intervening ancestor, Musina, the child of Demé and the mother of the four, was of no structural importance and had no fej, she was usually not mentioned in tracing descent lines. Her four children were referred to as Demé's children rather than his grandchildren.

The situation changed when a nonresident man, untitled but influential, came to the fej of Demé, a wealthy farmer named Wibé, and asked him for the land of Musina's brother Welde Sellasé. The twenty-four men who held the land of Demé, all of whom traced descent through Musina, held a meeting. They did so as members of a new minzir abbat's corporation, that of Musina, which had not previously had corporate existence, since it had no opposed segment.

The new corporation, subsuming the four corporations of Musina's children in the context of this case, needed a fej to represent their interests against the claim for Welde Sellasé's share of the land. Wibé, who was already the fej of Demé and who was unofficially considered the fej of Miskab as well, would normally have been a logical choice. The man selected to represent Musina, however, in this instance was Assegé, an aging nonresident who had both genealogical expertise and political influence deriving from his years of service in the administration of Dega Damot under Ras Hailu.

The fej and those he represented were faced with a serious problem. If they recognized the new claimant's rist rights through Welde Sellasé, they might eventually have to give him, and perhaps other men claiming similar descent, not a twenty-fifth of Demé's land, since he was one of twenty-five claiming members, but one-half of the land, as he would be the sole active member of the corporation which stands in a sibling relationship to that of Musina.

The Musina fej had either to call into question the legitimacy of the claimant's rist right or to come to some compromise settlement with him. Since the claimant already was plowing land held by a corporation of Welde Sellasé in a nearby parish, the fej did not argue that the claimant was not a Welde Sellasé descendent.

A compromise agreement was reached out of court. All of Demé's sections of land would be divided equally for Musina and Welde Sellasé in the future; for the present, however, only two of Demé's twenty-five fields would be divided, and Welde Sellasé's share of each of these fields would be given to the claimant. Two of Demé's hitherto undivided *yedenb* lands, held by men with questionable claims, were measured into equal sections, and the appropriate shares were allotted to the new claimant by lot. He, being an important man, promptly allocated his newly won land to tenants from Dereqé Maryam and friends from the neighboring parish. His friends, in turn, being important men themselves, allocated the land to tenants resident in Dereqé Maryam. Thus almost all the land continued to be plowed by previous holders, but they were now paying rent on the land that some of them had held before as rist. The claimant, of course, became the fej of the new minzir abbat's corporation of Welde Sellasé.

For the time being the dispute was settled and the corporation of Musina had no affairs. Its twenty-four active members individually plowed their lands and devoted their litigational talents to fighting other cases in which they happened to be involved through membership in other descent corporations. Even while the case was being disputed, the solidarity of the men plowing Musina land had not been very great. Some of them lived in other parishes and held only small amounts of land in Musina in any case. The main burden of the dispute had been carried by four or five elders.

The years passed and the claimant grew old and died, leaving no heir of equal political prominence. The men to whom he had given his Welde Sellasé fields continued to plow them, but those who had been his direct tenants did not pay rent any longer. Matters might have rested as they were, had not four members of the minzir abbat's corporation of Welde Sellasé from the nearby parish mentioned previously come to claim land through Welde Sellasé.

Once again, the interested members of Musina rallied. This time they were faced with what appeared to them as a more serious threat. The members of the corporation of Welde Sellasé in the nearby parish had been increasing in number. It seemed unlikely that they would long settle for a small fraction of the land which was now legally theirs, should they but come to claim it.

Though the consequences of the new claim were more serious, the claimants were individually of lower status than the previous opponent. It was decided to use a different line of defense. Assegé, the representative of Musina, decided to reverse the position taken earlier. Instead of trying to compromise with the claimants, he brought into question the legitimacy of their claim by an ingenious ploy. As in the earlier case, there was no legal doubt that the claimants were really descendents of Welde Sellasé. The fej therefore took the only alternative position and said that Welde Sellasé was not really the child of Demé after all. He alleged that Welde Sellasé was the child of Demé's wife by a previous marriage. Surely, he admitted, Welde Sellasé had been raised by Demé and was considered "as his child," but, according to the rule of land division and inheritance, a "mother's child" could not inherit rights from his stepfather.

The claimants from Welde Sellasé have not yet taken the case to court. Nor do they seem eager to do so before the old fej of Musina dies; for proving the biological paternity of a man who, if he ever existed, died perhaps a century and a half ago is a rather subjective and difficult task. One suspects, with the claimants, that it would prove a lengthy and expensive process, difficult to win against an opponent of Assegé's experience and remaining influence.

Case 6: Hetnora vs. Hiywetua

The case of Hetnora vs. Hiywetua concerns a protracted attempt by nontitled elders to have the *yedenb* lands of the minzir abbat Senbeta in Shoa Hayl (fig. 2) divided among her children. The case is complex because of the number of elders involved and because two distinct claims, only one of which concerned Senbeta, were eventually made in a single court action. The object of the plaintiffs in opening a double case was to save court costs.

Until 1942 the lands of Senbeta (see map 5) were all *yedenb*, or undivided. The more than three dozen men and women who held the lands as rist traced their descent lines through Hiywetua, Hetnora, or both. Though there had been no formal allocation between these children of Senbeta, it was evident to those who cared to find out that the descendents of Hiywetua held far more of Senbeta's *yedenb* lands than did those of Hetnora. It was thus to the advantage of an ambitious descendent of Hetnora to push for division by father between Senbeta's children.

In 1942 Aleqa Desta, an influential elder from the neighboring parish of Ziqwala Arbaytu Insesa, approached the fej of Senbeta, who at this time was Assegé, the same aging noble who figured as the fej of Musina in case 5. Aleqa Desta, the claimant, asked for the land of Hetnora through formal division by father. It would have been difficult to deny the legitimacy of the claim, for it was based on the fact that Senbeta was the wife of Akale Kristos of Ziqwala and mother of his two children, Hiywetua and Hetnora. Indeed, the land of Akale Kristos had been divided between their children for several decades. After consultation, the fej agreed to give the claimant three of Senbeta's thirty-odd fields as a compromise in lieu of dividing all the *yedenb* lands, as required by the strictest interpretation of the rule. The resulting situation was somewhat anomalous, for though the formal division of Senbeta's lands had begun and though the claimant was now the fej of Hetnora's corporation, not a single strip of Senbeta land had actually been measured into two parts. (Such situations cause endless confusion during interviews concerning the state of land division in Dega Damot.)

After some years, Aleqa Desta, the claimant, grew ill and died, leaving the three fields in the hands of his tenants. In 1965, shortly after his death, a new action was instituted by five nontitled elders, four of them resident on Shoa Hayl's land and the fifth from Ziqwala Arbaytu Insesa. The five claimants first asked the fej of Hiywetua, who was the same old noble that represented Senbeta, for the rest of Hetnora's lands through division by father. They also asked the fej of Nudé, a grazmach with no current office, to divide land for them in the name of Ayo. Nudé's land had not previously been divided officially by father.

The leader of the five claimants, the man from Ziqwala Arbaytu Insesa, assumed the position of fej for Hetnora and also became fej for Ayo. After deliberating with other leading men concerned, the fejs of Nudé and Hiywetua designated the lands held by ten men for division or outright assignment to the claimants. Three of the designated men were ordered to give up fields they held in Senbeta only, three were told to give up fields they held in Nudé only, and the other four were ordered to give up fields of both Senbeta and Nudé.

Two of the men asked to give up fields were former titled officeholders, long retired from official service and with the dwindling households that usually accompany old age. Another was the son of a titled former officeholder who once held extensive lands in the area. A fourth designee was the full brother of the *aṭbīya dañña* of Feres Bét, the parish in which the land of Shoa Hayl is located. A fifth was the elder full brother of one of the claimants. Three more were elderly men who had demonstrated little acumen at amassing land or attaining leadership, and the remaining two were young men who had inherited an unusual amount of land but had not yet achieved the standing in the community that would enable them to easily defend their rights in it.

It is interesting that neither of the largest holders of Senbeta land were asked to give up any fields. One of them was the fej himself, who is reported to have "begged" the claimants to leave him alone on the grounds that he would die in a year or two anyway and they could then take his land. This type of request is regarded by others as a veiled threat that the dying man will curse his younger opponents. At the same time, it should be borne in mind that the old noble was not yet devoid of influence in Dega Damot.

The other large holder of Senbeta land was the leading priest who stood accused as fej in case 4. In response to questions, informants said that the priest served the ark well and acted as soul father for many of the parishioners resident in Shoa Hayl. Since all priests in good standing perform these services, it may be surmised that his wealth and influence were important factors in protecting the priest from loss of land.

One of the elderly men and the two former officeholders agreed to divide some of their land with the claimants. The other seven men refused, were accused, and went to court. There each was asked, as defendant, to defend his right to the land he held. None of them claimed to hold the land by their own rist right.

The first older man said that he had a *wabī* for the land, his wife's brother, a man who happened to be the clerk of the Dega Damot district tax office. The other elder defendant said that he would not give up the land because he had not agreed to the appointment of Assegé as Senbeta's fej. As far as he was concerned, no one had been given the office legally since the death of the *fītawrarī* who had first brought Senbeta into Shoa Hayl (see case 7). The defendant who was a brother of one of the accusers said his *wabī* was his former wife's father. The land was his, he said, because of his son by the former wife. The wife's father was the *fītawrarī* and former officeholder who brought in Qusqo in case 7. One of the young defendants said that he had a *qeñazmach* for a *wabī* on his Nudé land and that the Senbeta land not only had been plowed by his father before him but was fertilized land and hence could not be divided. The other three defendants called *wabīs* of lesser distinction.

The judge ordered the *wabīs* to appear in court and said the lands concerned should be estimated. The high-ranking *wabīs* did not appear and the estimation took the better part of a year to complete, since the defendants never seemed able to get to court. Eventually the judge awarded all the land to the claimants and closed the case.

The defendants, however, refused to comply with the court order and would not permit the claimants to plow the land. The claimants then opened a criminal case against the defendants for illegally using their new lands. The judge decided in favor of the claimants once more, ordered the defendants to give up the land immediately and to pay a fine of $25 each. The defendants appealed their case to the higher court some seventy miles away.

> After incurring heavy expenses attending the higher court, the plaintiffs and defendants agreed to an out-of-court settlement that was to include the selection of new fejs to replace the fejs of Nudé and Senbeta, a remeasurement of all Senbeta's and Nudé's lands, and the allotment of land to the claimants. This agreement was being implemented at the termination of fieldwork in Dega Damot.

The speed and the completeness of land division by father is largely a function of the political power at the disposal of the plaintiff or plaintiffs. Both of the claims discussed above, for example, were opened by influential men without high office and resulted at first in compromise settlements. In each case the claims were raised again years later by a coalition of leading elders. Men with great secular power, by contrast, are more likely to force an immediate and complete redivision of the land, as in the three disputes discussed below.

The swift and dramatic entry of a new minzir abbat, and the attendant major redivision of descent corporations' estates, is an important political event not only because it is effected through the use of political power but also because it results in a reshuffling of the political loyalties of landholders as much as it does in a reallocation of land among people. The powerful men (or man) who control the fejship and the estate of the new corporation treat their newly acquired land more as a form of political patronage than as a potential source of economic profit. The fej soon begins to parcel out the corporation's land to those who have supported him in the past and to those whom he hopes will support him in the future. By recognizing remote and long-dormant pedigrees, the fej is able to give out the land as rist. The recipients, for their part, express their gratitude by small cash payments to the fej "to help defray his court costs," and by supporting him as their personal benefactor and patron. In some instances many of the men who receive rist land in the new corporation's estate have previously held land in the estate from which it has been created. For them, the dramatic shift in the structure of the first settler's descent corporation and in land division entails little more than the payment of a small fee in recognition of dependence on the individual who is the new fej. That the land of a newly created minzir abbat is widely distributed rather than given out in tenancy is attested to by the fact that today the number of rist-holders in Shoa Hayl's three new corporations—those of minzir abbats Senbeta, Kokeba, and Qusqo—is approximately the same as those holding the land of Shoa Hayl's three older minzir abbats, Teklé, Nudé and Gebré. The circumstances surrounding the entry of these three minzir abbats serve to illustrate well the role of political office and political power in claims for the division of land by father.

Case 7: The entrance of three minzir abbats in Shoa Hayl

Previous to about 1930 the estate of Shoa Hayl was divided into only three shares for Shoa Hayl's three presumed children: Teklé, Nudé, and Gebré. In about that year, a certain *fītawrarī* who had recently been given the court title of *agafarī*, or majordomo, and the office of *bilaténgéta*, or steward, over the gwilt lands personally held by the provincial ruler, Ras Hailu, approached the fejs of Teklé, Nudé, and Gebré. He said he was a descendent of Shoa Hayl through a fourth child, a daughter named Senbeta, and that he wanted her share of the land—one-fourth of all Shoa Hayl's land section.

The parish of Feres Bét in which the land of Shoa Hayl is found was at that time the *ganageb* of Ras Hailu and hence under the jurisdiction of the *fītawrarī* who now sought land. His authority was similar to that wielded by any gwilt *gež*, though his tenure in office was less certain. Thus many of the men who held the land of Shoa Hayl and who stood to lose land were subjects of the claimant.

Despite this tactical disadvantage, the fejs of Teklé, Nudé, and Gebré refused to give the *fītawrarī* the land of Senbeta, and the dispute went to court. The case was heard by another powerful noble, also a *fītawrarī*, who was governor of the district, which included what is now

Dega Damot. The claimant and the defendants each pledged a large container of honey to the judge, should they lose the case, as was the custom before the modern court system was instituted.

The claimant called as witnesses rist experts from the adjacent parish of Ziqwala Arbaytu Insesa. They testified that one of their ancestors, Akale Kristos, had married Senbeta, the daughter of Shoa Hayl, and had two children by her, Hiywetua and Hetnora. The claimant was also able to produce witnesses descended from two of the recognized minzir abbats, Gebré and Nudé, who acknowledged the legitimacy of the claim through Senbeta. Presumably these men were influenced by the claimant-lord, or they would not have testified against what would otherwise have been their own interest.

The judge ruled in favor of the claimant, the latter became the fej of the new corporation of Senbeta, and he was able to obtain one-fourth of all the lands of Shoa Hayl. In the years after the dispute, the winning lord let many of the previous holders stay on either as rist-holders or as his tenants. He gave other fields to men who claimed to be descended from Senbeta. In recent years, since the reorganization of Gojjam administration, the eclipse of Ras Hailu, and the death of the claimant, still other men have successfully asked for a share of Senbeta's *yedenb* lands.

A year or two after the successful entry of Senbeta into Shoa Hayl, another land dispute was brought by two titled officeholders. Both men had the rank of *grazmach*. One of them was the commander (*azzaž*) in charge of supplying Ras Hailu's army with provisions when it camped periodically near Feres Bét, where there were state storage bins.

The claimants said that they were descended from a fifth child of Shoa Hayl and were hence entitled to one-fifth of all his land. Once again, the claim was disputed and once again the claimants prevailed. The same governor judged the case, though this time sitting in the town of Adét, some thirty miles away, where he happened to have his military camp. One of the claimants became the fej of the new corporation of Kokeba, and the claimants apportioned the lands among themselves, their followers, and the previous holders. Over the years this land has passed into the hands of ordinary farmers asserting rist rights through Kokeba. The old lord who became fej has died. The other lord, the former commander of provisions, has become fej, but today holds no more land than other elders. He often dwells sadly upon the glory that once was Dega Damot and laments the dark days that have befallen it now that it no longer sees the tents of the provincial ruler.

Two years later a noble with the rank of *fītawrarī*, gwilt rights, and a post in the regional administration opened a case against the five fejs representing the five minzir abbats' corporations and asked for one-sixth of the land of Shoa Hayl in the name of a sixth child, Qusqo. He eventually won the dispute, though the case was appealed to Ras Hailu himself when he sat in Buré.

Disputes involving ancestors at such a high genealogical level, and hence so much land, are much less common than lower-level disputes. The rash of claims in Shoa Hayl probably had to do with the fact that Feres Bét, the parish in which it is located, had become a minor political center in Dega Damot under Ras Hailu. Not only was it the Ras's personal gwilt and the site of government granaries, it was also the location where the governors of Dega Damot most frequently situated the quasi-permanent military camps where they held court. Land in this politically central location seems to have been strongly sought after by officials stationed in the area. Indeed, a recent district governor resident in the town of Feres Bét found it expedient and possible to claim his rist land through five of Shoa Hayl's six children, though he had held no land prior to his appointment. Three years after his departure (under something of a cloud), he had lost almost all of the land.

9. Social Stratification and the Control of Land

That social mobility is a real possibility for the people of Dega Damot is indicated by the fact that a high proportion of the fields held by large holders are acquired by means other than inheritance. Figure 6a, which shows the relationship between fields held as rist and fields inherited by the men resident in Shoa Hayl about whose land the most complete and reliable data were collected, supports the opinion of Amhara elders and the writer that large holders have obtained a higher proportion of their land through their own efforts than have small holders.

The most important way in which upwardly mobile individuals acquire additional land is by successfully pressing claims lodged with a descent corporation. The importance of such claims to the holders represented in figure 6a is indicated in figure 6b, which shows the relationship between fields held and fields acquired from a fej. Since a man's ability to obtain land from a fej is closely related to his ability to press his case in court if necessary, it is to be expected that large holders are more litigious than small holders. This expectation is supported by data from intensive interviews with twenty-five household heads resident in Shoa Hayl. It was found that of the eleven large holders (defined here as men with more than seven fields) eight had been involved in two or more court cases concerning land during the twelve months prior to the interview; of the fourteen small holders only one had been involved in two or more cases during the same period. It could be argued that large holders are involved in more litigation over land simply because they control more

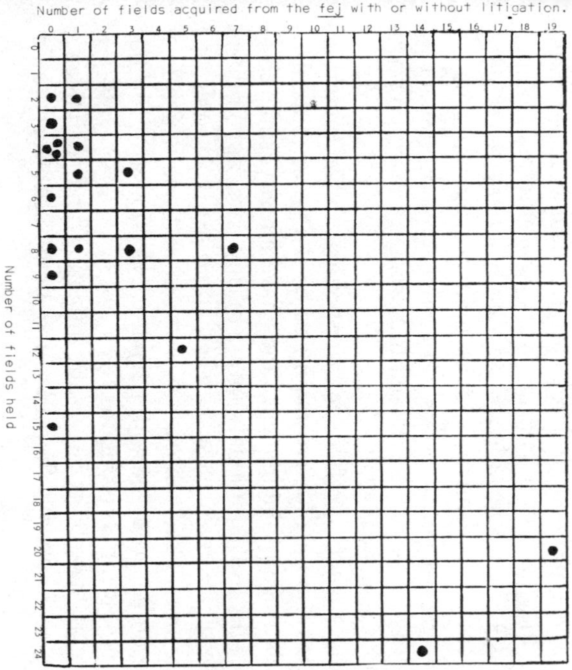

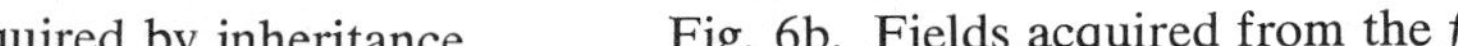

Number of fields acquired from the *fej* with or without litigation.

Number of fields held

KEY

Each dot represents a house hold head.

Fig. 6a. Fields acquired by inheritance

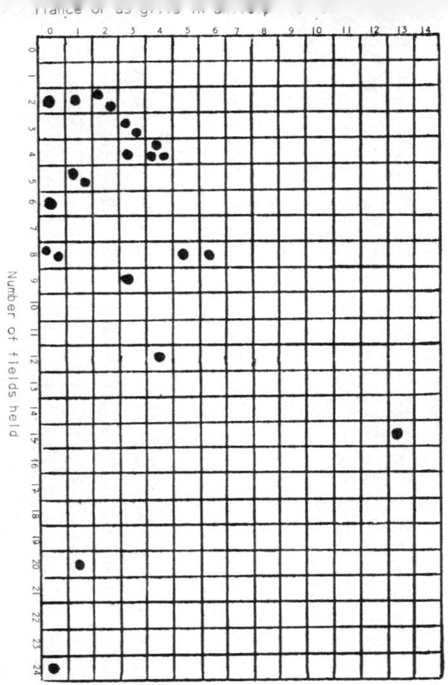

Number of fields held

Fig. 6b. Fields acquired from the *fej* of a descent corporation fields over which disputes arise at a more or less constant rate. That this is not so is suggested by the fact that of the six small holders involved in at least one land case during the one-year period, only two were involved in any case as plaintiff; of the nine large holders involved in at least one land case during the same period, seven were involved in at least one of these cases as plaintiff.

It is not, of course, a man's willingness to litigate that enables him to obtain land from the descent corporation, but rather his ability to litigate successfully. This ability is primarily a function of his political influence and power, that is, of his ability to influence witnesses, fejs, and judges.

It is thus crucial to examine more closely the dynamics of the relationship between political power and the control of land. More specifically, it is important to investigate how men can attain political power, how they can obtain additional land with this power, how they can use the land to further enhance their power, what prevents them from obtaining more land, and what happens to their land when they die.

The political influence through which some elders are able to claim more rist land than their fellow farmers is diffuse, localized and personal. In large part, it is usually based on the respect they have won over the years as arbitrators, counselors, and go-betweens in local community affairs. Particularly in the case of a *debtera* political influence may also be enhanced by an element of fear. An elder may also obtain influence by becoming a personal follower of a more powerful man such as a local gwilt *gež*.

Leading elders are frequently appointed to the minor administrative posts of *c̣hiqa shum* and *c̣hewa gebez*, but this is as much a sign of the influence they have already achieved as it is a source of additional power. In any case, appointment to these offices is, in most parishes, for a period of only one year. A more significant sign of success, and one which is of greater utility in the quest for land, is selection as fej in one or more descent corporations.

Through his ability to sustain litigation and to influence directly or indirectly the allocation of descent corporation land, a leading elder may obtain up to three or four times as much rist land as the ordinary farmer. To some extent, the possession of this land increases the holder's political influence or at least his litigational effectiveness and his ability to obtain and hold yet more rist land. It enables him to bring a poor boy into his household to help with the agricultural work, thus freeing himself to attend court more frequently. It also makes it easier for him to pay court fees, to make judicious gifts to court personnel, and to support the cost of appealing a case to a court distant from his and his opponent's home.

There are limits to the amount of land an elder without political office can acquire in this way; for in judging whether he has too much of a local descent corporation's estate the other landholders are primarily concerned with his secular authority and not with his wealth in land or money. After initial successes in obtaining additional land from a descent corporation, a man will find his claims opposed by an increasingly united group of landholders who feel that he already has too much of the land. His claims for land in more distant corporations' estates also bring him into conflict with an increasing number of widely scattered opponents. Furthermore, even if he obtains fields in some of these corporations' estates, he may find it difficult and even dangerous to collect rents from his new tenants. One resident of Shoa Hayl who has acquired through litigation numerous fields that once were held by his father's father, but not by his father, reports that he is unable to collect rent on fully half his newly won fields and that he is afraid to travel through the forests alone for fear of his enemies. He is also, interestingly enough, one of a small number of nonartisans generally said by his fellow parishioners to be a witch.

The estate built up by a successful elder does not generally outlast his lifetime. If he has several heirs it must be divided among them. Even if he has but one heir, it is unlikely that this heir will have the respect and the network of personal ties that enabled his father to acquire and defend so many fields of rist land. Inevitably some large holders pass to their children not only their land but also some of the special knowledge or skill which enabled them to obtain it. The son of a great wizard may become a wizard. The son of a fej well versed in genealogy may have an advantage in obtaining his deceased father's office. Even in such exceptional cases, however, it is more likely that the son will eventually build up an estate commensurate with that of his father than it is that he will simply take over his father's lands and status intact.

The most important source of the secular power which has enabled men to obtain large holdings of rist land has been political office, particularly the office of the local gwilt-holder, or gwilt *gež*. Traditionally, the power of the gwilt *gež* was pervasive and immediate since he served at once as judge, principal tax collector, and government representative. Even today, backed by the authority of the government from above and supported by his personal followers, the gwilt *gež* is able to exert considerable influence over the people resident within his neighborhood. This influence rests not only on the clearly prescribed duties of his office but also on his ability to help or harm his subjects when he carries out his duties.

A man who holds the position of gwilt *gež* for some years usually comes to hold more rist land in his neighborhood than anyone else. Even if he held no fields in the neighborhood at the time of his appointment, he can quickly build a respectable estate both within and outside of his neighborhood, provided, of course, that he has recognized rist rights in the area. It is relatively easy for him to obtain rist land for his rist rights even through remote and long unused pedigrees. The elders and fejs who manage the affairs of some of the local descent corporations are eager to have the new lord join their ranks; for he is sure to be a strong and effective supporter of their cause in future litigation. His support is particularly useful if the minzir abbat through whom he is claiming land has not yet been given the full share of the land to which he is genealogically entitled through division by father. In such cases, the men who hold the land of the descent corporation's estate may be able to increase their individual holdings through recognizing the claim of the gwilt *gež*. The gwilt-holder can also obtain rist land outside of his neighborhood through descent corporations that willingly recognize his claim in order to enlist his support in defending or enlarging their estates.

The gwilt-holder cultivates part of his lands with his own oxen and part with the aid of the labor and oxen provided annually by those farmers resident in his neighborhood. Still other fields may be given to tenants or, occasionally, to a poor man who lives in a house belonging to the gwilt-holder and who works as a tenant. Traditionally, the gwilt *gež* also received a land tax in kind from all those who cultivated land under his jurisdiction. The produce that the gwilt *gež* obtained from his rist land, together with the produce he received as land tax, was essential to the maintenance of his prestige and power. It supplied provisions for him and his followers when he attended his lord's court or accompanied him to war. It also enabled the gwilt-holder to provide for the needs of his large household and the many feasts which, as a big man, he was expected to give.

The ability of the gwilt *gež* to acquire rist land should not be overestimated, for it was and is limited. The same type of descent group politicking which enables a gwilt *gež* to obtain land in other men's neighborhoods enables them to obtain land in his. Members of descent corporations which are in danger of losing land to corporations which the gwilt *gež* is supporting can actively seek to recruit powerful men from other neighborhoods. These powerful non-residents, often themselves gwilt-holders, serve to reestablish a balance of power and prevent or forestall further shifts in land division. Because powerful outsiders recruited under these circumstances are usually asked to represent the corporation as fej, it comes about somewhat paradoxically that, though one of the primary tasks of a fej is to reject the claims of nonresidents, a great many fejs are themselves nonresidents! If, despite these checks, a gwilt *gež* succeeds in manipulating the distribution of descent corporation rist land too flagrantly to his and his friends' advantage, he will find the resident population of his neighborhood and hence his personal power and prestige dwindling. In the last analysis, it is control over men and not control over land that gives a man honor and power in Dega Damot.

The impression that the local gentry is an hereditary group whose status rests on the possession of land has been created, in large part, by the tendency of the gwilt *gež* and the people he governs to regard his office as hereditary; this despite the fact that provincial rulers have insisted on their right to give gwilt rights to the man of their choice. In a sense, both claims are correct; for to have an hereditary right to the office of gwilt *gež*—that is, to consider gwilt rist-gwilt—one must only be accounted a descendent, in any line, of the first gwilt-holder. The number of eligible candidates from which the ruler can select an "hereditary" gwilt *gež* is thus very great.

The critical question, then, is to what extent the office of gwilt *gež* actually has passed from a man to his son or close collateral kinsman. Although a definitive answer to this question must await further research, present evidence indicates that, in the present century, gwilt has passed from father to son less than 50 percent of the time. Instances in which it passes to either a son or a close collateral kinsman are more common (Hoben 1970b).

Dramatic changes in the disposition of gwilt rights are often associated with major shifts in the provincial power structure as a new ruler tries to reward the followers who have brought him to power. In unsettled times it is thus more difficult for an hereditary gentry to form. In the present century Gojjam has certainly seen political turmoil, but not more than it experienced in the previous two centuries. It thus can be said conservatively that great and enduring "families," owing their high status to succession to office and the possession of *rist* land, were the exception and not the rule in Dega Damot. As there has been rapid upward social mobility into the gentry, so there has been swift downward mobility out of the gentry for office holders' sons who failed to distinguish themselves as leaders of their people and servants of their lord.

Traditionally the most important officeholders in Dega Damot were the governor, his court officials, the *līqekahinat* in charge of church administration, and the heads of large monasteries. Most high secular officials also held several neighborhoods as their personal gwilt or rist-gwilt. They were thus able to obtain widespread rist land in their neighborhoods like ordinary gwilt-holders. They were also able to obtain widespread rist lands in other neighborhoods; for though the power that flowed from the possession of high office did not in itself often directly affect the day-to-day lives of ordinary peasants, it enabled those who exercised it to engage very effectively in the type of descent-group manipulations already described.

To these powerful and landed men of Dega Damot, the quest for land, with its constant involvement in dispute and intrigue, has been as much a political as an economic activity; and the land itself has been as much a form of political as economic capital. In order to attract retainers to his court and cause, a great officeholder had to be able to feast them at his table, to reward them periodically with clothes, and eventually, if he were a great man and they served him well, to help them obtain control over land, particularly gwilt, with which, in turn, they could hope to build a following of their own. Without such a cadre of loyal followers attracted by land and the fruits of the land, a great officeholder could not enforce his rule over those who were nominally under his jurisdiction, protect his interests against his peers who were inevitably rivals, and provide the support expected of him by his superior lord; for it was characteristic of the traditional Amhara polity that a man's political power derived more from his ability to help or harm individuals under his control than from his occupancy of a clearly defined position of command in an enduring political organization.

Neither a great lord's rist and gwilt lands nor the political privileges which enabled him to acquire and hold them normally passed undivided to a single heir; for there was no rule of succession by which any of his kinsmen were promoted to his vacant position. On the contrary, a powerful man's death was regularly followed by an intense struggle for his court duties, prerogatives, emoluments, offices, and lands, all of which would probably never again be held in the same combination by a single individual.

A son, a son-in-law, a brother, or a nephew of the deceased who succeeded in reconsolidating a large part of the deceased's political base and in attaining his most impressive political office is often spoken of as his heir, a usage which overlooks the competitive and precarious nature of Amhara succession. The ideology of hereditary succession is further enhanced by the tendency of Gojjamis to refer to any man who has risen to power as a member of the "ruling" family so long as it is possible to relate him through a bilaterally traced pedigree to Ras Hailu the first, a shadowy figure who is said to have ruled Gojjam several centuries ago.

The following brief life sketches have been included in this chapter in order to illustrate more concretely the way in which the many factors discussed may affect a single individual's quest for land and improved social status. Three of the sketches were selected from a series of intensive interviews with residents of Shoa Hayl and the fourth is based on interviews carried out during an earlier period of research. Two of the men are commoners and two are titled. The commoners, Molla and Dersih, were chosen because they are of the same age but differ in their "political standing" and status within the community and in their success at acquiring new rist land. The titled men are Grazmach Admasé, the *aṭbiya dañña* of Feres Bét Mikael, who has the sixth largest holding in Shoa Hayl's land, and Līqekahinat Assegé, the former chief clerk of Dega Damot and the largest landholder in Shoa Hayl.

Life History 1: Molla

Molla lives with his wife and his brother's ten-year-old son in a simple homestead near the stream that separates Dereqé Maryam from Feres Bét Mikael (homestead 1, on map 3). He has one ox, two calves, one horse, and five sheep, and by all accounts is neither wealthy nor an influential elder. In 1966 he reported that he was forty years old.

Molla was born in Shoa Hayl, the fourth of eight children including six boys, two of whom were his elders. He lived with his family in Shoa Hayl until he was ten years old, when his father died. Soon after her husband's death, Molla's mother moved with her children to the nearby parish of Shangi Maryam in order, she said, to be farther from the Italian cantonment in Feres Bét. During the occupation, Molla remained in Shangi Maryam under the authority of his mother and his oldest brother. After the war Molla's mother moved back to Shoa Hayl in Feres Bét Mikael. She never married again. Molla's oldest brother and one of his sisters had both married in Shangi Maryam, however, and did not return. Soon after the return to Shoa Hayl, his other elder brother married and built a homestead on his new wife's rist land, leaving Molla as the oldest male in his mother's household.

A few years later Molla married and, after living with his mother for one year, built a new homestead nearby on her rist land. Two of his younger brothers also married, eventually, and established homesteads in Shoa Hayl. His younger sister married locally also, and the other brother died at the age of fifteen while attending church school and studying to become a priest. The number of his siblings and, equally important, their failure or inability to disperse more widely is undoubtedly one reason that Molla and his brothers have been notably unsuccessful at acquiring additional fields of rist land.

Molla still lives with his first wife, who has borne him a son, a daughter, and four other children who died in infancy. His son has married twice and now lives in the parish of Dereqé Maryam. The daughter, now fifteen, is married and lives near the other end of the parish of Feres Bét.

Molla has had no church school education, has never been chosen for public office, such as hamlet representative or *ch̩iqa shum*, and has never served as fej for a descent corporation. His only legal activity during the year preceding the study was of being one of the defendants in case 6 above. By any measure, Molla's political standing in the community is low.

The first field Molla acquired is in the parish of Shangi Maryam. It had been used by his father, then by his oldest brother. When Molla became old enough to plow, he cultivated the field for his mother's household, of which he was a part. After his marriage and departure from the house, he continued to use the land for the exclusive benefit of his new household.

In 1951 Molla built his present house on pasture land (field M1 on map 3) that was considered the *yedenb* land of Qusqo, and began to plow about three acres of land around it. He has no recognized descent line from Qusqo and admits that he simply has possession without rist right. He says that his sister has a child by a man with rights in Qusqo and that he would call this man as his *wabī* if challenged.

In 1960 Molla asked the fej of a minzir abbat's descent corporation in Dereqé Maryam for rist land through a descent line he traced through his wife. He needed the land, he said, so that his married son, Tilahun, could build a homestead on it. The request was granted. In 1966 Molla and his son tilled the land together and shared the produce equally. Molla says that the land is really his through his wife because, after all, it was his request that obtained it. The son, Tilahun, while not openly disagreeing with his father, points out in private that it is really his field since it is his "mother's rist." In fact, the field was previously held by a man who was not considered a kinsman of Molla or his wife, though he was, of course, the latter's *dirrib*, or codescendent.

The next year, 1961, lots were cast to divide a previously undivided, or *yedenb*, land of Shoa Hayl. Molla obtained a field (M2) at this time. He claims the land as "mother's rist" but some men say he really holds the land for the time being in the absence of a more influential holder.

In 1964 he plowed a field (M3) in a comparatively infertile section of pastureland that had been assigned to Senbeta following a dispute some years before. He did not ask the fej for the land. The following year the fej told him to give it up. He refused and became one of the seven Senbeta defendants in case 6, discussed in the previous chapter.

Life History 2: Dersih

Not far to the east of Molla lives Dersih, along with his wife and ten-year-old daughter (homestead 2 on map 3). With three oxen, two calves from cows that died earlier in the year, two geldings used as pack horses, one mare and her colt, Dersih is considerably more wealthy in livestock than Molla, though the two men are of approximately the same age. Dersih also controls more rist land than Molla and commands more respect as an elder and arbiter of others' disputes.

Dersih was the last of six children and has three older brothers. His eldest brother died while in church studies at a distant monastery. The following brother is a farmer living in Shoa Hayl. The next child, a girl, died without having children. The other sister is now a nun and the other brother died after marriage but before having children. Since his mother did not have children by any man other than his father, Dersih had to share land and land rights with only one sibling.

Dersih was born, raised, and married off by his mother and father in Shoa Hayl. After this comparatively uneventful childhood, he married and lived with his parents for a year. At the end of this time his father asked him to build his new homestead near his own. Dersih objected, respectfully but firmly, saying that there was not enough land near his father's homestead and that it would be better for all if he moved farther away to the other end of the hamlet. His father eventually acquiesced. Dersih's new home was built on land held by his father but located at the opposite end of Shoa Hayl's estate.

Dersih still lives with his first wife, who has borne him six children. The firstborn child died in infancy, the second, a boy, is married and has established his own household. The third is a student in government school at the provincial capital of Debre Markos. The fourth, a girl, is married. The fifth lives with him, and the last child, a boy, died at the age of three years. Dersih went to church school for a total of five years in two parishes before he gave up his studies and married. Today he is the tax collector, or *teṭerī* (see chapter 10) for Shoa Hayl; he helps the *c̣hiqa shum* and *aṭbīya dañña* and often arbitrates the minor disputes of others. He does not serve as fej for any descent corporations, though he says he hopes to.

During the year preceding the study, Dersih was involved in three court cases. The first was case 6, in which he was one of the plaintiffs. The second concerned another man't attempt to plow up part of the land which Dersih used as a cattle path from his home. Dersih was the winner in this case also. In the third case Dersih was the defendant as guarantor for another man's business transaction. He lost and was forced to pay his opponent an ox.

Dersih was more fortunate than Molla in inheriting land from his father. He has also been more successful at acquiring additional fields of rist land. Before his marriage, Dersih was assigned the responsibility of cultivating two fields. One was a field of Senbeta (D1 on map 3) which his father had been using through Dersih's mother's rist right. The other was a field in Mahelbét, a *goṭ* in the parish of Gesagis Maryam. The produce of these fields went towards the support of his father's household.

When Dersih married and established his own homestead, his father let him continue to use these two fields rent-free and gave him three Nudé fields (D2, D3, and D4) in return for a share of the crop. On one of these Dersih built his house. At his father's death Dersih assumed full control over all these fields.

Some years later, in 1951, Dersih asked the fej representing Gebré for a share of Gebré's land as his wife's rist. The fej acknowledged the legitimacy of the claim and ordered that two men share some of their land with Dersih. The designated men stalled for some time until Dersih threatened to take them to court. An out-of-court settlement was then reached and Dersih received one field (D5) of Gebré land.

In 1956 Dersih complained to his older brother that the latter held more than a fair share of their father's lands. After some quarreling, the brother gave him two fields (D6, and D7) from Kokeba. His father had used the field as wife's rist before Dersih's brother had taken it over.

In the following year Dersih acquired two more fields. The first was pastureland which he simply plowed without asking anyone. Later, when lots were cast to divide the area, which had been Shoa Hayl *yedenb*, this field was given to Dersih as Kokeba land. He says the elders gave it to him undivided to help him, since it was near his house. Dersih acquired the other field from a stranger by asking the fej of Nudé's husband's descent corporation in the *goṭ* of Mahelbét in Gesagis Maryam, where he already held one field he had acquired from his father before marriage.

In 1959 Dersih asked the fej for more rist land in Mahelbét. The fej told him to take two fields used by a certain weaver. The weaver refused to give up the land. Dersih went ahead and began to plow the fields. The weaver sued him, and Dersih countersued the weaver. Eventually the dispute was ended by an out-of-court agreement. The weaver retained the larger of the two fields while Dersih took possession of the smaller.

In 1963 Dersih, together with two other elders, opened a case to bring in a new minzir abbat in the *goṭ* of Indibego

> in Gesagis Maryam. After much litigation, a favorable decision, a second criminal case, a second victory, and an appeal to the subprovincial court, the plaintiffs made an out-of-court settlement and received about ten acres of unfertilized land, from which Dersih obtained one field.
>
> In 1966 Dersih was actively pursuing the quest for more land as a claimant in another case. He speaks hopefully of the future and says he will become a rist expert in time. He seems to take great pleasure in the process of getting land as well as in its possession. Like all men in Damot, he regards the fields he acquires through litigation as his rightful due, and he is one of the most adamant defenders of the inherent justice of the rist system of land tenure.

Because Dersih and Molla are ordinary farmers of about the same age and are residents of the same hamlet, differences in their landholdings are informative. These differences are summarized in table 4a. It is evident that Dersih holds much more land formerly held by his father than Molla holds of his father's land, though it should be remembered that, to get two of his fields, Dersih had to quarrel with his older brother. It is also evident that Dersih has been more successful than Molla in acquiring rist land from descent corporations. Furthermore, while Molla has no recognized right in the field he has built his house on and has been told by the fej to give up the other field he simply plowed as pastureland (one of the two fields listed on table 4a under "fields obtained in other ways"), Dersih was able to obtain as Kokeba rist a field which he first plowed when it was undivided

TABLE 4a Fields Held by Molla and Dersih

	Total fields	Fields inherited directly or through brother	Fields obtained through *fej* upon request or through division by lot	Fields obtained in other ways
Molla	5	1	2	2
Dersih	12	7	5	0

pastureland. Finally, Dersih was engaging in litigation to obtain more land at the time of study, while Molla was engaged in litigation as a defendant trying to retain what land he had.

Since Dersih is the kind of elder who can easily acquire additional fields of rist land and Molla is not, it is interesting to examine more carefully differences in their position in the community as reflected in their daily activities. Records of the major daily activities of Molla and Dersih were kept for sixty-two consecutive days during the spring of 1966. Activities were grouped into six major categories and one miscellaneous. The first category, agriculture, includes: plowing, tending the village flocks, bringing hay or straw to the house, threshing, working on irrigation, and searching for lost livestock. The second category is house-building, for this is the time when old houses must be readied for the rains and new houses built. The third category, ritual, includes: going to mass; abstaining from work because of a personal religious vow; activities involved with death, burial, and funerals; attending church feasts. The fourth category, commercial, includes: going to market, buying goods for the household, and visits to trade partners. The fifth category, legal and administrative, includes: assisting public officials such as the *aṭbīya dañña*, the *c̣hiqa shum*, or fejs; attending public inquests; appearing in court; acting as arbitrator for other men's disputes.

Table 4b shows the number of days on which each man engaged in one or more activity in the appropriate major category. Since more than one activity may take place on a single day, each man's total activities add up to more than sixty-two, the number of days recorded. The proper way to read the first cell in table 4b, for example, is: "During the sixty-two day period, Dersih engaged in agricultural activities on nineteen days, Molla on eighteen."

The two men engaged in economic (agricultural and commercial) and ritual activities with approximately the same frequency. Dersih spent more time than Molla house-building, socializing, and in legal-administrative activity. The higher level of Dersih's house-building and "socializing" were related to the preparation of his son's wedding feast.

TABLE 4b COMPARISON OF ACTIVITIES OF MOLLA AND DERSIH FOR 62 DAYS

		Agri-culture	Building	Ritual	Com-mercial	Legal Adminis.	Socia-bility	Misc.
Dersih	#	19	19	12	11	11	30	32
	%	30.6	30.6	19.4	19.3	19.3	48.7	51.6
Molla	#	18	9	14	13	5	19	10
	%	29.6	14.6	22.6	21	8.1	30.6	16.3

NOTE: The upper row of numbers in each of the cells indicates the number of days during the 62-day period on which the man engaged in the specified activity. The lower row of numbers in each cell indicates the percentage of days during the period in which he engaged in that activity.

The most significant difference in activity is in legal and administrative activity—a kind of activity which, in Dega Damot, might well be called petty politicking. Dersih was called upon three times to settle the disputes of others; Molla was not asked at all. This is, in itself, probably the best index available of the higher social esteem in which Dersih is held by others in the community. Influential as he is for his age, however, Dersih, unlike the next individuals to be considered, lacks the authority and ability to obtain rist land that accompany political office.

Life History 3: Grazmach Admasé

Grazmach Admasé is the son of a nontitled common farmer. The forty-seven-year old Admasé was born in Shoa Hayl, the second of eight children Yet in 1966 he was the *aṭbīya daññа* of the largest parish in Dega Damot, had a title, and lived in a complex of three buildings (homestead 3, on map 3) with his fifth wife, her four-month-old baby girl, a fifty-two-year old servant woman who is his wife's father's father's brother's daughter, an eighteen-year-old youth whose parents were Nilotic slaves and who does not expect to have his marriage provided for by Admasé, and a blind old nun who is of no service to the household but whom Admasé says he keeps "for his soul." The homestead also houses two oxen, three cows, four calves, two pack horses, ten sheep, and a fine riding mule.

Two years after his first marriage, Admasé's father died, and he stayed on with his wife and mother for another two years. After this he built his new homestead immediately adjacent to his widowed mother's. When the Italians came, Admasé took to the forests as a patriot. By the end of the war he was the leader of a small guerrilla band and had been given the rank of *grazmach* by Gojjam's leading patriot. After the occupation, the rank was confirmed by the emperor. Later, Grazmach Admasé was appointed to look after Feres Bét Mikael.

The *grazmach* acquired only one field, part of A1 on map 3, at his father's death. All of his other eighteen fields, many of which are valuable fertilized land, were previously held by men who were not his close kin and were acquired through litigation or implied threat of litigation.

In 1947, shortly after he rose to authority, Grazmach Admasé successfully claimed seven fields in Shoa Hayl (A2, A3, A4, A5, A6, A7, and part of A1). The fields include the land of Senbeta, Qusqo, and Kokeba, but Admasé, who does not fancy himself a rist expert and who says sardonically, "I plow with my rifle," states, with rather grand vagueness, that all of the land is Shoa Hayl *yedenb*. In the same year, Admasé acquired six fields in the parish of Gidiliñ Medhane Alem through litigation. None of his ancestors in recent generations had held land in Gidiliñ.

In 1953 Admasé acquired two more fields in a nearby parish by asking the fej. There was no litigation. In 1957 he received two more fields in the parish of Feres Bét Mikael in the land section of Qusqwamawīt. There was again no litigation. Admasé says that the fej simply gave it to him, saying, "You are our judge; you must have your land." One suspects that there was more to the matter than this.

Life History 4: Līqekahinat Assegé

Līqekahinat Assegé (formerly resident in homestead 4 on map 3), like Grazmach Admasé, was born to an ordinary peasant family. Yet in 1962, some years after his official retirement from the powerful office of chief clerk of Dega Damot, he remained the largest landholder encountered in this study and, after the governor, the most influential single individual in the district.

Assegé was born in Ziqwala Arbaytu Insesa in the last decade of the nineteenth century. At the age of seven he began church studies at his local parish church. As a church student, he was occupied literally day and night with study and was not able to spend much time herding the family livestock, as other young boys do.

Assegé showed promise as a student, learning the syllabary alphabet and moving on to study the psalms within his first year. His teacher, who had been hired on a yearly contract by the people of the parish, left at the end of the year, and another teacher came. Assegé continued his studies. When the new teacher also left, Assegé went with him, leaving his family behind. For three years Assegé studied with the teacher in the parish in Ṭelim Mikael, some six kilometers from his home. At the end of this time he decided to go to the most famous monastery in Dega Damot, Washera Maryam, to study a highly specialized type of Ge'ez poetry called *qiné*. After two years at Washera, Assegé moved on to study in Gonj with a teacher who was noted for his excellence in a branch of *qiné* poetry. Three years of study in Gonj brought Assegé himself to the standards of a teacher. Following this, Assegé returned to his former teacher in Ṭelim Mikael as an assistant teacher and a continuing "graduate student" in certain books on which his former teacher was an expert. When the teacher decided to leave Dega Damot altogether and go to another part of Gojjam some eighty kilometers to the east, Assegé went with him. During this time he was troubled with eye disease, but he did not leave his studies and return to his parents' home, as sick church students normally do. After passing six years away from Damot, serving as a teacher and pursuing his studies at the same time, Assegé finally left school.

At the age of twenty-two with fifteen years of grueling study behind him, Assegé set off for Addis Ababa to see the only bishop in all Ethiopia. He carried with him letters of introduction from church and civil authorities in Dega Damot. His letters, hours of patient waiting near the gates of important officials, luck, and his considerable erudition brought him success at last. At the age of twenty-three, Assegé was appointed to be administrative head and judge of all the secular clergy (*līqekahinat*) in Arefa subdistrict of Dega Damot. The office was not without its rewards in the form of presents, power, and honor. After holding the office for eleven years, Assegé was able to have himself appointed to the powerful office of chief clerk of Dega Damot, a position which he retained until 1954, when he was succeeded by his son. In a country where full literacy is rare, the position of chief clerk has great importance. In many ways it might be more accurately described as deputy governor. In addition to receiving many gifts, Assegé received two parishes as rist-gwilt. One of them was Dereqé Maryam.

During his long years of study Assegé held no rist land. Today he holds thirty-two fields, many of them above average in size, in seven parishes. About two-thirds of his fields are in the two parishes which are his gwilt or in Feres Bét Mikael, in which he is resident. His holdings in Shoa Hayl are shown on map 3.

Some of Assegé's rist-holdings and one of his two gwilts can be attributed to his late and successful marriage. His first and only marriage was contracted when he was forty years old. His political office and concomitant wealth enabled him to marry a noblewoman who would have been far above his station had he married at the usual age. His wife's father was an important nobleman who distributed his five gwilts among his children, including Assegé's wife. The gwilt technically remains hers, but her husband acts for her as lord of the parish.

Most of the land Assegé claims through his father is through a single ancestor, Welde Raguél. He is the fej for this ancestor in four parishes and is so strongly identified with Welde Raguél's interests that none of the less important landholders dared to reveal the genealogical structure of the corporation for fear of incurring Assegé's wrath. Each member was willing to tell his own descent line but would not expand on any of the collateral lines. When questioned, the members invariably recommended that Assegé be asked about the genealogy.

Assegé's tenants, even those who do not live in his gwilts, are also his followers, and he expects them to come to see him often. If they stay away for more than a reasonable period of time, he will suspect that they are plotting against him or currying the favor of some other important man.

In 1962 Assegé, who then claimed he was seventy-eight, was thinking of the next world. Despite his failing eyesight, he was often to be found sitting on a hill behind his homestead reading the Bible. Once he was found musing over a written "record" of his pedigree from Adam in 138 generations via most of the pre-Gondarine imperial line! Nevertheless, Assegé had not dropped out of competition for land. Four times during the two-year period of fieldwork he mounted his mule and made the difficult journey, some of it on foot, to Debre Markos, the provincial capital, in order to fight a land case involving a few acres of land.

In 1966, during the second period of research, Assegé was found to have aged greatly. He had moved to the town of Feres Bét, seldom left his bed, and was in the process of losing his fej-ships. He had not lost any of his rist land; for "who wants to risk a dying man's curse?" Nevertheless, though people still spoke of him with great respect, it was clear that he no longer exercised his former political power. Metaphorically, at least, the old man's claim that he was ninety-nine, an increase of twenty-one years since 1962, was not devoid of meaning.

10. Changing Patterns of Land Tenure in Dega Damot

Despite the devotion of the people of Dega Damot to the rist system, there have been a number of changes during the past four decades in the way it functions, and still greater changes seem inevitable in the future. The changes which have already taken place are related to changes which have occurred in the natural and institutional environment of the rist system rather than in its formal rules. Specifically, they are the result of increased population pressure on the land and the displacement of the political and economic institutions associated with the traditional feudal order and their replacement by a modern bureaucratic form of government. Future changes may be brought about by reformative legislation directly altering the rules of land tenure.

The object of this chapter is to examine the effects of these demographic and institutional changes on the rist system, to assess the probable effects on it of future land-reform policies, and to illuminate the attitudes of the people of Dega Damot towards these changes and policies of reform.

The effects of ecological and demographic change

According to all reports, the uncleared forest lands of Dega Damot have diminished greatly during the present century. It is also universally maintained, though this is more difficult to document, that population density has increased while the fertility of long-cultivated land has declined. The most important effects of this increased population pressure on available land are greater fragmentation of landholdings, increased conflict over land, and a decrease in the density of kinship bonds between the members of a local community.

As land becomes scarce and is no longer available for clearing, young men are increasingly forced to move out farther from their fathers' homesteads and to claim land in the estates of descent corporations where their fathers have not previously held land. There is thus an increase in the number of claims for land brought against the fejs of descent corporations and a consequent rise in the frequency of litigation. As a result of this greater competition for land, the process of division by father is carried to lower genealogical levels, land becomes further fragmented, and the land of each descent corporation becomes divided among more men. The dispersal of sons away from the parental homestead also reduces the interaction between people who are close kinsmen. It is possible, though it is difficult to obtain evidence of this, that the reduction in the extent to which kinship provides a basis for day-to-day interaction also reduces the already weak sense of community cohesion still further.

While the people of Dega Damot are aware of the increased pressure on land and the resulting level of conflict, they generally do not express personal anxiety over the effect of future increases of population; as they assure the investigator, they have extensive rist rights which they can use to obtain more land when necessary. Even when pressed on this point, men were hesitant to admit that an indefinite increase in population under the same conditions of production would lead to insurmountable difficulties.

The breakdown of the feudal order, the growth of bureaucracy, and tax reform

Traditionally there was very little differentiation of governmental tasks in Dega Damot. The same set of unspecialized quasi-military officials carried out most of the rather limited administrative, judicial, and taxational functions of government. During the past four decades the military elite that formerly ruled Gojjam and Dega Damot, and the institutions on which it depended for its support, have been progressively eroded and replaced by a functionally differentiated bureaucracy under the direct control of the central government in Addis Ababa. This process of political and administrative change, which is as yet far from complete at the local level, has begun to affect land tenure in Dega Damot in several ways. It has weakened the position of the gwilt-holder, it has increased the economic and decreased the political significance of land, it has affected to some degree the circumstances under which men can acquire rist land through the courts, and it has radically changed the way in which land is taxed.

During the first part of the present century the rulers of Gojjam, Negus Tekle Haymanot and, after him, his son Ras Hailu, enjoyed almost complete autonomy from the central government in the administration of their province. Political and administrative organization remained essentially unaffected by the first attempts at governmental modernization which were just beginning in Shoa.

In 1933 Ras Hailu was arrested in Addis Ababa for conspiring against the emperor and placed under detention until he was freed by the Italians. Ras Imru, a Shoan and a relative of the emperor, became governor of Gojjam where he ruled with the support of paid Shoan troops rather than the gwilt-holders of Gojjam. The latter were by no means neglected. On the contrary, to win their support Ras Imru granted many of them prestigious military titles. They were not, however, given commensurate offices. It thus came about during this period and again after the war that there was a great increase in the number of titled men and a consequent dissociation of title and actual power. The Shoan occupation of Gojjam may have contributed to the later introduction of administrative reforms by putting an end to provincial autonomy and weakening the older nobility through dilution, but it did not in itself bring change to the intermediate or local levels of provincial administration.

Only four years after their occupation of Gojjam the Shoan armies lost control of the province to the invading Italians. The Italian period, lasting five years, was also indecisive from the point of view of modernization. Partly because of its terrain, partly because of the low value of its exports in the eyes of the Italians, and partly because it was the center of intense guerrilla resistance Gojjam remained administratively and economically undeveloped in comparison with some other provinces. Of the utmost significance, however, was the construction of a road bridging the Blue Nile and linking the provincial capital of Debra Markos with Addis Ababa in Shoa. The importance of this road to the institution of bureaucratic reforms after the Second World War was fully appreciated by conservative Gojjamis some of whom attempted several times without success to dynamite its major bridge.

Following the reconquest of Ethiopia by allied forces and the restoration of Haile Selassie to the throne, Gojjam was divided into its present administrative units, and a bureaucratic form of administration was introduced. Though the governor at each level retains great power, he must work with officials representing and responsible to various ministries in Addis Ababa. In Feres Bét, the administrative center of Dega Damot, these officials included, in 1966, two judges, a police sergeant, a tax collector, a school director, and a medical worker. Below the district level of administration, however, there is still no bureaucratic differentiation. For most people most of the time the gwilt *gež*, in his modern role as the *aṭbīya dañña*, remains the main intermediary with and agent of the central government.

The weakening of gwilt

In view of the broad powers and crucial interstitial role of the gwilt-holder in the traditional order, it is scarcely surprising that efforts at bureaucratic modernization have, in part, been directed at weakening and eventually at abolishing his position. The first step in this direction was the reduction in the military importance of the gwilt *gež* already noted. Even more fundamental changes were brought about by postwar changes in taxation which abolished payments in kind and service to the gwilt-holder and made taxes payable directly to a representative of the Ministry of Finance at the district level. The gwilt-holder was responsible for seeing to it that taxes on his neighborhood were paid, in return for which he received a small part of the tax money back from the government, but he no longer had the power he had formerly held as assessor and collector. During the same period, religious institutions which held gwilt lost most of their former autonomy with regard to the secular administration of those who lived on their lands.

The significance of the gwilt-holder was further diminished by Proclamation of 90 of 1947 which established a system of local judges, or *aṭbīya daññas*, throughout Ethiopia. Under Proclamation 90 the judicial powers traditionally enjoyed by the gwilt-holder, subject to a financial limitation of Eth. $25 in civil cases and Eth. $15 in criminal cases, were placed under the jurisdiction of the newly created office of *aṭbīya dañña*. In neighborhoods which were not currently rist-gwilt or which were under the control of a monastery or a local parish church, the elders were to elect a candidate for appointment to the new office. The full impact of the change was not immediately evident since, according to Article 7 of Proclamation 90, the holders of rist-gwilt were automatically appointed as *aṭbīya daññas*. The gwilt *gež* of Dega Damot were thus apparently regranted much of the judicial authority that they had held all along. In fact, by creating a legal separation between gwilt and the judicial powers formerly associated with it, Proclamation 90 obviates the necessity of appointing a new gwilt *gež* when, after the death of a gwilt-holder, a dispute arises concerning succession to his position. An increasing number of neighborhoods which formerly were ruled by a gwilt *gež* are today under the jurisdiction of a local elder who is *aṭbīya dañña* but not *gwilt gež*.

Despite the erosion of their former powers, the gwilt *gež* of Dega Damot still, as has been noted, enjoy a marked degree of power and prestige within their neighborhoods. It is clear, however, that it is the intention of the government to abolish their position altogether as soon as is practical. In fact, Proclamation 230 of 1966, which strips gwilt-holders throughout the country of all taxational rights, is generally interpreted as having removed the legal authority for the existence of gwilt as a type of land tenure. The provision of Proclamation 230 which would no longer permit rebates of tax money to gwilt-holders has not yet been enforced in Gojjam where, according to officials of the Ministry of Finance, their assistance in enforcing tax payments is still essential.

The increasing economic importance of land

Traditionally there was relatively little separation between political power, the control of land, and wealth. Men who enjoyed high positions of secular authority usually controlled much land. They were also at the apex of a redistributional economic organization. They collected tax and tribute from those over whom they held authority and expended a large portion of it again on the feasts and followers that were essential to the maintenance of their political power and their legitimacy in the eyes of their subjects. In contrast to this redistributive economic system in which political considerations ultimately had primacy, trade and voluntary exchange of goods were comparatively weakly developed. For men who have sought to increase their power and status, land has been as much a political as an economic commodity in the way in which it has been acquired and the way in which it has been used.

Today the politically dominated redistributive economic organization of Dega Damot has been greatly weakened. The tribute and tax formerly received by government officials from their subjects has been replaced by a cash salary from the central government. With their authority backed to a greater extent than ever before by the force of the central government, officeholders are no longer willing or able to feast their followers and reward their favorites as in the past. Indeed, modern officials are frequently criticized in Dega Damot for being stingy and selfish as well as for being unresponsive to the problems of their people. Land, power and wealth, under these changing circumstances, are becoming increasingly distinct. An officeholder, through his political influence, can still obtain more land than ordinary men, but the control of land and its produce no longer plays its former role in the maintenance of his position.

Though the breakdown of the redistributive organization has not been accompanied by an equally rapid growth in the exchange economy of Dega Damot, there are signs that gradual increases in the price of some crops are beginning to affect the ways in which people seek and utilize land. At least in the area from Feres Bét to the road, rents payable to the landholder on both fertilized and unfertilized land are said to have risen somewhat since World War II. It was also claimed by some ambitious and successful farmers around Feres Bét that they are more interested in opening cases to obtain rist than in the past because with these rising rents land is becoming more valuable. It may also be, though again it is difficult to document, that these ambitious farmers, who are often referred to by others as *rist fellagī* or rist-seekers, are relying increasingly on money rather than political influence when engaging in litigation over land.

The effect of changes in the administration of justice

Paradoxically, the greater independence of the judiciary and greater commitment to legal principles than to political matters seem to be increasing the amount of land litigation and the fragmentation of landholdings. As a legal system, the rist system, with its overlapping and unbounded claims, is unworkable. The more men are encouraged by the greater impartiality and efficiency of the courts to claim their "rightful" land through remote descent lines, the more cases are opened and the farther division by father and fragmentation proceed.

At present, judges interpret the new Civil Code as congruent with customary land law. Remote claims are upheld so long as a descent line can be established. To a large extent, it is the expense of litigation and the inability of the courts to enforce their decisions that discourage still more men from attempting to claim the land they think is rightfully theirs through long-unused pedigrees. Future improvements in the functioning of the courts unaccompanied by changes in the interpretation of the law itself are likely to further exacerbate the conflict over and fragmentation of land.

The effect of changes in taxation

The postwar tax reforms which weakened the position of the gwilt-holder have also been the object of great concern to the holders of rist; for in the absence of any government registration of land ownership, the land tax constitutes the sole link between the government and the land upon which the government's subjects depend for a major part of their subsistence. The payment of the land tax has traditionally been regarded both as the obligation of the rist-holder and evidence of ownership. In light of this close association of ownership and taxation, it is scarcely surprising that the landholders of Dega Damot regard tax reform as a part of or a prelude to land reform and that their attitudes towards changes in taxation reflect their attitudes towards changes in their system of land tenure. In reality, the changes which have been introduced in land taxation do not, as yet, appear to have had a significant effect on land tenure. They have, however, invariably provoked reactions which illustrate clearly the apprehensions of Damotian taxpayers concerning land measurement, land registration, and land reform.

Before the Italian occupation there was no uniform system of taxation in Dega Damot. In most neighborhoods the most burdensome tax, the *gibir*, was assessed annually in the fields by the gwilt-holder along with three local elders and the *c̣hiqa shum*. In other places the *gibir* for the entire neighborhood was commuted to a payment in salt bars which was fixed and did not vary with the harvest from year to year. The obligation to pay the tax in salt was divided among the neighborhood's descent corporations and their respective minzir abbats, according to the principle of division by father. The other major tax, the *asrat*, was paid everywhere by the owners of oxen at the rate of one Maria Theresa dollar per ox. In no instance in Dega Damot was a tax paid in accordance with the area of land controlled.

During the occupation the Italian administration did not have sufficient control of the countryside in Dega Damot to collect taxes on a regular basis. Leaders of patriot bands exacted tribute as best they could from the peasants in their locality, a privilege for which they not infrequently quarreled with one another.

After the defeat of the Italians and the restoration of the Ethiopian government, land taxes were reimposed throughout the empire. The new taxation system was radically different from the prewar system. Its major objectives from the beginning were to convert all tax payments to cash and, as has been noted, to weaken the power of gwilt-holders (and holders of similar rights) by having taxes paid directly into the government treasury. Both of these objectives are clearly presaged in a proclamation issued by the emperor in 1941, shortly after his return to Ethiopia. It is interesting that the proclamation first touches upon a traditional theme—that the payment of land tax is a privilege, since it confirms "ownership" of the land.

> After the Italians entered our country, they considered the land of Ethiopia as their own and intended to exterminate our race, putting their own people in their place. To achieve their purpose they abolished the payment of taxes. But the payment of tax in blood was a common occurrence.
>
> So that your government may live long, your liberty may be safeguarded, your standard of living may be raised, and your land may remain in your hands, it is necessary to pay taxes to the government without discrimination of age or wealth.
>
> Whereas we have understood the difficulties that befell you during the past five years, we are permitting you to pay only half the taxes you paid before. Henceforward the payment of tax will be in money. The amount to be paid will be announced later.
>
> Manual labour, firewood, grass, contribution for annual feast days, and miscellaneous dues and taxes are abolished. However, *desta, gindibel,* and such other lands which give a tax of manual labour will be entitled to pay tax in

the same way as other landowners. The new administration entitles all governors and government officials to salaries; and the above-mentioned taxes will be paid to the government treasury.

(Gebré-Weld-Ingida Worq 1962:325)

In the first postwar years, taxes were paid in kind and sold by government officials to convert them to cash. Then, in 1944, the changes adumbrated in 1941 were systematized in the Land Proclamation No. 70. The basic principle embodied in Proclamation 70 is that taxes were to be paid in Ethiopian currency according to the amount and quality of land held. The estimation of area was to be in *gashsha*, an unstandardized unit of land measurement introduced in 1879–80 in Shoa by the Emperor Menilek. Each *gashsha* was then to be classified as fertile, semifertile, or poor. To maintain a sense of continuity with tradition, the tax levied per *gashsha* on each quality of land was divided into two parts: a tax in lieu of the *gibir*, which is still commonly called the *gibir*; and a tax in lieu of the *asrat*, still commonly termed the *asrat*.[1] To these basic taxes an education tax was added by Proclamation No. 102 of 1948 and a health tax by Decree No. 36 of 1959.

In recognition of economic and political difficulties it would create, the system of taxation introduced by Proclamation 70 of 1944 was not standardized throughout Ethiopia. Taxing rist land seems to have presented a particularly difficult problem. Special low rates were established in Proclamation 70, for example, for what is referred to as "land, known as 'rist' in the district of Shoa Amhara."

The lands of the northern provinces of Gojjam and of Tigre and Begemdir, where rist systems similar to that of Dega Damot are most widespread, were exempted altogether from measurement and classification. Proclamation 70 states

1. The tax schedule for Shoa (with the exception of the district in which the rist system predominates), Harar, Arussi, and Wello was standardized. The rates for fertile land were: *asrat* $35 and *gibir* $15. The rates for semifertile land were: *asrat* $30 and *gibir* $10. The rates for poor land were: *asrat* $10 and *gibir* $5. All figures are in Ethiopian dollars.

that, "In these three provinces the tax shall be paid in money at the rate which was in force in 1927 [Ethiopian calendar], plus the estimated tithe in money." Since historical records concerning prewar taxation in Gojjam are scanty, to say the least, Proclamation 70 left much to the discretion of provincial administrators and the Ministry of Finance. The new system of taxation thus had little immediate effect on taxation in Dega Damot.

It was not until 1950 that the rist land of Gojjam was estimated, classified, and assessed according to a tax schedule similar to that in use in the central and southern provinces. Curiously, there is no legal authority in the Negarit Gazette (the Ethiopian government's official reporter of legislation and administrative regulations) for these changes. In fact, the Health Tax Decree No. 36, written nine years later, still exempts Gojjam from the new tax system and levies the health tax according to the prewar formula laid down in 1944.

The tax reforms of 1950 aroused deep suspicion throughout Amhara Gojjam and, in some areas, were met with armed resistance. A delegation of Gojjam elders went to Addis Ababa and begged the emperor to allow their people to pay the tax "in the old way." The governor of Gojjam was removed, minor concessions were made concerning taxation, and an amnesty was given to those who had rebelled; but in the end, under continuing government pressure, the new system was at least formally instituted.

Opposition to the tax change of 1950 was primarily based on the incorrect but widespread belief that the measurement of land which it was thought to require was a first step towards the abolition of the rist system and the alienation of land to outsiders, particularly "Shoans" and "Gallas." Specifically, what Gojjamis feared was that their rist would be reclassified as *qelad* or *sīso*—types of tenure established by the Shoan rulers in conquered non-Amhara regions of central and southern Ethiopia during the nineteenth century. Under these systems of tenure the lands of peoples defeated by the Shoan armies were measured with a rope, or more crudely estimated, and the resulting land units, known as *gashsha* or *qelad*, were apportioned (sometimes in thirds, or *sīso*) among officials and soldiers, the crown, and selected leaders of the vanquished population. The conquered common folk usually continued to cultivate most of the land that they had held before, but on much of it they were henceforth share-cropping tenants and not independent landholders.

The way in which the land tax was eventually estimated in Gojjam served to allay the worst fears of the farmers. In the end there was no measurement of land, and the crude estimates of size and quality recorded in the government tax records were based on the estates of first settlers or minzir abbats and not on individually held fields. In Dega Damot the estimates were made by the district governor along with his clerk, the district tax collector, representatives of the Ministry of Finance from the subprovincial seat at Finote Selam, and three elders, known as *mirṭ* or *widd*, chosen from each of the neighborhoods estimated. The assessment committee viewed the land of each neighborhood in turn from a hilltop and estimated the area in *gashshas* and the fertility of each of its constituent first settlers' estates. Estates which were considered large were broken down into minzir abbats. The names of the first settlers and, where relevant, the minzir abbats were entered into the tax book according to neighborhood, and taxes were assessed accordingly.[2]

In keeping with tradition, lands which had formerly been held as gwilt by a monastery or which had been the priest land of a local church were classified as church land. A part of the tax assessed on such lands, usually the gibir, was then granted to the appropriate monastery or church. The taxes granted to religious institutions are not, however, usually collected by government or church officials. Tax rates on land which happens to be church land are thus lower than on other land. It is supposed that this lower rate of taxation offsets the expenses incurred by the landholder in fulfilling his special service obligations to the church (see chapter 4).

2. The tax schedule used in Gojjam differed somewhat from that used in Shoa, Harar, Arussi, and Wello. The rates for fertile land were: *asrat* $16, *gibir* $32, and education $14.40. The rates for semifertile land were: *asrat* $11.67, *gibir* $23.33, and education $10.50. The rates for poor land were: *asrat* $4, *gibir* $7, and education $3.60. All figures are in Ethiopian dollars.

It is difficult to obtain an overall picture of how accurately the assessment of land in Dega Damot was carried out. It is also difficult to see how a group of men, most of whom had no idea of the size of a *gashsha*, could have estimated the land visually with much precision. On the basis of an aerial photograph it appears that one of the most intensively studied first settlers' estates, estimated to be 160 acres, in reality covers more than 1,000. A decade after the assessment was carried out, elders generally maintained that the new tax system, as such, was good but that the assessment was unfair, some estates having been overestimated, some underestimated, and a few not recorded at all.

The tax system introduced in 1950 did not establish a direct link between rist-holders and the district tax collector's office, for a single individual, appointed from among the rist landholders, is responsible for bringing in the money due annually from each estate listed in the tax records. This unpaid official, known as the *teṭerī*, or "one who is called," may or may not be the fej of the descent corporation, but, in any case, he must be a respected elder. The position of the *teṭerī* is not entirely enviable, since he is imprisoned by the district governor if he is delinquent in paying the tax. On the other hand, it is generally suspected that the *teṭerī* is able to turn a profit by overcollecting the tax.

The tax burden falling upon a descent corporation's estate is divided among its landholders according to the same two principles used in the division of the land itself, division by father and division by allotment. According to the first principle, the money owed by the first settler's estate is divided equally among his minzir abbats. Each minzir abbat must then also have an official responsible for collecting his share of the tax. The total tax paid on the land of Wendim, for example, is Eth. $220. The corporations of each of Wendim's children, the minzir abbats Demé and Gubeno, are therefore responsible for $110. Each of Gubeno's minzir abbats' corporations are similarly responsible for the payment of $27.50. Below this level the money is gathered by agreement in proportion to the amount of land individually held. In some estates, however, the entire tax is divided by allotment in accordance with the way land is held by living men, even though the estate itself has been divided by father. In Shoa Hayl, for example, the entire tax of Eth. $160 is divided by allotment. Shoa Hayl's *teṭerī* has a list of all the people who give him tax money, but this list does not include all the landholders in Shoa Hayl's estate, for nonresidents, women, and small holders often give their share of the tax money to their kinsmen who, in turn, give it to the *teṭerī*. Though there are 119 men and women who hold land in Shoa Hayl's estate, only 65 names appear on the *teṭerī's* list.

The extent to which the people of Gojjam fear changes in land tenure and the difficulty of administering such changes were again demonstrated by the disturbances that accompanied the abolition of the *asrat* and the introduction of a new agricultural income tax in 1968. The object of the tax change, introduced by Proclamation No. 255 of 1967, was to tax individuals according to their agricultural income rather than according to the area and quality of the land they held. Its purpose was to increase government revenues from areas where cash crops, particularly coffee, are grown. It was not intended to increase tax rates in the agriculturally poor areas of the northern provinces.

According to Proclamation 255, a tax is to be paid on income from all agricultural activities (excluding forestry, processing, and cattle breeding) regardless of whether such income is derived from rent, share-cropping, or an individual's own production on his own land. Gross income derived from "renting" land or giving it to a tenant for a share of the crop is taxed progressively according to one schedule (Schedule B). A second tax schedule (Schedule D) applies in a similar way to gross income from all other agricultural activities, reduced by: the amount of any land taxes payable by the taxpayer; the amount of rent payable in cash or kind by the taxpayer; and a deduction of one-third of the gross income in lieu of an assessment of production expenses.

According to the proclamation, the income of farmers who are not required by law to keep books of accounts and records—and this includes all the farmers of Dega Damot—is to be assessed by local committees. Each committee is to consist of two members "elected from among the residents of the locality" and one official of the district. The meetings are to be arranged and regulated by a representative of the Income Tax Authority.

The representative of the Income Tax Authority is to present to the local assessment committee a list of all the persons within the jurisdiction of the committee who appear to be liable to tax. If it appears to the committee that an individual's taxable income derived from agricultural activities does not exceed Eth. $300 he is to be assessed the minimum tax of $1.50. If it appears that a taxpayer's income may exceed $300, the committee is to estimate his gross taxable income. This estimate is to be based on: the harvest on the farmland from which the income is derived; the types of crops and the produce from such farmland; and local prices of such crops and produce. These estimates are to be based on a "normal year." This gross income, reduced by the deductions listed above, is then taxed according to the appropriate schedules. Unless the Ministry of Finance determines otherwise, the assessment made in this way is to remain in force for a period of five years.

The implementation of the agricultural income tax in Gojjam was fraught with difficulties from the outset. In some areas local assessment committees were formed consisting of two elected elders, the subdistrict governor, and a representative of the Ministry of Finance sent from Addis Ababa. A list of residents was obtained from the *aṭbīya dañña* of each neighborhood. Accurately assessing individual income, however, proved to be difficult. The elders selected did not have accurate knowledge of their fellow residents' agricultural production, particularly on lands which were located in another neighborhood. Many people were registered several times, once for each neighborhood in which they farmed. Furthermore, however accurate the elders' knowledge might be, it was widely feared and rumored that the elders, the subdistrict governor, and the ministry representative were accepting bribes and favoring their friends.

In Dega Damot, as in much of Amhara Gojjam, attempts to introduce the agricultural income tax triggered armed resistance which continued intermittently for over a year. There were a number of secondary factors which contributed to the readiness of the people to oppose the new tax policy. Prominent among these were the belief that the district receives fewer government services than its tax money should pay for and the complaint that, though household heads have been pressured by their governors to make "voluntary" contributions for the construction of a road from Debre Markos to Dega Damot three times, there is, at present, no sign of the road or of the money. Fear of increased taxation in itself does not seem to have been an important source of apprehension. On a number of occasions peasant representatives are reported to have said, perhaps with less than total candor, that they would gladly pay higher taxes if only they could pay them in the "old way." What they objected to, they said, was this new tax—it was a dangerous thing. Some people did voice the suspicion that the tax would be raised inordinately in the future. "One-fifty this year, one hundred and fifty next year," went the slogan. The meaning behind this phrase, however, was that taxes would be raised to a point where people would not be able to pay them, and their rist land would then be alienated by the government.

There can be no doubt, however, that the primary and immediate cause of the revolt was the conviction that the government intended to measure land and alter or abolish the rist system of land tenure. What was most threatening about the agricultural income tax proclamation was that under its provisions tenants were to be given tax receipts and that there was to be an assessment of individual income, which was mistakenly taken to mean the measurement of individual landholding. The former provision was feared because it was thought that the tax receipts would be used by the tenants to establish ownership over the land they worked in tenancy. Measurement was thought a prelude to the establishment of the *qelad* system. The following summary of the events that accompanied the introduction of the agricultural income tax in Dega Damot illustrates the attitude of its people toward what they conceive of as land reform. At the same time, it reveals the difficulty of introducing even minor changes in land tenure under present administrative conditions.

> News of the new tax proclamation reached Dega Damot early in September 1967. Two days later, elders from all parts of Dega Damot were assembled near the Feres Bét marketplace to hear the proclamation read by the district governor, the subdistrict governors, and the district tax collector. Fearing that the rist system was to be changed and the *qelad* system introduced, the elders refused to comply with the proclamation without time for further study. The governor suggested they study the document and meet with him again on September 16, 1967. The elders replied after consultation that they preferred to meet privately on September 16 and to give their answer to the government officials on the twenty-third. The governor agreed.
>
> On September 16 the elders met and, after much discussion, decided not to pay the new tax without first discussing the matter with leading men from surrounding districts. On September 23 the people's representatives told the district governor of their decision. The governor, for his part, asked them to select two elders from each neighborhood, in accordance with the proclamation, and to have them start estimating each resident's agricultural production. The people's representatives replied that they could take no action before meeting with men from other districts on September 30.
>
> On the thirtieth of September, men from several districts met and swore a solemn oath that they would not select elders for the estimation. The next day, the district governor was ordered to go to the subprovincial capital at Finote Selam, where he was told to produce the elders required for the tax estimation. The district governor hurriedly chose five of his supporters who had accompanied him to Finote Selam. These men were reportedly

delighted with their appointment and its salary of $4 per day.

Early in November, after traveling to the provincial capital and Finote Selam several times, the district governor called a meeting of *atbīya daññas* and leading elders in Feres Bét. Those called refused to assemble. The district governor reported to his superiors that the people had refused to carry out his orders, had denied the authority of the delegated elders, and no longer recognized his authority. Shortly after this, he was recalled from office, and one of the subdistrict governors was appointed to replace him.

The new governor, a native son of Dega Damot, was, at first, well received. He soon confirmed his popularity by preparing a great feast featuring beer, hydromel, and the slaughtering of an ox. For the next two months Dega Damot remained quiet and the new tax remained unassessed.

On February 1, 1968, the governor asked an assembly of elders once again to pay their tax. Again they replied that they would not do so until the other surrounding districts had done so. The governor thereupon sent the elders who had been chosen by the previous governor to the subdistricts of Dega Damot to begin tax assessment. Representatives from each subdistrict were sent to the district governor again protesting that there could be no assessment or payment of the tax until other districts had complied.

Whatever the governor's reply to the representatives may, in fact, have been, he is universally quoted as having said, *Sinkwan merétun mīstun asgebrewalluh*, or, "Not only will I make them pay their taxes, but their wives as well!" Such hostile phrases are normally attributed to unpopular figures in Gojjam and serve as focal points for rallying opposition.

On February 7 upwards of one thousand men armed with spears and rifles gathered near the marketplace in

Feres Bét to consider their next move. Under the emerging leadership of a middle-aged titleholder with no office, it was decided to send the new tax collectors out of Gojjam and to urge people of other districts to do likewise.

On February 20 another militant meeting was held near Feres Bét. It was attended by men from a neighboring district as well as from all over Dega Damot. It was the consensus of the meeting that the new district governor, the subdistrict governors, and the gwilt *gežs* should be removed from office, and that the five elders who had accepted positions as tax assessors should be tried. The latter were notified in writing that, since they had agreed to help change the land of Dega Damot from rist to *qelad*, they must come and stand trial before the people. If they did not surrender themselves for trial voluntarily, they were told, their homesteads would be surrounded, their houses and crops burned, and when they came running out of the flaming houses they would be shot dead.

On the following day the men appeared and pleaded that they had been tricked into signing the paper on false pretenses. "If we had no children and households," added one elder, "we would have fled forever in shame. But, blessed be the Almighty, we are now back in our country amidst our own people and ready to stand trial." Then each of the defendants was ordered to give a guarantor to ensure that he would no longer act as tax assessor. After this someone shouted that he had seen his subdistrict governor and another man estimating land in his home parish. After much heated debate, it was decided to march to the subdistrict governor's compound and burn his house down.

The next morning about five hundred men armed with rifles set off for the governor's home some twenty kilometers away. As they left, they sent a message to the district governor, telling him that unless he left Dega Damot he would cause a "disturbance of the peace." Upon hearing this, the governor armed loyal militia men (*neçhçh lebashī*) and readied his troops to defend the town of Feres Bét. He also sent a group of elders and churchmen as intermediaries to dissuade the rebels and their leader from attacking either the subdistrict governor or himself. The intermediaries' mission met with success and the rebels disbanded for the time being.

On February 25 another meeting was called by the rebel leadership at a parish some kilometers to the east of Feres Bét. After deciding to order the people of a certain parish to hand over a resident militiaman who had supported the district governor, the assembled men decided to elect their own administrative officials. Eventually the noble who had assumed leadership of the revolt was elected district governor and other men were selected as subdistrict governors. More than fifty other men were elected from various neighborhoods to replace the government-appointed *aṭbīya dañña*s. These officials were known as *gobez aleqas*, or "strong chiefs." The main qualifications for office seem to have been the possession of a gun and the will to oppose the tax.

The first acts of the new "government" were to threaten those peasants, both in Dega Damot and in surrounding districts, who agreed to pay the new tax. In some instances the peasants' cattle were killed. The rebel governor and his followers then decided that Dega Damot was not big enough for two district governors—and that he (the rebel) was not leaving. The government-appointed governor refused to leave Feres Bét. The rebels gave him three days to change his mind. Outgunned and under pressure from elders who did not want fighting to break out, the governor withdrew to the subprovincial seat at Finote Selam.

Nearly two months went by before the district governor, accompanied by a large number of police, returned to Feres Bét. He entered the town on Easter Sunday. Once again, he prepared a feast and killed an ox. The *gobez aleqas* elected by the rebels were invited, but they did not attend.

On May 9 the rebels assembled once more and again ordered the governor to leave. After fruitless negotiation, he took refuge in the police station and finally agreed to leave town, which he did shortly after nightfall.

For the next two and a half months the rebel government ruled in Dega Damot. There was one near-confrontation with the government when a contingent of Damot rebels set off to prevent the peasants in a nearby district from paying their tax. They were met by a commission including the bishop of Gojjam. A list of complaints calling for the removal of the provincial and subprovincial governors was sent to the emperor. Finally, after more delegations had come and gone, a commission from the central government was sent to Feres Bét.

On August 27 the commission, headed by the Minister of the Interior, landed by helicopter in Feres Bét. The peasant representatives repeated their demand that the governors above them be changed and that they not be forced to pay the new tax. They said that they did not want to pay an "additional" $1.50 in taxes (the minimum tax). The minister replied that the governors would be removed, but that the government tax proclamation could not be changed. An elder is reported to have said, "Bring an airplane and kill us here, as we are assembled; for we will not pay the tax."

The provincial and subprovincial governors were duly removed and replaced with men more acceptable to the local people. The new governor of the subprovince in which Dega Damot is located was a *dejazmach* who is undoubtedly the most successful and powerful man claiming Dega Damot as his home. He had been a governor in other areas and a senior senate official for a number of years.

On September 2 he was welcomed home to Feres Bét with singing and dancing. Three days later he read a proclamation in the marketplace granting the people of Dega Damot a full amnesty for what they had done, provided they paid their tax by January 10, 1969. Henceforth, he assured them, they would be held responsible for their crimes.

Three days later, the great man paid the tax for the fields of rist land he still personally held in a nearby parish. He induced the *aṭbīya dañña* of another parish to follow suit. The rebel leader, infuriated, gave the *dejazmach* and the subprovincial police chief who had accompanied him until September 13 to leave Dega Damot. They left on the fourteenth.

With the departure of the governor the situation deteriorated. On September 22 a small group of rebels, along with their leader, broke into the police station and took guns and ammunition. On October 15 a group of rebels organized to attack the police station in the town of Dembeçha, some fifty miles away on the road. On October 17 skirmishing broke out between the rebels and a special heavily armed police squad sent from the provincial capital of Debre Markos. Between fifty and a hundred men were reportedly killed in the fighting that followed. Eventually jet fighters were sent to disperse the rebels.

In the ensuing two weeks the *dejazmach* recruited additional militiamen, and on October 31 he reentered Feres Bét and ordered the people to pay their tax. People from Shoa Hayl and Dereqé Maryam began to pay the tax. The rebels sought to punish them, and fighting broke out again on December 15. The fighting became worse, and the *dejazmach* radioed for jet strikes.

In the following air attacks a dozen or so houses were burned. The rebels dispersed in fear. On December 18 an imperial proclamation announcing another amnesty and

> once again ordering people to pay their taxes was dropped by air.
>
> On December 21 a delegation of notables from Addis Ababa once again landed by helicopter in Feres Bét. Their leader told a large assembly of peasants that he, too was a Gojjami and that never would he stand by idly while the rist of his natal country was changed to *qelad*. He also explained that the new tax of $1.50 replaced, not supplemented, the *asrat*. Taxes would, in fact, be lower than before. The question of assessment was forgotten for the time being, and the people agreed to pay their taxes. Within the next two weeks most of them had done so.

The image of a ragged band of Damotian farmers, armed with ancient rifles, a few rounds of ammunition and spears, setting out to defend themselves and their rist against the modern forces of the Imperial Ethiopian Government may seem quixotic. Pathetic would be a more apt term; for the men of Dega Damot did not expect to win. Their attitude towards their land and their chances of successfully defending it were summed up in the slogan of the hour: "Die for your rist!"

Prospects for land reform in Dega Damot

It is evident that the attitude of people in Dega Damot towards land reform is informed by a deep-seated, if ill-founded, suspicion that their land will be taken away from them. It is useful, however, to disregard this mistrust of government intentions and to consider the prospects for the type of land reform measures that are in fact contemplated in government and advisory circles.

The long-term goal of the Ethiopian government, as set forth in the *Third Five-Year Development Plan* (*1968–73*), is to encourage peasants to grow and market more crops so as to raise their standard of living, increase their contribution to and participation in the national economy, and increase government tax revenues. Recognizing the difficulties inherent in developing the peasant sector at the present time, the plan envisages virtually no per capita improvement in the current plan period except in three limited regions of concentrated development (TFYDP, p. 193). The plan states that "subsistence production is expected to grow by 1.8% per annum, which is about the rate of increase of the population engaged in this sector" (TFYDP, p. 44).

With regard to longer term planning, land reform is singled out as an area of prime importance. It is stated that:

> Very little progress in agrarian reconstruction and development, particularly in peasant agriculture, can be made under the existing conditions of tenure and farm size. The immediate concern of land reform is to overcome the apathy of the agricultural population, caused by traditional inequitable land tenure patterns, concentration of land ownership in a small group, insecurity of tenure, and exorbitant rent or sharecropping arrangements (TFYDP, p. 195).

With particular regard to the "communal system of land ownership prevailing in the northern part of the country," a reference which includes the Amhara rist system as well as several rather different systems found in Tigre and Eritrea, the plan asserts that:

> [The system of communal tenure] eliminates the possibility either of mortgage credit or of transactions in land. It also seriously obstructs farmers from investing in productive farming operations and particularly from safeguarding against soil and water erosion. The Ministry of Land Reform and Administration during the TFYDP period must complete necessary studies to formulate a tenure pattern which would solve the problem (TFYDP, p. 197).

It is also often said among planners in Addis Ababa that both fragmentation of holdings and the high rate of litigation over land characteristic of rist areas result in wasted time for many farmers.

While the object of this discussion is to evaluate the effects of specific land reform measures in Dega Damot and not the prospects there for general economic development, several of the premises upon which land reform policy is being based require comment. First of all, the assumption that land is inequitably distributed and that it is concentrated in the hands of a small group is not applicable to Dega Damot. Second, while insecurity of tenure associated with the rist system might discourage people from improving their land in the future, there is no evidence that it does so under present conditions. On the contrary, the fact that fertilized land is not subject to reallocation by the descent corporation fej unless the holder has no recognized rist right in the corporation may encourage farmers to improve their land. Similarly, the impossibility of selling land and the consequent difficulty of establishing agricultural mortgage credit will only become an impediment to investment when other barriers to development, particularly the inaccessibility of national markets, are removed. Finally, while much time is certainly spent traveling to and from scattered fields and litigating over land, it is not clear, under present conditions of underemployment, whether this time could be used, in itself, to increase production.

Proposed policies intended to implement the goals of land reform in areas with communal tenure are, broadly speaking, of two types: those which are intended to establish a more truly communal, cooperative, or collective system of land tenure; and those which are intended to "individualize" the rist system; that is, to replace it with a system in which individuals would hold land in freehold tenure. The Third Five-Year Development Plan, unlike earlier plans which favored individualization, does not favor any policy.

Those who favor the first type of reform policies have variously made proposals to establish a system in which all members of the community would be allocated equal shares of the land, as is at least ideally the case in some Eritrean and Tigrean systems; to encourage farmers to cooperate in marketing and in the mechanized cultivation of land they individually hold under the present system of tenure; and to establish collective ownership and cultivation over some unit of land, such as the neighborhood or parish. Since these rather diverse recommendations have not been translated into specific reform measures or proposed legislation, it is difficult to assess their possible effects. It should be noted, however, that there appears to be little traditional basis in Dega Damot for collective ownership of land or voluntary large-scale cooperation in agricultural activity. As was noted earlier, group activities, including the cultivation of state farms, or *hudad*, were always organized by a powerful authority figure rather than through a voluntary and cooperative effort for the mutual benefit of the members as a group. A number of small holders with whom the matter was discussed were favorably disposed to the idea that the land of each parish or neighborhood be equally divided among its resident household heads. Large holders and ambitious men, however, strongly opposed such reform.

Proposals to individualize land tenure are, in effect, proposals to abolish the rist system and the descent corporations through which each person has inalienable potential rights to a share of numerous, widely scattered first settlers' estates, and to replace it with a system of freehold tenure under which people would have alienable rights to specific pieces of land. The measures through which this change would be brought about are a cadastral survey, the registration of individual title to land, and the instituting of land sale.

The attitudes of farmers towards these proposed measures are inconsistent. Land measurement is, of course, opposed as a prelude to the *qelad* system. If the possibility that the *qelad* system will be introduced is ruled out, their responses are different. They generally wax enthusiastic over the prospect of having their rist land registered in their own name in the government tax book, since they feel this would help them defend it against the claims of others; but they are appalled by the suggestion that they should lose their rist rights in estates where they currently do not hold rist land. Similarly, they welcome the suggestion that only their own children should be allowed to inherit the lands they hold; but not if legislation to this effect would also prevent their children from claiming a share of the land held by collateral relatives.

The possibility of land sale, on the other hand, is almost universally opposed. Rist, unlike moveable property, it is argued, is the inalienable birthright of every child. It would be a social as well as a moral evil if parents could sell this birthright for the love of money and personal advantage, and it is assumed that at least some of them would.

An assessment of the direct and indirect effects of radically altering or abolishing the rist system must take into account what it accomplishes in its present form. From a demographic and social point of view, rather than an individual point of view, the rist system is not merely a way of allocating land to people. It is also a way of allocating people to available land in accordance with their social and political prominence. It serves to move people from estates and parishes which are densely populated to ones which are not, and, at the same time, it allocates to individuals with unusual political skills lands commensurate with their political attainments. It thus adjusts the ecological realities of an agrarian society to the political realities of a competitive and fluid feudal polity, and does this without producing a large class of landless and alienated peasants.

In principle, the reallocative functions of the rist system would be replaced by the transfer of land through sale, which would enable the young and ambitious to buy additional land in accordance with their skill as farmers. The establishment of individual freehold tenure would thus, in theory, replace time-wasting political and legal activity with productive farming activity as the prime mode of acquiring additional fields and would complete the process of making land an economic rather than political commodity already begun by the breakdown of feudal institutions.

As a part of a comprehensive program of rural economic development, land reform may be both desirable and necessary. There is no evidence, however, that in the absence of secondary roads and other marketing facilities, changing the rules of land tenure would, in itself, stimulate production or encourage the sale of land or enable hard-working farmers to acquire land. On the contrary, there is a real danger that land reform, unaccompanied by a substantial growth of the cash economy, would have highly undesirable effects on the distribution of land and the welfare of the people of Dega Damot.

In the absence of another mechanism for allocating land to people and people to land, the transformation of rist to freehold through a cadastral survey and the registration of individual title to land as it is currently held would, in effect, freeze a transitory pattern of landholding and social stratification at one moment in time. It would convert a fluid system of individual inequalities into a permanent pattern of economic and social stratification. Following the "individualization" of landholding, demographic inequalities, differences in net reproduction, would create economic and social inequalities between families and between larger communities. Sons from large families would no longer be able to move away from the parental homestead to another parish where, by virtue of residence and their latent rist rights, they could commence to put together a new household estate. Nor would the able and ambitious men be able to acquire additional land and improve their social status in their communities.

Not only would the restricted inheritance rules of freehold tenure increase the number of households permanently dependent for most of their livelihood on tenancy arrangements, but the greatly improved security of title to land would, for the first time, make possible absentee landlordism on a large scale. Large holders would be able to leave their land in the hands of tenants, without fear that in their absence their relatives or their tenants themselves would claim the land as their own rist.

Unless there is a fundamental change in the opportunities of farmers to market their crops and a related shift in their attitudes towards the sale of land, it appears that instituting freehold tenure might well result in: greater and more enduring inequalities of landholding than presently exist; an increase in the importance of tenancy; an increase in absentee landlordism; and a possible increase in migration out of Dega Damot and political unrest on the part of people with no land.

If the analysis presented here is substantially correct, the "individualization" of land tenure through a cadastral survey and the registration of individual title to land will not, in itself, contribute to increased agricultural productivity or a more equitable distribution of land in Dega Damot. What is even more evident is that, at the present time, a reform program based on the measurement of land is unacceptable to the vast majority of Damotians and that it will be met with armed resistance.

Paradoxically, it appears that the first step towards attaining the goals of land reform in Dega Damot is not to reform land tenure but to encourage extra production for the market and thus, over time, to bring about a change in the meaning of land to farmers and to create among them a demand for changes in the rules of tenure.

11. Conclusion

In the preceding chapters I have described and analyzed the interrelated set of Amhara conceptions, rights, expectations, interests, and actions, which together I termed the rist system, and have examined the practical implications of this analysis for land reform policy in Dega Damot. In this, the final chapter, I would like to return to some of the more general themes discussed in the introduction and to place this narrowly focused and detailed case study in a broader comparative and theoretical context. The discussion has three closely related aims: to summarize the features of the rist system which are of most interest in the comparative study of cognatic descent; to assess the place of the rist system in the study of land tenure and social stratification in traditional agrarian societies; and to comment on the utility of the analytical perspective I have adopted in writing this book.

First, I want to comment on an issue which has received a considerable amount of attention in the literature on descent. This is whether, and in what sense, cognatic descent is a meaningful anthropological concept. I have avoided this issue up to now because I believe that prior to the foregoing substantive analysis of the Amhara rist system, treatment of the issue would have been rather sterile. I raise it now because it serves to focus the discussion on just those aspects of cognatic descent systems, or whatever else one may choose to call them, which from a comparative point of view are most interesting: overlapping membership, choice of affiliation, and flexibility of function.

The central issue underlying the controversy over cognatic descent is the question of to what extent it is comparable to unilineal descent and hence susceptible to analysis by the same concepts. Murdock, for example, holds that cognatic descent groups (he calls them ambilineal descent groups, or ramages) are "the precise functional equivalents of lineages" (Murdock 1960:11); and Firth (1960) speaks of the Maori *hapu* as functionally equivalent to a lineage. Fortes, Freeman, Goody, Leach, and Schneider, on the other hand, consider the differences between unilineal and cognatic descent to be so great that referring to them both as systems of descent can only lead to confusion.[1] The differences that these latter writers stress are related to the fact that cognatic descent systems do not assign people to mutually exclusive categories on the basis of kinship principles alone. Speaking of cognatic kinship systems, Fortes writes:

> In these societies, kinship connections, whether taken in the narrow sense or in the wider connotation of including affinal relations, are potentially unlimited in range. Structural boundaries cannot be generated from within the kinship universe, and non-domestic corporate organizations *delimited by kinship criteria,* do not occur in such systems. (Italics mine.)
>
> (Fortes 1969: 122)
>
> "Descent," in the commonsense interpretation of taking cognizance of personal pedigrees reckoned by steps of filiation to forbears antecedent to parents, is recognized. . . . But this recognition of "descent" does not align persons whose pedigrees converge in common ancestors into permanent and *exclusive units* of social structure. (Italics mine.)
>
> (Fortes 1969: 136)

Similarly Leach, in a rare moment of agreement with Fortes, writes:

1. For a comprehensive recent exposition of this point of view see Fortes (1969: chap. 14). See also Schneider (1965).

> To be pedantically accurate one might perhaps say that, in such situations [Leach is here referring to the Samoan *aiga sa* and *fatelama* as described by Davenport (1959)] the potentiality of kin-group membership is based on an ideology of descent, but, since descent does not in itself specify who is or who is not a member of any particular group, it is here misleading to describe the operative corporations as "descent groups." For in such groups, not only is it the case that membership derives from choice rather than from descent, but the membership itself is at all times ambiguous. . . . It is because this kind of ambiguity and choice does not automatically arise in true (that is, in unilineal) descent systems that Fortes and others have found it satisfactory to analyse unilineal descent systems as structures of jural obligations. In contrast, the analysis of any kind of cognatic kinship structure invariably ends by throwing the emphasis upon mechanisms of individual choice.
>
> (Leach 1962: 132)

In the absence of a more apt and widely accepted term I will refer to the rist system as a system of cognatic descent, for, having attained some currency, the term at least has the virtue of inviting comparisons with a broad range of similar cognatic structures elsewhere. It should be evident from my introductory discussion of descent, however, that in most respects I am in agreement with Fortes and Leach concerning the very important differences that exist between cognatic and unilineal descent as role-structuring principles.[2] In that

2. I agree with these writers that there are important differences between unilineal and cognatic descent as formal or logical ways of assigning people to categorical membership, but I find that differences between the actual operation of unilineal descent systems and cognatic descent systems are somewhat less marked. I also find enough similarities between both types of descent as indigenous theories or cultural paradigms of social organization to justify their grouping under the same very general heading. It is true, as Fortes notes, that the active, that is, the landholding membership of Amhara descent corporations is not delimited out of the kinship universe by kinship criteria alone. Nevertheless, it represents a subset of a category of persons delimited by kinship criteria, namely, descent

introductory discussion I commented at some length on the peculiar organizational problems of cognatic descent systems relating to overlapping membership, the restriction of

from a common ancestor, and I can find no way of describing the active membership of the group without reference to this fact.

It is also true, as Fortes points out, that Amhara whose pedigrees converge in common ancestors are not aligned into exclusive units. Nonexclusiveness may make Amhara descent corporations very different from the groupings that interest unilineal descent theorists, but it does not make them intrinsically less interesting. Nor, as Keesing (1968:84; 1970) has pointed out and the present monograph has demonstrated, does it make them "unworkable"; for people's roles and interests are sorted out in the context of the specific situations in which they are relevant.

Leach's contention that the analysis of a cognatic structure throws emphasis upon the mechanisms (and, I would add, the institutional contexts) of choice is certainly borne out by the Amhara case. I would not, however, as Leach does, say that "membership derives from choice rather than from descent," for the choices available to the actor are themselves defined by descent. Furthermore, I find that if we consider the way people actually behave instead of the abstract models constructed by anthropologists, individual choice with regard to such crucial issues as land utilization, residence, and political affiliation in times of crisis are by no means absent in African societies such as the Tiv and Nuer in which unilineal descent plays a major organizational role. (This tendency of some writers to compare cognatic systems as they are observed to operate with anthropologists' idealized models of unilineal descent is discussed by Barnes [1962:5].)

Finally, as a cultural paradigm, as a system of Amhara ideas, the rist system is grounded in an ideology of descent. The men and women who use the land bearing the name of a particular ancestor do so because they recognize one another to be his descendents (*tewellaj*, sing.), and the way they divide the ancestor's land is justified by reference to a genealogical charter of descent. Insofar as the issue is terminological, I hold no brief for "cognatic descent," but do not find the other terms which have been suggested particularly apt for describing the Amhara rist system. Cognatic stocks, for example, a term used by Freeman (1961:200) and suggested by Fortes (1969:287) seems appropriate, as these writers define it, for cognatic kinship systems like that of the Lozi of Zambia (described by Gluckman 1941, 1943, 1950, 1955, 1963), in which an individual is always considered to belong to eight partially overlapping categories, each composed of the descendents of one of his eight great-grandparents. It does not, however, describe the Amhara case, in which the same remote ancestors serve as fixed genealogical reference points for corporate landholding groups generation after generation, and in which a person may trace his descent lines through only a few of his great-grandparents, never through all eight of them. For this reason, I would prefer to call the Amhara descent groups ambilineal, but I have chosen "cognatic" because it is the most widely accepted term for the general phenomenon with which I am concerned.

membership by criteria other than kinship, and the role of choice as it affects the form and the functions of cognatic descent systems.

I believe that the main contribution of this monograph to the comparative study of cognatic descent has been to show in detail how these organizational problems are met in a contemporary, truly cognatic descent system characterized by comparatively great generational depth, structural differentiation, and overlap of membership.[3] The Amhara case is of particular interest because it has not been subjected to a century or more of alien political control, judicial reform, and land registration. In this respect it differs from cognatic descent systems in other complex societies such as the Ondo Yoruba of Nigeria (Lloyd 1962) and the Sinhalese of Ceylon (Leach 1961; Obeyesekere 1967).

In a sense it is misleading to say that the rist system has resolved the organizational problems inherent in the overlapping membership of unrestricted cognatic descent categories; as the preceding chapters have made abundantly evident, the ambiguous nature of *rist* rights fosters chronic suspicion and engenders endemic conflict amongst kinsmen and neighbors. The rist system is not a system of solidary corporate groups providing men with a set of nesting economic, political, and ritual loyalties to one another in opposition to successively more remote groups; it is rather a system of structured ambiguities which tends to keep men apart from one another except to form temporary alliances on the basis of frank self-interest.

3. In their ideology and remembered genealogy, Amhara descent charters, in contrast to the charters of most other similar cognatic descent systems, place truly equal emphasis on links traced through males and females. The Choiseulese and Kwaio descent systems, for example, give ideological emphasis to the agnatic line but permit the tracing of links through women. The Sinhalese system, according to Obeyesekere, was not cognatic but agnatic until the British colonial regime enforced the bilateral inheritance rules of Roman Dutch law under the mistaken impression that their Dutch predecessors had already done so.

The cognatic stocks of the Lozi (Gluckman 1941, 1943, 1950, 1955, 1963) and the Iban (Freeman 1955, 1958, 1960, 1961) are also truly bilateral; in other important respects, however, as I noted above, they are dissimilar to the Amhara.

If the rist system fosters ambiguity of membership and conflict of interest, it also limits them in formal terms to the narrow and highly specific context of land tenure. As I noted in the introduction, restriction in cognatic descent groups is generally related to the geographical localization of their estates or territories. What is distinctive of the Amhara rist system, in contrast to many other cognatic descent systems, is not that descent groups are organized in relation to a particular territory but that controlling land is almost their sole manifest function. The rist system is first and last a system of land tenure. In many other cognatic systems descent groups have overt political, social, and religious functions as well as control over usufructuary rights in land.

In the Gilbertese case described by Goodenough, for example, the most inclusive and theoretically unrestricted descent category, the *oo*, functions only in relation to property. The smaller groups, or *bwoti*, which are composed of only those members of the *oo* who actually hold particular plots of the *oo*'s land, however, function as formalized meetinghouse councils (Goodenough 1955:73–74). In the Choiseulese case described by Scheffler (1965), members of the cognatic descent group resident in its territory constituted a political community. The comparatively unrestricted cognatic descent groups of the Kwaio of Malaita, British Solomon Islands, described by Keesing (1965, 1966a, 1966b, 1967, 1968, 1970) have important ritual functions as well as functions relating to land use and residence. Finally, the cognatic landholding Sinhalese groups of Ceylon described by Leach (1961) and Obeyesekere (1967) are also kinship groups in the sense that their members are considered to be bound by the rules and sentiments of kinsmen.

Among the Amhara, by contrast, neither the people who share a first settler's estate of rist land nor those of them who live on it constitute a political community or a congregation. Nor do these codescendents make up a kin group in the usual sense of the term. In fact, while relations of kinship and descent are always analytically distinct from one another, the disjunction between cognatically traced ties of kinship (which have not been discussed at length in this book) and ancestor-oriented lines of cognatic descent is a striking feature of Amhara social organization.[4]

Membership in Amhara cognatic descent corporations is not restricted by formal rules, for rist rights are, in Amhara theory, inalienable and inextinguishable. Nevertheless, it is striking that neither the active (that is, landholding) membership in a descent corporation nor the number of descent lines through which individual men trace their pedigrees to founding ancestors normally increases with the passage of successive generations. This is a reflection of the fact that, though a man's rist rights are very extensive, his chances of successfully claiming rist land in a descent corporation are restricted by several kinds of pragmatic considerations. Most important of these, as I have said, are: whether his close kinsmen, particularly his parents or grandparents, have held land in the corporation's estate; whether he is a resident elder in the parish where the estate is located; and whether he has political influence or power. The analysis of these three types of restriction in detail led to an examination of the institutional contexts in which decisions about rist land are made: household, community, and polity.

The processes through which membership in descent corporations is restricted also shape and restrict the descent lines or rist rights available to the individual. At birth each person has two arrays of rist rights; one traced through his father and one traced through his mother. Each consists of a set of pedigrees tracing his descent from a first settler. Only full siblings have identical arrays of rist rights, and even their rights normally become differentiated when they marry and gain access (in trust) to their wife's mother's and father's rist rights which they indiscriminately refer to as wife's rist. From an analytical point of view, then, socially recognized procreation brings together four sets of rist rights, the mother's and father's rights of both the child's parents. From the child's point of view, these four sets of rights are recategorized into only two sets of rist rights, mother's and father's.

4. An excellent discussion of the distinction between cognatic kinship and cognatic descent is to be found in Keesing 1970.

Rist rights are forgotten as well as merged in each generation, despite the Amhara ideology to the contrary. The process through which they pass into oblivion is not, however, so precise and predictable as that by which they are merged. The process begins anew in each generation whenever, usually to avoid excessive fragmentation, the land a man holds in a particular descent corporation's estate is not apportioned to all his children. All of them still retain rist rights in the estate, but those who do not hold land lose their immediate interest in it and take no part in the descent corporation's affairs.

Rist rights for which rist land is not held are not immediately forgotten. If they remain unexercised for two or three generations, however, they begin to pass out of awareness. This process of "forgetting" is closely associated with the fact that, though Amhara kinship is bilateral, most men are not aware of the number or the names of all their lineal ancestors beyond the grandparental generation. There is no definite point either in years or generations at which rist rights are irretrievably lost to memory. A man may not know of the rist rights he theoretically has through his mother's father's father, but he may have a mother's brother who does, or perhaps there is a rist expert who could be consulted, should the occasion arise. On the average, however, the range of rist rights which men are aware of does not increase from generation to generation, despite the fact that, according to the basic bilateral rule of inheritance, it should.

Viewed abstractly, a man's known rist rights can be thought of as fiber-like descent lines coming to him in bundles through some, but not all, of his lineal ancestors. The bundles of descent lines merge with others as they descend to him and finally reach him in two large bundles through his mother and father. Having passed through him, the bundles of descent lines become increasingly differentiated once again in subsequent generations as they are sorted out among his descendents. The descent lines of greatest importance to an individual are those by virtue of which he holds rist land. Next in importance are those through which his parents and grandparents held land but through which he does not. Least important are those long unused descent lines, many of which will be cut off from his descendents by a slowly descending curtain of genealogical forgetfulness.

The rist system is a land-tenure system. Because of the central role of land in Amhara social organization, however, it also has important latent ecological, demographic, and political consequences. In all of them it exhibits the type of "flexibility" that is characteristic of cognatic descent; a flexibility that is closely related to the ways in which descent corporation membership is restricted.

From an ecological perspective, the Amhara descent system serves to allocate people to available land by enabling them to move from one parish to another and still claim land with comparative ease. Similarly, from a demographic perspective, it helps to mitigate the economic effects of uneven population growth by enabling sons from large families or men from fertile communities to move away and claim land through other descent corporations.[5]

From a comparative point of view, I believe the most interesting function of the rist system has been to introduce an element of flexibility into the feudal polity and its associated system of social stratification. This flexibility has been manifest both in the fluidity of ties between peasant and lord, and in the relative ease of social mobility.

The rist system, unlike the gwilt system, is not a part of the formal political structure of Amhara society. In processual terms, however, the rist system and the traditional political system interpenetrated one another. In part, this was because both systems were grounded in the same territorial framework. The comprehensive division of the countryside into estates of gwilt provided the territorial framework of administration in the traditional Amhara polity. All the men and women who held rist land within an estate of gwilt were

5. In many other agrarian societies, variations in family fertility produce marked intergenerational variations in wealth and hence often in status as well. This process is well illustrated in Bailey (1957: chap. 4).

obligated to pay taxes to the gwilt-holder, and, in some cases, to aid him in administration. All those who lived on an estate of gwilt were the gwilt-holder's subjects as well.[6] When a person gained or lost rist land within an estate of gwilt or moved from one community to another, he might well alter his relationship with one or more gwilt-holders.

From an analytical point of view, then, the rist system distributed people to the land-based administrative structures of the Amhara polity. The flexibility of the rist system as a way of allocating land to people and people to land was translated into a flexible relationship between the peasantry and the gwilt-holding officials who were responsible for their administration. In many other traditional agrarian societies, peasants have been bound more tightly to a territorially based administrative framework either through the law, as in parts of feudal Europe, or because of a land-tenure system that made it more difficult for them to change their residence or shift their holding.

The other way that the rist system and polity have interpenetrated one another in processual terms has been that strategic decisions men make as members of one system are greatly affected by their position and their interests in the other. Most important, by seeking rist land and leadership positions in an increasing number of descent corporations, men have been able to convert newly acquired political power into a personal estate of "hereditary" land commensurate with their new status. The rist system also facilitated downward social mobility. In the absence of a politically successful heir,[7] the rist land amassed by a powerful individual was soon broken up by the inheritance rule that gave land, at least in theory, equally to all children. Often the dissolution of a powerful man's holding after his death was accelerated by the inability of his heirs to hold together and utilize his widely scattered lands. The net result of these processes was

6. In the area I studied in Gojjam, estates of gwilt are always composed of an integral number of descent corporations' estates. In other areas I visited this is not always the case.

7. Virtually no office and no title was hereditary in a strict sense in traditional Amhara society.

a rather fluid relationship between land, power, and honor in Amhara society.

The rist system, with its overlapping and ambiguous land rights, its ever-present possibilities for upward mobility at the expense of others, and the premium it places on political expertise, produces what, in comparison with many other agrarian systems, appears to be a high degree of endemic competition for and conflict over land. In the feudal systems of western Europe, by contrast, particularly in regions where the open-field system of land tenure prevailed,[8] competition for land and social mobility among peasants were curtailed by the more or less well-institutionalized cultural principle that society should consist of a finite number of strata and that jurally equal members of the farming class should enjoy equal landholdings, or tenements, in their lord's estate. In some parts of Tigre and Eritrea, conflict over land is partly limited by the principle that land belongs to the resident members of a descent corporation or of a village and should be periodically redistributed in equal shares to all household heads.[9]

In Tokugawa Japan, on the other hand, as in Dega Damot, there were many gradations in peasant status corresponding, in large part, at least in the earlier part of the period, to differences in the amount of land held. In the Tokugawa case, however, upward social mobility was severely restricted by the fact that a large part of all the agricultural land in most villages was attached to a relatively few great and enduring households. Control over most of the land was attached to one of these great households, and was passed from its head, the *oyakata*, to his principal heir. The heir's collateral kinsmen were either supported as dependents in the great household or were given small amounts of land through a process of highly unequal partitioning.[10]

8. An excellent discussion of the open-field system in thirteenth century England and of its relationship to social stratification is to be found in Homans (1960).

9. Nadel (1946); Bauer (1972).

10. For a perceptive discussion of the Tokugawa village land-tenure system, see Smith (1959).

In Dega Damot, by contrast, none of these limiting conditions obtain. Not only is there no principal heir, as in Tokugawa Japan and many parts of feudal Europe, but land must be shared among children of both sexes. Nor is it held, even as an ideal, in Dega Damot that all peasant farmers should have equal status or equal amounts of land. Indeed their households' lands vary greatly. At the same time, the extensive rist rights held by each individual, far from resigning him to his present position, or to his father's in the community, encourage him to believe that he holds less than his "rightful" amount of rist land.

The frequency and virulence of conflict over land in Dega Damot tends to obscure the fact that its people, peasant and officeholding official alike, are deeply committed to the rist system and the polity with which it was until recently associated. In the rist system they see the guarantee of the liberties and opportunities they most cherish. In their eyes the system enables them in time of personal adversity to move to another parish and still be accounted hereditary landowners. It enables their children, no matter how numerous, to become independent landowning farmers. It enables them to increase their personal estate and community standing, and finally it holds before them the possibility that they or their children, with good fortune, may obtain the gwilt rights once held by a remote ancestor and an appropriate large estate of rist land. However unrealistic this assessment of the rist system may appear to the observer, there can be no doubt that at present Damotians do not desire to change the rules by which they compete with one another for land and status.

The rist system has also generated commitment to the traditional polity and enhanced the legitimacy of its ruling elites in several ways. Historically it has enabled peoples conquered by the expanding Amhara kingdom's armies to become Amhara rather than remain ethnically distinct, economically disadvantaged, and politically disaffected subjects. With the passage of but a few generations and with intermarriage, it became possible for most of the descendents of the non-Amhara (often Galla) conquered population to trace pedigrees selectively to Amhara invaders and hence to claim rist rights and Amhara status.[11]

The rist system also helped commit the peasants to the political order, with its blatant inequalities of power and prestige, by holding forth the possibility that they or their children may attain office, honor, and an abundance of their hereditary rist land. This belief has been reinforced in the face of statistical probability by the fact that many of the more remote ancestors through whom pedigrees are traced were themselves titled office holders. In this way the rist system with its widely ramifying descent lines has created a sense of common identity between the Amhara within a region, commoner and noble alike. Ultimately all the people of Dega Damot have the same ancestors. It is only chance of birth, political aptitude, and luck that differentiates them from one another in their opinion, and not innate worth.

Land tenure and land reform are widely considered to pose pressing, if little understood, problems for Ethiopian development. Consequently, many educated Ethiopians and foreign observers took an active interest in my research. Most of them were kind enough to say they were favorably impressed by the results of my in-depth study. Almost invariably, however, they asked me whether my findings are representative of Amhara in other provinces or even in other districts in Gojjam.

In order to answer this question, I have tried, rather unsystematically, to obtain information about land tenure from other regions of northern Ethiopia. During the rainy season of 1962 I spent six weeks traveling by car through the provinces of Wello, Tigre, and Begemdir. With the aid of most helpful letters from the Ministry of the Interior, I was able to interview government officials and elders from many districts in these provinces. The data I gathered in this way were generally qualitative rather than quantitative.

11. The process of Amharicization continues today in many parts of Ethiopia. Any child with an Amhara parent can have himself accounted Amhara.

From the end of 1968 until the beginning of 1970, I carried out a second intensive microstudy 110 air miles to the northeast of Addis Ababa in the Gra Midir district of Menz in Shoa province. This study was not primarily concerned with land tenure. Nonetheless, I was able to gather a considerable amount of comparative data from several parishes in this region. Finally, an excellent study by Wolfgang Weissleder (1965) has provided us with a description of land tenure in a parish near Ankober, formerly the seat of Shoan monarchs on the southeastern frontier of the Amhara area.

Throughout most of the long-settled Amhara heartlands I found the rist system to have the same basic features I observed in Dega Damot.[12] To be sure, there are also regional variations of several kinds. There are variations in the terminology people use to talk about the rist system. There are variations in the landholding pattern resulting from regional historical differences in the ecological, demographic, and political parameters of the rist system. Perhaps most important of all, there are variations in the formal rules of the rist system. A substantive discussion of these variations is beyond the scope of this book.

The point I want to make here is that underneath these regional variations in form, the rist system has the same structural features and performs the same basic functions.[13] Everywhere it is grounded in a system of territorially based cognatic descent corporations. Everywhere children of both sexes can inherit land from both their mother and father. Everywhere most men in each generation must actively strive to put together anew estates of rist land to support their households. Everywhere the rist system functions to create a

12. By Amhara heartlands, I mean a contiguous area comprising northern and eastern Gojjam, northern Shoa, western Wello, and southern and eastern Begemdir. The Ankober area discussed by Weissleder is on the fringe of this area. Its land-tenure system differs in some important respects from the rist system found in the more central regions.

13. To avoid confusion, it should be remembered that the Amharic term "rist" is used to mean land held in freehold in areas that do not have the rist system as understood here.

comparatively fluid relationship between land, status, and power in Amhara social organization.

The Amhara themselves clearly recognize the underlying unity of the rist system. In fact they are apt to overemphasize it. What appear to the anthropologist to be significant differences are either disregarded or explained away as minor deviations from a formerly widespread, more pure form of the rist system. In the absence of any detailed historical accounts of Amhara land tenure, it is impossible to prove or disprove the last assertion.

There is no reason to consider the communities I happened to study in Dega Damot particularly typical Amhara communities; nor is there any reason to consider the form of the rist system in these communities especially typical of the Amhara rist system as a whole.[14] I would argue that the concept of typicality is not a useful one in this context; for Amhara land tenure and Amhara social organization, of which the rist system is an important part, exhibit variation not only from region to region but even within a region. What are constant are not the exact patterns of landholding and of social relationships but the underlying institutional features and the processes out of which these patterns are generated.[15]

In this book I have tried to do two things. I have tried to describe the land-tenure system I observed at a particular time and place. I have also tried to analyze the institutional elements out of which and the processes through which this system of tenure is created and sustained. The detailed de-

14. The Feres Bét area of Dega Damot was, in fact, selected after a two-week trip by mule and on foot, from among several possible sites suggested by Ato Taye Retta, director of the Imperial Ethiopian Government Mapping and Geography Institute. The main criteria by which it was chosen were that it be far enough from the road to have escaped the major impact of the national market system (most of Gojjam is), high enough to be free of malaria in the rainy season, and under the jurisdiction of a district governor who would not oppose the study.

15. A full analysis of Amhara social organization in these terms is beyond the limited scope of this book. An excellent example of this approach to typicality is to be found in an article on form and variation in Balinese village structure by Clifford Geertz (1959).

scription of land tenure presented in the preceding chapters may or may not fit other communities in other Amhara areas. I am reasonably certain, however, that the analytical model of the rist system which I have constructed here will be useful to those who wish to investigate form and variation in the rist system throughout the Amhara region.

appendix: amharic titles

The Amhara penchant—one might almost say passion—for receiving and using honorific titles (*maireg*, sing.) has been noted by many observers of the Ethiopian scene past and present. Indeed, this intense interest has led to a great proliferation of titles and considerable variation in their usage and relative importance from region to region and from epoch to epoch. Here, however, my aim is not to give an exhaustive or comparative account of Amhara titles but only to explain the significance of the titles mentioned in this book.

For present purposes it is useful to distinguish two broad classes of titles: those which give their recipient membership in the elite and those which do not. Titles which give elite status, in turn, are of three types: quasi-military titles, courtly titles, and ecclesiastic titles. Each of these types requires comment.

Quasi-military titles have reference to positions of leadership in the traditional armies of the emperor and the great regional rulers. They are not, however, military offices, and the men who hold them do not necessarily have any military responsibilities. The quasi-military titles referred to in this book, in order of importance from highest to lowest, are:

Title	*Reference*
Neguse Negast	king of kings, or emperor; hence, commander of many armies
Negus	king, and hence commander of several armies

Ras	commander of an army
Dejazmach	commander of the (ruler's) gate
Fītawrarī	commander of the vanguard
Qeñazmach	commander of the right wing
Grazmach	commander of the left wing
Balambiras	commander of a fortress

Courtly titles have reference to services performed for the king or ruler. While the recipient might indeed be called upon to perform the services entailed in his title, courtly titles were not, first and foremost, offices, for a man retained his title for life, even if he was no longer serving at court; and even while he was at court he might be called upon for a variety of services not entailed in his title. The only courtly titles mentioned in this book are *Bilaténgéta*, or steward in charge of the ruler's estates of gwilt land; *Agafarī*, a court official performing the functions of a *majordomo*; and *Azzaž*, or commander—in this case, the commander in charge of provisioning the provincial ruler's army when it camped in Dega Damot.

Ecclesiastic titles implied learning and, in some instances, sanctity, but their primary reference was to authority within the administration of the Ethiopic church. Like all Amharic titles they are retained by the recipient for life, whether or not he continues to occupy the office with which they are associated. Ecclesiastic titles mentioned in the text either in Amharic or their English equivalent are:

Title	*Reference*
Abuna	bishop. Formerly there was only one bishop for all Ethiopia. Today there is a bishop for each province, including Gojjam.
Līqekahinat	an official learned in church law who acts as administrator and judge for the clergy in a district or subprovince.

Memhir	the head of a monastery (also see below).
Aleqa	the head of an endowed church center (also see below).

The same individual might be honored with more than one type of title and might well hold office and gwilt land as well. All titles were retained for life even if the recipient fell out of favor or joined a rival lord. An extreme test of this principle is an elderly man of Dega Damot who was given the title of *dejazmach* (and a trip to Rome!) by the Italians during the occupation as a reward for his collaboration. Though the emperor has not, for obvious reasons, confirmed him in his title, this elderly gwilt-holder is still referred to as *fītawrarī* by Damotians, apparently on the theory that his title is not quite as legitimate as it should be.

In the past, quasi-military titles were given to few men and carried a correspondingly high degree of prestige. In 1900 there was but a single titled man in all Damot, and he was only a *grazmach*. In the course of the present century quasi-military titles have been given more freely, first by Ras Imru, Gojjam's first Shoan governor, in the early 1930s; then by the Italians; and, most important, by the emperor, who confirmed numerous patriots in the titles they had been granted by their own wartime leaders and who subsequently bestowed titles rather generously in the decades since the Second World War.

This great increase in the number of men who hold quasi-military titles and the fact that many of them have never held any office higher than that of gwilt *gež* has diminished their prestige. For the most part, the titled men of Damot who are referred to both individually and as a class in this book should be thought of as a local gentry, usually enjoying authority in their local communities as gwilt-holders and honor throughout the district.

In addition to the titles that give their bearer elite status, there are a number of minor titles which appear in the text. The commonest secular title of this type is *aleqa*, or "chief" (not to be confused with the title of a high ecclesiastic official, discussed above), which may be given to any man who holds or has held the office of *chiqa shum*. On the religious side there are the clerical titles discussed in chapter 4: *qés* (priest), *diyakon* (deacon), *debtera* (chorister-scribe), *memhir* or *merīgéta* (church school teacher), and *qése gebez* (head priest of a church).

glossary

Only those Amharic words used as technical terms in the text or those used in case material have been included here.

abbat — literally, "father"; also used for any ancestor.

agafarī — a court title. See Appendix.

aleqa — the head of an endowed church center; also, a title prefixed to the name of anyone who holds a minor secular administrative office, such as that of *ç̣hiqa shum*.

asrat — a tax (literally, a tithe); in Gojjam commuted to a tax on oxen. Also used to refer to one of the postwar land taxes paid in cash.

aṭbīya — neighborhood; a recently introduced territorial unit of administration which, in Gojjam, corresponds to a traditional estate of gwilt land.

aṭbīya dañña — an unpaid official with minor judicial and peace-keeping responsibilities over a neighborhood.

ato — an honorific term corresponding to "Mister" which precedes a man's name. Its use implies that the person designated is a respected elder or an official.

awrajja	an administrative division of a province.
azzaž	a courtly title literally meaning "commander." See Appendix.
balambiras	a minor quasi-military title. See Appendix.
beabbat	refers to the division of land according to the *per stirpes* rule. Literally means "by father."
beyažish	refers to possession of land without rist right. Literally means "by holding."
bilaténgéta	an official appointed by the ruler of Gojjam to look after his estates of gwilt land. See Appendix.
c̣hewa gebez	a minor official chosen annually from among the rist landholders in a parish to look after the secular affairs of the church.
c̣hiqa shum	a minor official appointed for a one-year term from among the peasant elders in each estate of gwilt to act as intermediary between the gwilt-holder and the other peasants. Similar to the reeve in thirteenth-century England. Literally the "mud chief."
debir	1) a major religious center with a large church, daily service, a large number of specialized church offices, and an endowment of gwilt land; 2) also used to refer to any parish, particularly when it is being distinguished from a neighborhood that does not have a church.
debtera	a chorister-scribe; a learned but unordained cleric. Some are thought to use their esoteric knowledge for magical purposes.

dejazmach	an honorific quasi-military title. See Appendix.
fej	a representative, such as the representative of a descent corporation or of a hamlet (*yemender fej*).
fītawrarī	an honorific quasi-military title. See Appendix.
ganageb	gwilt land held personally by the ruler of Gojjam.
gashsha	a Shoan unit of land measurement used for assessing the postwar land tax.
gashsha merét	first settler's estate added to a parish subsequent to the founding of the parish, often constituting a separate estate of gwilt.
gebez	either of two types of minor church official: *qése gebez*—a priest responsible for the ordering of a parish church's service; *c̣hewa gebez*—a church official chosen from among the holders of church land to administer the secular affairs of a parish church.
gibir	a land tax; traditionally the tax paid in kind to the gwilt *gež*. Today, a tax paid in cash to the government.
goṭ	a neighborhood or estate of gwilt land that does not include a church within its boundaries.
grazmach	an honorific quasi-military title. See Appendix.
gwilt	land held as a fief or benefice.
gwilt gež	the official who holds gwilt rights over an estate of gwilt in Gojjam. The term is not generally used in other provinces.

hudad	statute labor. Also, land temporarily set aside from the rist system and worked by statute labor for a few seasons for the benefit of a governor.
immahoy	an honorific title used for a nun.
iṭa merét	land that has been assigned to an ancestor by casting lots.
kahinat	clergy; or pertaining to the clergy.
kisara	a punitive payment the courts can order a litigant to give to his adversary when the litigant fails to appear at a hearing on the appointed day.
līqekahinat	a church official in charge of enforcing church law among the clergy in the area under his jurisdiction.
memhir	the head of a monastery; a type of church-school teacher.
merīgéta	a kind of church-school teacher.
mesno	literally, "irrigation." In this book, however, following my informants, I use it to refer to a species of barley grown on fertilized land without the use of irrigation.
mikittil wereda	an administrative subdistrict.
minzir abbat	a divisional ancestor; an ancestor in whose name land has been divided by father and who is hence the apical ancestor of a segment of a descent corporation.
qeñazmach	an honorific quasi-military title. See Appendix.
ras	a high honorific quasi-military title. See Appendix.
rist	inherited land-use rights.

rist-gwilt	a grant of gwilt which is, in principle, hereditary. A grant of gwilt over land in which the recipient also has rist rights.
shī belo	pasture land which has not been divided by father.
wabī	one who has given his rist land to someone else and who hence may be called to defend the land, should the recipient's right be challenged.
wanna abbat	the apical ancestor in a descent corporation's genealogical charter. The first settler. Literally, the "principal father."
was	a guarantor.
wekīl	a steward or bailiff.
wereda	an administrative district.
wetadir	literally, "soldier"; used today as a title for policemen or soldiers.
yedenb	portion or share. Land of an ancestor which has not been subdivided in the names of his children.

bibliography

Alvares, Francisco

1961 *The Prester John of the Indies: a true relation of the lands of the Prester John*. Published for the Hakluyt Society, Cambridge.

Bailey, F. G.

1957 *Caste and the economic frontier*. Manchester: Manchester University Press.

1960 *Tribe, caste, and nation*. Manchester: Manchester University Press.

1970 *Strategems and spoils*. Oxford: Basil Blackwell.

Banton, Michael

1965 *The relevance of models for social anthropology*. A.S.A. Monograph 1. London: Tavistock Publications. New York: Frederick A. Praeger.

1966 *The social anthropology of complex societies*. A.S.A. Monograph 4. London: Tavistock Publications. New York: Frederick A. Praeger.

Barnes, J. A.

1962 African models in the New Guinea highlands. *Man* 62:5–9.

Bauer, Dan F.

1972 Land, leadership and legitimacy among the Inderta Tigray of Ethiopia. Doctoral dissertation, University of Rochester. University microfilms, Ann Arbor, Michigan.

Beattie, J. M. H.
1964 Bunyoro: an African feudality? *Journal of African History* 5:25–36.

Bender, Donald R.
1967 A refinement of the concept of household. *American Anthropologist* 69:493–504.
1971 De facto families and de jure households in Ondo. *American Anthropologist* 73:223–41.

Bender, M. L.
1968 Amharic verb morphology: a generative approach. Doctoral dissertation, University of Texas at Austin. University Microfilms, Ann Arbor, Michigan.

Bloch, Marc
1961 *Feudal society*. Chicago: The University of Chicago Press.

Bruce, James
1790 *Travels to discover the source of the Nile*. Edinburgh: J. Ruthven.

Caquot, A.
1957 La royauté sacrale en Éthiopie. *Annales d'Éthiopie*, 2:205–19.

Clapham, Christopher
1969 *Haile Selassie's government*. London and Harlow: Longmans, Green.

Coult, Allan D.
1964 Role allocation, position structuring, and ambilineal descent. *American Anthropologist* 66:29–40.

Davenport, William
1959 Nonunilinear descent and descent groups. *American Anthropologist* 61:557–72.

Fallers, Lloyd A.
1961 Are African cultivators to be called peasants? *Current Anthropology* 2:108–10.

Firth, Raymond

1963 *Bilateral descent groups: an operational viewpoint.* Occasional Papers of the Royal Anthropological Institute 16:22–37.

Fortes, Meyer

1966 Introduction. In *The Developmental Cycle in Domestic Groups*, Jack Goody, ed. Cambridge Papers in Social Anthropology, no. 1:1–14. Cambridge: Cambridge University Press.

1969 *Kinship and the social order.* Chicago: Aldine.

Freeman, J. D.

1955 *Iban agriculture: a report on the shifting cultivation of hill rice by the Iban of Sarawak.* London: Her Majesty's Stationery Office.

1958 The family system of the Iban of Borneo. In *The Developmental Cycle in Domestic Groups*, Jack Goody, ed. Cambridge Papers in Social Anthropology, no. 1. Cambridge: Cambridge University Press.

1960 The Iban of western Borneo. In *Social Structure in Southeast Asia*, G. P. Murdoch, ed. Viking Fund Publications in Anthropology 29:65–87. Chicago: Quadrangle Books.

1961 On the concept of the kindred. *Journal of the Royal Anthropological Institute* 91(2):192–220.

Gamst, Frederick

1970 Peasantries and elites without urbanism: the civilization of Ethiopia. *Comparative Studies in Society and History* 12(4):373–92.

Gebré-Weld-Ingida Worq

1962 Ethiopia's traditional system of land tenure and taxation. Translated by Mengesha Gessesse. In *Ethiopia Observer* 5(4):302–39.

Geertz, Clifford

1959 Form and variation in Balinese village structure. *American Anthropologist* 61:991–1012.

Gluckman, Max

1941 *Economy of the central Barotse Plain.* Rhodes-Livingstone Paper, no. 7. Northern Rhodesia: Rhodes-Livingstone Institute.

1943 *Essays on Lozi land and royal property.* Rhodes-Livingstone Paper, no. 10. Northern Rhodesia: Rhodes-Livingstone Institute.

1950 Kinship and marriage among the Lozi of Northern Rhodesia and the Zulu of Natal. In *African Systems of Kinship and Marriage*, A. R. Radcliffe-Brown and Daryll Forde, eds. London: Oxford University Press.

1955 *The judicial process among the Barotse of Northern Rhodesia.* Manchester: Manchester University Press.

1963 *Order and rebellion in tribal Africa.* New York: Free Press.

Goodenough, W. H.

1955 A problem in Malayo-Polynesian social organization. *American Anthropologist* 57:71–83.

1961 Review of social structure in southeast Asia. *American Anthropologist* 63:1314–47.

Goody, Jack

1963 Feudalism in Africa. *Journal of African History* 4:1–18.

1966 *The developmental cycle in domestic groups.* Cambridge Papers in Social Anthropology, no. 1. Cambridge: Cambridge University Press.

Hoben, Allan

1963 The role of ambilineal descent groups in Gojjam Amhara social organization. Doctoral dissertation, University of California, Berkeley. University Microfilms, Ann Arbor, Michigan.

1970a Social stratification in traditional Amhara society. In *Social Stratification in Africa*, Arthur Tuden and Leonard Plotnicov, eds. New York: The Free Press.

1970b Land tenure and social mobility among the Damot Amhara. *Journal of Ethiopian Studies*, Proceedings of the Third International Conference of Ethiopian Studies, held in Addis Ababa, April 1966.

Hoben, Susan

1972 Situational constraints on semantic analysis: an Amharic case. Doctoral dissertation, University of Rochester. University Microfilms, Ann Arbor, Michigan.

Homans, G. C.

1960 *English villagers of the thirteenth century*. New York: Russell and Russell.

Keesing, R. M.

1965 Kwaio marriage and society. Doctoral dissertation, Harvard University.

1966a Kwaio kindreds. *Southwestern Journal of Anthropology* 22:346–53.

1966b Kwaio descent groups. Offset monograph, Center for South Pacific Studies, University of California, Santa Cruz.

1967 Statistical and decision models of social structure: a Kwaio case. *Ethnology* 6:1–16.

1968 Nonunilineal descent and contextual definition of status: the Kwaio evidence. *American Anthropologist* 70:82–84.

1970 Shrines, ancestors, and cognatic descent: the Kwaio and the Tallensi. *American Anthropologist* 72:755–75.

Kroeber, A. L.

1948 *Anthropology*. New York: Harcourt, Brace.

Leach, E. R.

1961 *Pul Eliya*. Cambridge: Cambridge University Press.

1962 On certain unconsidered aspects of double descent systems. *Man* 62:130–34.

Levine, Donald

1964 Legitimacy in Ethiopia. Paper read at the September 1964 meeting of The American Political Science Association.

1965 *Wax and gold*. Chicago: The University of Chicago Press.

Lloyd, P. C.

1962 *Yoruba land law*. Published for the Nigerian Institute of Social and Economic Research, Ibadan. London: Oxford University Press.

Maquet, Jacques

1961 *The premise of inequality in Ruanda*. London: Oxford University Press.

1970 Ruanda castes. In *Social Stratification in Africa*, Arthur Tuden and Leonard Plotnicov, eds. New York: The Free Press.

Mayer, Adrian C.

1966 The significance of quasi-groups in the study of complex society. In *The Social Anthropology of Complex Societies*, Michael Banton, ed. A.S.A. Monograph 4. London: Tavistock Publications. New York: Frederick A. Praeger.

Murdock, G. P.

1949 *Social structure*. New York: The Macmillan Co.

1960a *Social structure in southeast Asia*. Viking Fund Publications in Anthropology, no. 29. Chicago: Quadrangle Books.

1960b Cognatic forms of social organization. In *Social Structure in Southeast Asia*, G. P. Murdock, ed. Viking Fund Publications in Anthropology, no. 29. Chicago: Quadrangle Books.

Nadel, S. F.

1942 *A black Byzantium*. Published for the International African Institute. London: Oxford University Press.

1946 Land tenure on the Eritrean plateau. *Africa* 16(1):1–21.

Obeyesekere, Gananath

1967 *Land tenure in village Ceylon*. London: Cambridge University Press.

Pankhurst, Richard
1961 *An introduction to the economic history of Ethiopia from early times to 1800*. London: Lalibela House.

Peranio, Roger D.
1961 Descent, descent line, and descent group in cognatic social systems. In *Symposium: Patterns of Land Utilization and Other Papers*, Viola E. Garfield, ed. Proceedings of the 1961 Spring Meeting of the American Ethnological Society. Seattle: University of Washington Press.

Perham, Margery
1948 *The government of Ethiopia*. London: Faber and Faber.

Pitt-Rivers, J. A.
1961 *The people of the Sierra*. Chicago: The University of Chicago Press.

Rattray, R. S.
1929 *Ashanti law and constitution*. Oxford: The Clarendon Press.

Scheffler, Harold
1965 *Choiseul Island social structure*. Berkeley: University of California Press.

Schneider, David M.
1965 Some middles in the models: or, how the system really works. In *The Relevance of Models for Social Anthropology*, Michael Banton, ed. A.S.A. Monograph 1. London: Tavistock Publications. New York: Frederick A. Praeger.

Smith, Thomas C.
1959 *The agrarian origins of modern Japan*. Stanford: Stanford University Press.

Trimingham, J. Spencer
1952 *Islam in Ethiopia*. London: Oxford University Press.

Tuden, Arthur, and Plotnicov, Leonard
1970 *Social stratification in Africa.* New York: The Free Press.

Ullendorff, Edward
1955 *The Semitic languages of Ethiopia: a comparative phonology.* London: Taylor's Foreign Press.

Weissleder, Wolfgang
1965 The political ecology of Amhara domination. Doctoral dissertation, University of Chicago.

index

ALLAN HOBEN is assistant professor of anthropology and research associate in the African Studies Center at Boston University. He has published articles on the Amhara in various scholarly journals. This is his first book.

[1973]